An Introductory Guide to Artificial Intelligence for Legal Professionals

An Introductory Guide to Artificial Intelligence for Legal Professionals

Edited by

María Jesús González-Espejo
Juan Pavón

Wolters Kluwer

Published by:
Kluwer Law International B.V.
PO Box 316
2400 AH Alphen aan den Rijn
The Netherlands
E-mail: international-sales@wolterskluwer.com
Website: lrus.wolterskluwer.com

Sold and distributed in North, Central and South America by:
Wolters Kluwer Legal & Regulatory U.S.
7201 McKinney Circle
Frederick, MD 21704
United States of America
Email: customer.service@wolterskluwer.com

Sold and distributed in all other countries by:
Air Business Subscriptions
Rockwood House
Haywards Heath
West Sussex
RH16 3DH
United Kingdom
Email: international-customerservice@wolterskluwer.com

ISBN 978-94-035-0943-3

e-Book: ISBN 978-94-035-0982-2
web-PDF: ISBN 978-94-035-1030-9

Editors

María Jesús González-Espejo is a jurist who has specialized in law firm's management and innovation, as well as in Legal Tech. She is the managing partner at Instituto de Innovación Legal and Vice-president at the European Legal Technology Association.

Juan Pavón is a Professor at the Faculty of Computer Science of Universidad Complutense Madrid (Spain), where he leads the UCM-GRASIA research group and the Institute of Knowledge Engineering.

Contributors

Moises Barrio Andres, J.D., PhD, is a Legal Counsel for the Council of State in Spain. In addition, he has been a practising lawyer since 2004, and he is a senior advisor to several public administrations, both in Spain and Latin America.

Paloma Aparicio is an in-house lawyer, currently practising law as a solo corporate advisor, mastered in personal data protection and with a practical business approach.

Michał Araszkiewicz is an assistant professor at the Jagiellonian University, Kraków, Poland, Department of Legal Theory. He specializes in legal philosophy, argumentation and in computational modelling of legal reasoning.

Ignacio Arnaldo is a chief data scientist at PatternEx, whose focus is to use machine learning to solve cybersecurity challenges.

Caroline Chetrit is an expert in business strategy and innovation with over fifteen years of experience. She is also a jurist and the current Managing Director of an international network of law firms.

Virginia Dignum is a professor at the University of Umeå, Department of Computer Science, and heads the Research Group on Ethical and Social AI.

Javier Martín Fernández is the Managing Partner of Ideo Legal. He is also a professor of Financial and Tax Law at the Complutense University of Madrid.

Grzegorz J. Nalepa is a full professor at the Jagiellonian University, formerly at the AGH University of Science and Technology, in Kraków, Poland. He is an engineer with degrees in computer science – artificial intelligence, and philosophy.

Bárbara Román is CEO of NOLEGALTECH.

Julia Suderow is founding partner of 3C Compliance and associate professor at the University of Deusto, Spain, and head of the Osservatorio Antitrust of the University of Trento in Spain.

Summary of Contents

Table of Contents

Preface

PRESENTATION

This book's collective authorship is far from coincidental. It responds to the necessity of building up a discipline that due to its novelty requires the pooling of knowledge and experiences of many: from Artificial Intelligence (AI) and its legal framework, as well as its relationship with the field of Law and more specifically the legal professions.

As editors of this volume, we have had the privilege of coordinating the work of some well-respected experts in the field, all of them pioneers in the analysis of AI and its impact on legal professionals and the law. In fact, during the selection of contributors, we have applied two essential criteria: first, all contributors needed to be experts in their subject, and second, they had to be able to offer the possibility to show readers an international view on the subject. As a result, this volume features a wide range of authors from different countries and professional areas, including academia, government, law firms and legal/industrial consultancy.

The main goal of this book is to comprehensively introduce readers to a discipline that might still be alien to them, but that in our view will become indispensable in the coming years for any jurist. We are convinced of the urgent need to be able to understand its potential impact in all spheres of our lives: as citizens, clients or legal professionals. There are many AI-based tools being developed that can help lawyers to become more efficient at their work and can replace them in some of their tasks, like, for example, public institutions' chatbots built with the aim of informing citizens about regulations and procedures. AI is equally interesting for lawyers because advising on its legislative framework and assisting those who are developing this kind of technology can be an excellent source of new income. Furthermore, AI is present in our lives in several ways (from e-commerce platforms, fraud prevention tools, decision-making tools for banking and insurance companies, etc.) and we lawyers in our role as citizens also need to understand it.

During the last few months, the references to AI in multiple publications (both specialized magazines and mainstream media), as well as various legal sector training and information forums, has only increased in frequency. We have witnessed all kinds of statements being made concerning AI. Whilst some embrace AI's potential, others warn about the inherent risks and dangers that its use may raise as well as its impact on legal professions. Often mentioned is AI's capacity to substitute judges in their judging duties,[1] or to transform the Tax Authorities into an even more invasive organisation. However, when one searches libraries in an attempt to find solid foundations with a scientific basis to support these statements, what one encounters is a rather uncultivated field, but with great potential for legal research by curious law professionals. There is a clear lack of academic research to validate the aforementioned statements, a gap that this volume aims to tackle by introducing AI in a simple, fast and intelligible style and offer the reader as many practical examples and business cases as possible so that they are able to understand the real application of this technology and its impact on their jobs and lives.

AI: ORIGIN AND CONCEPT

The first chapter of this volume, written by María Jesús González-Espejo and Juan Pavón, offers an introduction to the concept of AI and its main techniques. To that end, a historical overview properly illustrating the evolution of the discipline is provided. We will find out that AI is not as young as commonly thought, given that it dates back to the 1950s. Yet, it must be acknowledged that the increase of computer capacity to handle the huge amounts of data that are being generated in these last few years has led to a significant technological advancement in AI's development and thus to a vast social and economic impact.

AI is an umbrella term for various technologies of differing nature and characteristics. In the first chapter, we will *see* how multiple technologies are lumped under this term, and their names often swapped indiscriminately and misinterpreted: *machine learning, deep learning, reinforcement learning, artificial neural networks, data analytics and data mining*. All these technologies share the commonality that they allow a machine to learn in an autonomous or semi-autonomous way using varied data as a source in order to do tasks considered to be only performable by humans, such as distinguishing objects visually, understanding spoken languages or making decisions.

From the above terms, three are worth mentioning because of their extended use in the legal sector. First, techniques for Natural Language Processing (NLP), which facilitate processing substantial amounts of text or communicate with people using natural, written or even spoken language. The other two terms that we should start getting acquainted with are: Machine Learning (ML) and Deep learning (DL). These two techniques could be applied to perform Natural Language Processing (NLP), an area that has experimented consistent progress in the last years. In chapter 1, we will analyse what they mean.

1. In March 2019, Wired informed that the Estonian Ministry of Justice had made an assignment to a group of developers to design a 'robot judge' that could adjudicate small claims disputes of less than EUR 7,000 (about USD 8,000). Read more here: https://www.wired.com/story/can-ai-be-fair-judge-court-estonia-thinks-so/, accessed 17 Dec. 2019.

With the ultimate purpose of classifying them in a comprehensible manner for non-experts, AI technologies tend to be grouped into three broader categories. First, *superintelligence* refers to technology capable of executing tasks which surpass the capacities of the human mind. Technology belonging to this category tends to raise suspicion and generate fear towards the idea that it might 'stop obeying' one day, albeit superintelligence's existence is still a distant possibility. Next, *strong* or Artificial General Intelligence (AGI), which does not yet exist either, would be able to carry out any task human beings perform. Finally, *weak AI* is able to perform very specific tasks, usually much better than human beings, and this is the one being developed and available for use as of today and, therefore, that legal professionals should familiarize themselves with (or at least understand) and eventually use.

In the first chapter, we will also see that many of the current AI tools are based on the integration of three key processes: information gathering, information analysis and drawing of conclusions for decision-making.

THE IMPACT OF AI IN THE LEGAL SECTOR

As pointed out at the beginning, the potential impact of the different technologies grouped under the umbrella of AI is relevant for both legal professionals and justice itself. We have articulated this impact under three main headings:

1. AI as a transformative technology of the labour market and training.

The impact of AI on the labour market will be positive in terms of its development, implementation and use, which will conversely demand professionals with new skill sets. The development of AI requires an understanding of how it works. While it is not necessary for all of us to become computer experts, it is essential to learn how to work with those who can develop AI and provide them with what they need to know in order to create tools that respond to the needs of society and comply with the legal framework.

With regards to tools for the legal sector, lawyers should be able to identify what the specific needs of their sector are, such as the automatization of those processes that AI could perform better than the human brain.

AI will require new specialists like people capable of identifying the rules and procedures that the algorithm must reflect, feed it with the appropriate data, and understand how it works. Additionally, it will be necessary to introduce training activities in all public and private organizations and, more importantly, in professional associations and universities. As the European Commission itself points out '...EU countries face a shortage of IT professionals and lack higher education programs specialized in AI. That is why the Commission, together with European countries, supports advanced degrees in this field through specific scholarships. The Commission will also continue to support digital skills development and lifelong learning for society as a whole, and especially for those workers most affected by AI, as set out in its AI strategy. With regard to the anthropocentric development of AI, it is also important that

AI be included in the educational programs of other disciplines, such as Law.' In fact, many higher education institutions already offer fairly extensive courses on AI.[2]

It is obvious that due to AI, some jobs will disappear, but it is also foreseeable that they will not be the most coveted positions and will rather be those that are generally undervalued.[3] Nevertheless, it is more than reasonable to expect that due to AI, new jobs will emerge. For instance, within the field of Law, and imagining the future, the figure of the 'legal robotizer' might appear, with functions such as helping the AI developer to automate processes, design workflows and check that the development engineer turns them into an AI tool by means of appropriate verification and validation techniques. Correspondingly, the 'legal chatbotter' could be a lawyer capable of defining the content and workflow of a 'chatbot' that provides service on some legal subject, and the legal data scientist will be the professional capable of managing data of a legal nature and of legal organizations. These are just but three examples among many that we could imagine in terms of those new job profiles that will be required by the legal sector.

Another logical consequence of AI's existence is that young lawyers will have to be trained in a different way. If machines do end up carrying out the simple, more repetitive and automatable tasks that were traditionally done by these lawyers, they cannot continue to be trained as before, and it is paramount to think about how they can continue to acquire the solid knowledge they need.[4] We believe that this knowledge will be different than it is today.

2. AI: An economic and business sector in need of legal advice.

Conversely, AI is a productive sector that has been identified as having enormous potential in the economy of most developed countries (Germany, Canada, South Korea, USA, France, Japan, United Kingdom, among others), which have included it in their strategic plans and have decided to allocate significant budgetary funds to foster this industry. Likewise, on 7 December 2018,[5] the European Union (EU) presented a

2. To know more about who is already offering training in AI to legal professionals, it is interesting to check these two articles from Paulius Astromskis (January 2019), A Systematic Review of Law & Technology Master Programs in Selected European Union (EU) Universities, SSRN Electronic Journal, https://www.researchgate.net/publication/333692109_A_Systematic_Review_of_Law_Technology_Master_Programs_in_Selected_European_Union_Universities.And this other from the same author, A systematic review of law & technology master programs in selected EU universities (pilot research report), Law review, Jan 2019, https://www.researchgate.net/publication/334699375_A_systematic_review_of_law_technology_master_programs_in_selected_European_Union_universities_pilot_research_report. We also recommend the index created by Dan Linna: https://www.legaltechinnovation.com/ last accessed 17 Dec. 2019.
3. As pointed out in *The future of Jobs report* available at: https://www.weforum.org/reports/the-future-of-jobs-report-2018, last accessed 19 Dec. 2019. *See also The future of Employment*, available at: https://www.oxfordmartin.ox.ac.uk/downloads/academic/The_Future_of_Employment.pdf, last accessed 19 Dec. 2019.
4. On a similar note, check: https://www.legaltechnology.com/latest-news/deloitteinsight-100000-legal-roles-to-be-automated/ and this: https://www.lawsociety.org.uk/news/documents/horizon-scanning-artificial-intelligence-and-the-legal-profession/, last accessed 19 Dec. 2019.
5. The digital program on AI available at: https://ec.europa.eu/commission/news/artificial-intelligence-2018-dec-07_en, last accessed 19 Dec. 2019.

coordinated plan that has been prepared with the Member States to promote the development and use of AI in Europe. The plan proposes joint actions to achieve closer and more efficient cooperation in order to increase investment, the amount of available data, foster talent and ensure trust. The main objective is to make Europe the leading region in the world for the creation and implementation of cutting-edge, ethical and safe AI.

Therefore, AI will generate work for many lawyers: for those lawyers that offer their services to the developers of AI tools; for those who use them; and also for those who will defend the rights of people who suffered any kind of damage from the use of AI. Moreover, AI will require experts to develop specific regulatory standards, as well as interpret and apply these standards. It will also require experts in defence of fundamental rights because AI's misuse may result in violations that will need to be challenged.

3. A sector in need of regulation.

AI requires a clear legal framework that in virtually all of its aspects is still in a rather embryonic state. In chapter 2, Moises Barrio analyses the legal framework and explains his view on the need to regulate this technology better. While this framework becomes mature, an ethical approach to limit AI has become the interim solution. In chapter 3, Virginia Dignum explains the ethical and social issues around AI.

The book includes one chapter for each of the legal disciplines that will possibly be shaped by this future legal regime in one way or another, namely, Tax law, Labour Law, Competition Law, Industrial and Intellectual Property (IP) Law, Data Protection and Liability Law. Additionally, the relationship between AI and Cybersecurity is also analysed in chapter 9. Finally, a chapter is dedicated to the use of AI in the judiciary, where, as we will see, several solutions are already in use.

AI might be a lethal weapon to free competition and for the very survival of a market composed by operators with different profiles. Robots that are capable of monitoring prices and even reaching agreements between them, vertical portals that annihilate competitors or the monopolistic control that certain operators have over businesses such as online advertising, are phenomena that must be understood by lawyers and will indeed generate work for many in the coming years. We will discuss this in depth in chapter 6 on AI and Competition Law, a chapter written by Julia Suderow and Bárbara Román.

The World Intellectual Property Organization (WIPO) and the national IP Offices are exploring the areas of activity in which AI can add value to industrial and IP. They include automatic classification of patents and trademark applications for goods and services; search for state-of-the-art patents and the figurative elements of trademarks; control of compliance with the requirements for the granting of trademarks and patents; technical assistance services (automatic responses to the client); automatic translation, linguistic and terminology tools and lastly, data analysis for economic research. On the other hand, there are discussions about authorship and AI. In chapter 7, Caroline Chetrit analyses the different issues that arise in relation to industrial and IP and AI.

None of the studies that have been carried out, which are far from few, doubt the important impact that robots will have on employment and point out to the need of seeking mechanisms to compensate for the consequences that the loss of these incomes will have for some countries. Less income, fewer taxes, translates into less capacity to maintain infrastructures, pay pensions or health expenses. Figures of all kinds are being considered, and some of them are utterly shocking. The reality is that it is impossible to know with certainty how many jobs will be lost, or the impact that this reduction in income can have on the tax collection of countries. What is clear, however, is that the use of AI will have an impact on state revenues and, consequently, it is necessary to reflect on what repercussions this reduction may have while considering alternatives to increase tax revenue. One of the solutions is for robots to pay taxes. Prominent figures, such as Bill Gates have supported this initiative in order to compensate for those jobs that will be destroyed by the incorporation of robots. Yet, detractors hold that only companies' profits should be taxed, and not the means to obtain them. The chapter on AI and taxation aims to address this critical issue thoroughly. In summary, tax systems, as they have been articulated until now, might be obsolete for the challenges derived from AI. This and other relevant questions relating to taxation and AI are reviewed in chapter 5, written by María Jesús González-Espejo and Javier Martín.

On another note, one of the main ingredients of AI is data and, in many cases, data that belongs to private individuals. This is why the development and use of AI give rise to challenges related to privacy, and therefore, there are numerous bodies that are already working to deliver recommendations that mitigate the risks related to privacy for those responsible for AI development. Specifically, it will be necessary to review the use of personal data in the training of algorithms, in the application of AI for decision-making and in the use of AI to extract other personal information from data sets that apparently do not contain personal data. Hence, we felt it was crucial to include a chapter on AI and personal data protection, and in chapter 10, Paloma Aparicio has analysed the main questions that arise relating to data protection and AI.

The three remaining chapters of the book, in turn, delve into three major themes: ethics and AI by Virginia Dignum (chapter 3); the responsibility of AI by Grzegorz J. Nalepa and Michał Araszkiewicz (chapter 8); and the relationship between cybersecurity and AI by Ignacio Arnaldo (chapter 9).

Finally, in chapter 11, María Jesús González-Espejo has analysed how AI is being used or could be used in the judicial field. She analyses key concepts as probability or prediction tools, legal open data, black box and bias through the description of several cases. She has also analysed the concept of robot judges.

AI has a peculiarity: since it is a technology that, in some cases, will take on human behaviour, it is vital that it also adheres to a series of ethical principles. This is currently being debated in the political and academic spheres, and interesting initiatives are being developed to publish guidelines and ethical principles for AI by public institutions, such as those of the European Parliament and the OECD, as well as private companies such as Alibaba, Amazon, Facebook, Google, Microsoft, and Telefónica.

In order to understand the state in AI, it becomes pressing to contemplate the principal element of the current debate: ethics. There is a discussion and reflection on the feasibility of having an ethic which should be imposed on AI for it to be 'good'. There are those who believe that an ethical code is a way, but there is a growing group of people who promote a legislative framework instead because they believe that there can be no ethics, given that ethics is something personal, not national or universal. Virginia Dignum explains in chapter 3 the differences between the so-called ethics by design, ethics in design and ethics for design, the three key perspectives when considering the diverse questions that arise when analysing ethics in relation to AI.

As we shall see, if harm were to result from the use of AI, someone would have to answer and be liable. Who should this be? Whoever provided the data? Who developed the algorithm, funded the development of the solution, marketed or distributed it, or who used it or applied the results? In the AI value chain, there are, as can be seen, a multitude of operators and ideally, each of them should have a clear view of their own liability.

In order to better understand responsibility and liability, it is necessary to think about the different roles that intelligent systems exercise. For example, a robot that produces works of art, literature, etc., has to be responsible for the originality of its productions, and not commit plagiarism. On the other hand, a robot helping to pilot an airplane will be responsible for guaranteeing the safety of passengers and a satisfactory journey. Another interesting example of AI liability is that arising from anti-competitive behaviour as a result of the possible fixing of an agreement by the robots whose task is to monitor the prices published by online platforms. Finally, another interesting example might be that of enforced liability of a citizen who is sentenced to a penalty based on a trained system fed with biased data, as has happened in some cases in the United States and the United Kingdom. There, it was found that the applications developed to support the judge in setting a sentence contained algorithms that had been fed with historical data that wronged citizens belonging to certain racial minority groups.

Conversely, cybersecurity has become a major challenge for governments and businesses. Chapter 8 will analyse the relationship between liability and AI.

Finally, fighting cybercrime requires having tools at one's disposal that can face complex challenges, and AI is probably the best-suited technology. It is also the technology that is increasingly used by cyber-criminals. In chapter 9, Ignacio Arnaldo delves into the topic of AI and Cybersecurity.

A USEFUL TECHNOLOGY FOR LEGAL SECTOR OPERATORS

The legal sector faces many challenges amongst which are internationalization; the need to embrace transparency, sustainability and to make the law more understandable and of better quality; the impact of technology; the pressure brought by clients on prices; the need to report and control efficiently; more demanding clients asking for immediate responses or the increasing complexity of regulations; the need to give a solution to an increasing amount of conflicts, many of them with an international component and related to issues with an innovative character. AI can certainly help to tackle many of them.

AI will have a profound impact on the way in which judges, lawyers and other jurists will do their jobs. It has the potential to perform many of the tasks that are now carried out, providing greater neutrality, efficiency, speed and security. AI-based tools will be for sure in no more than five years from now fundamental allies of legal professionals.

The application of AI in the legal sector is relatively recent and is already being used to help lawyers perform their work and manage their organizations adequately. However, AI technology is not of simple usage, and it requires a considerable investment in terms of time, work and money that are still far too high for most organizations. In fact, one of the risks that may arise from the development of this technology is that the existing gap between large and small businesses/firms will further increase. At present, only a handful of businesses have the financial capacity and access other necessary resources to develop certain types of AI-based applications, which, in turn, allow their owners to obtain a competitive advantage that is virtually impossible to achieve by those who do not have the means.

Through the media, we know that some of the biggest law firms are developing and/or testing AI-based solutions. However, aside from this particular category of firms, there are virtually no other examples. Therefore, it could be concluded that AI-based technologies are not at this point in time in a mature state, and their price is inaccessible for small- and even medium-sized legal organizations. In other words, to date, we can state that AI is a subject limited to large organizations or those with significant financial resources and staff.

Another challenge derives from the languages for which AI is being developed. Those tools based on natural language generally respond when they are the result of private initiatives to one or more languages, normally those for which there is potential business. This may eventually imply that languages such as English, Chinese or Spanish, the most broadly spoken, would probably enjoy a wider assortment of AI natural language-based tools than other languages. If this is so, in the long term, this could cause a technological gap between these two groups of communities: the ones with a widely spoken language and those with minority languages.

In any case, for the sake of truly understanding the usefulness of this technology, it is best to analyse significant use cases, among which there are some very interesting ones today.

– Analytical Tools

The tools in this category stand out for their data analysis and conclusion extraction functionality. Legal professionals frequently have to analyse large amounts of information. This occurs, for instance, in the processes of buying and selling companies in the so-called Due Diligence or in highly complex legal proceedings. It has already been proven[6] that AI is capable of performing this task much faster and more efficiently than any professional.

6. LawGeex has carried out an experiment with the universities of Standford, Duke Law and Southern California, in which twenty American lawyers competed against an AI tool. Their task

Another tool with a similar purpose is one designed to appraise if a Non-Disclosure Agreement is legally correct or needs some improvements. The application is used by the law firm that invested in its deployment, which uses it as a marketing tool to target clients more effectively by offering its advisory services in those cases where the output of the ML tool recommends the reviewing of a clause.[7]

Analytics is equally important for the management of the organizations in the legal sector: law firms, professional associations, etc. The massive handling of data, also called Big Data, which can be done through AI, can assist in the improvement of financial management, accounting, sales, people or knowledge management.

– Tools for Result Prediction and Improved Strategy Determination

This category of tools includes those that, based on data extracted from sources such as legal judgments, allow the user to identify an appropriate strategy. This same category is possibly the one with the most operational and tested products. Apart from the diverse applications developed by the great publishing houses of the sector, it is interesting to mention here one of the first cases of use that entered the world of public opinion: the tool that, based on natural language processing techniques, is capable of predicting whether or not a case will prosper in the European Court of Human Rights.[8] The authors based their research solely on textual content. They formulated a binary classification task where the input of the classifiers was the textual content extracted from a case, and the target output was the judgment as to whether there has been a violation of an article. The accuracy of their model was impressive; the court's decisions could be predicted with 79% accuracy on average. They discovered as well that formal facts of a case are the most important predictive factor and that the topical content of a case is another important feature in this classification task.

In the field of IP, AI is being used by professionals that want to file applications with more certainty that they will be accepted by the examiner. There are solutions that help to appraise the viability of a patent application, building its results on the previous decisions made by the examiner to whom the application has been assigned. It has also been proven particularly useful as a tool that helps the examiners themselves in the time-intensive but critical task of searching prior learning to determine whether, at the time of patent filing, the invention claimed was novel and non-obvious.[9] And last but not least, it is also a technology that offers interesting business opportunities to those

consisted of identifying in four hours, a series of errors in five Non-Disclosure agreements (which had more than 3,000 clauses and 152 paragraphs). The result was that whilst lawyers identified 85% of the mistakes, the AI system identified 94%. Additionally, whilst the fastest lawyer revised all contracts in 51 minutes, the rest needed an hour and a half; the AI just took 26 minutes. Access information here: https://www.lawgeex.com/resources/AIvsLawyer/.

7. NDA LYNN (https://www.ndalynn.com/), built with BIG ML technology.
8. Aletras N, Tsarapatsanis D, Preoţiuc-Pietro D, Lampos V. 2016. Predicting judicial decisions of the European Court of Human Rights: a Natural Language Processing perspective. *PeerJ Computer Science* 2: e93 https://doi.org/10.7717/peerj-cs.93.
9. *Arti K. Rai*, Machine Learning at the Patent Office: Lessons for Patents and Administrative Law, Iowa Law Review, 2019, https://ilr.law.uiowa.edu/print/volume-104-issue-5/machine-learning-at-the-patent-office-lessons-for-patents-and-administrative-law/.

who advise and file patents, since as stated already, large amounts of investment are being put into AI developments that logically end up applying for IP protection.[10]

- Information Classification Tools

This group of tools includes those that assist in the classification of all types of legal documents (contracts, judgments, rules, etc.) through the use of NLP techniques. Classification with this type of technology is faster and more accurate.

- Tools for Organisational Improvement

This type of tools analyses past data and identifies guidelines in them in order to define the best possible strategy for the future. In countries like Colombia or Spain, authorities in charge of security are already using this kind of tools to better organize police presence and provide a better service to citizens, preventing the commission of crimes.

- Monitoring Tools

Through public information, like that provided by Google, alerts can be created in order to detect topics of interest that have changed, such as a rule, a law or a resource, which might be relevant for a specific case. An interesting example of this kind of AI tools is the one developed by the Spanish Ministry of Internal Affairs to detect hate speech on social networks.[11] *HaterNet*, as an intelligent system currently being used by the Spanish National Office Against Hate Crimes of the Spanish State Secretariat for Security that identifies and monitors the evolution of hate speech on Twitter. The tool introduces an intelligent system that monitors and visualizes, using social network analysis techniques, hate speech in Social Media. It has been trained with a public dataset on hate speech in Spanish consisting of 6000 expert-labelled tweets.

- Customer/Citizen/Professional Service Tools

This group is composed of the so-called chatbots, a technology which is based on NLP and allows users to get answers to the questions they pose. There are many tools for developing chatbots for the most popular online platforms; a well-known example in the legal sector is Ross,[12] a technological solution created at the University of Toronto back in 2014, which is able to help a lawyer find an answer to their question in a matter of seconds using NLP. This category of tools is being increasingly applied to offer information to citizens in public services, such as tax agencies and other governmental services.

In conclusion, AI foreshadows a source of new opportunities for lawyers: for lawyers who specialize in counselling, for those who develop tools of this kind, for

10. https://www.wipo.int/tech_trends/en/artificial_intelligence/story.html, last accessed 17 Dec. 2019.
11. Pereira-Kohatsu, Carlos; Quijano-Sánchez, Lara, Liberatore, Federico; and Camacho Collados, Miguel in *Detecting and Monitoring hate speech in Twitter.* https://www.mdpi.com/1424-8220/19/21/4654, last accessed 17 Dec. 2019.
12. https://rossintelligence.com/.

those who use them, and for those who, somehow, are damaged from their use. AI will demand experts in charge of developing, interpreting and applying specific regulatory standards. It will also require experts in defence of fundamental rights, as it has already been mentioned, for violations as a result of AI's misuse.

THE FUTURE OF AI IN THE LEGAL SECTOR

The vast majority of the tools being developed as of today are essentially based on ML technology and are useful for analytical and information extraction in order to save time and effort or to improve decision-making. Our diagnosis for this type of applications is in line with that of experts like Marchant:[13] its use is becoming democratized thanks to cost-reduction, training and increased availability and quality improvement of relevant data for the legal sector and jurists' deeper awareness on the role of data and need to control it and the improvement of systems. Another key factor for its implementation will be the decision taken by governments to use it for different purposes, such as a more participative and transparent legislative development, which will result in regulations of better quality, crime prevention, trends detection or the direct supply of all types of information to citizens.

On the other hand, tools based on language analysis also have great potential. The analysis of what is being said on social media or other kinds of textual content and their classification are fields where AI may add significant value to legal professionals. The development of NLP has a great potential to help in bringing legal language closer to the real needs of clients, citizens or consumers.

Additionally, AI will play an essential role in matters where it is necessary to prevent risks such as compliance or data protection. The combination of big data with this type of technology will give rise to programs that will automate the tasks of supervision, surveillance and risk control There is the possibility of an authentic Robot Compliance Officer and Robot DPO, despite what Aguilera Gordillo[14] contends: 'The use of big data or AI lacks a logical and direct link with Criminal Law, which can generate inconveniences when considering it from a technical-legal perspective or when using it to base or explain the legal basis of the attribution of responsibilities.'

Finally, although surely the companies dedicated to robotics (design, construction, operation and use of robots, as well as computer systems for their control, sensory feedback and information processing) have a preference to bring into life automatons of nurses, doctors, social workers, psychologists and other highly demanded profiles, maybe one day they will also decide to create the perfect robot-lawyer, empathetic, patient, sympathetic, wise, adherent to deadlines, committed, punctual in information delivery, honest in terms of fees, a communicator capable of choosing the right registry

13. Marchant, gary e., Artificial intelligence and the future of legal practice, https://www.americanbar.org/content/dam/aba/administrative/litigation/materials/2017-2018/2018-sac/written-materials/artificial-intelligence-and-the-future.authcheckdam.pdf, last accessed 17 Dec. 2019.
14. Aguilera Gordillo, Rafael, *Compliance penal. Régimen jurídico y fundamentación analítica de la responsabilidad penal de la persona jurídica y el compliance program.* https://helvia.uco.es/xmlui/handle/10396/16714, last accessed 17 Dec. 2019.

so that the client understands them, exactly that lawyer that we all aspire to have at our disposal.

CONCLUSIONS

AI is one of the technologies that will have the greatest impact on the future of the legal profession and the life of each individual and society as a whole. Hence, the opportunity of this book, which we have attempted to structure in such a way that the reader can readily grasp the key aspects of this technology and what differentiates it from others, the advantages and disadvantages of its use, the risks arising from its misuse and the relationship of AI with the legal disciplines of competition Law, Tax Law, Labour Law, Privacy Law, Intellectual and Industrial Property Law) and other aspects that affect the use of AI by legal specialists in the exercise of their professions, such as ethics, cybersecurity and liability. We have seen that the legal framework of AI still requires the development and that we are dealing with a business sector that is going to need the support of experts in Law, in other words, an area of specialization that offers opportunities to the lawyer who decides to explore this area.

In addition, we have reviewed the different categories of tools through the analysis of several interesting use cases. But there is still great potential for those who wish to develop tools based on this technology. Whoever chooses to order custom developments will have to identify the tasks that can be automated: locating the data sets, designing the processes to which they will be subjected and what results they want to obtain. And all this, of course, can only be done by lawyers with the support of AI specialists.

We hope that after reading this book, your view on AI is more accurate, and we are quite sure that this is a field of great potential. We invite you to reflect and express your views on the future of AI in the legal profession, which still needs to be defined. We jurists have a special responsibility in helping AI to mean a better future for mankind.

María Jesús González-Espejo and Juan Pavón
Madrid, March 2020

List of Abbreviations

3D	3 Dimensions
4IR	4th Industrial Revolution
AI	Artificial Intelligence
AIaaS	Artificial Intelligence as a Service
AGI	Artificial General Intelligence
AIS	Autonomous Intelligent Systems
ANN	Artificial Neural Network
AVIVA	Asistente Virtual de IVA
CI	Computational Intelligence
CEPEJ	European Commission for the Efficiency of Justice
DFKI	Deutsches Forschungszentrum für Künstliche Intelligenz (German Research Centre for Artificial Intelligence)
DL	Deep Learning
DoD	Department of Defense
EAD	Ethically Aligned Design
EU	European Union
GDPR	General Data Protection Regulation
GPS	General Problem Solver
HLEG	High-Level Expert Group (on Artificial Intelligence)
JAIC	Joint AI Center
KBS	Knowledge-based system
KMS	Knowledge Management System
IoT	Internet of Things
IP	Intellectual Property
IPR	Intellectual Property Rights
IS	Intelligent System (or AI system)

MCNL	Minimal content of natural law
ML	Machine Learning
OECD	Organization for Economic Co-operation and Development
OCR	Optical Character Recognition
PSA	Public Safety Assessment
Q&A	Question and answer
R&D	Research and development
US	United States
VAT	Value-added tax
WIPO	World Intellectual Property Organization
XAI	Explainable Artificial Intelligence

Acknowledgements

To Gwen de Vries for allowing us to water the plant of AI in a desert.

To Chris Sykes for helping us to adapt the book to the standards of Shakespeare.

And to our families for supporting our dreams one more time.

María Jesús González-Espejo and Juan Pavón

CHAPTER 1
Fundamentals of Artificial Intelligence

Juan Pavón & María Jesús González-Espejo

§1.01 A BRIEF HISTORY OF AI

Many common devices around us today make use of Artificial Intelligence (AI). Your smartphone is probably your closest companion. It allows you to find almost any kind of information by using text, voice, or images. It can help you to identify a song by tune or look for a nearby restaurant that fits your tastes. It also allows you to take a picture of a text in a foreign language and obtain the translation in real-time. It converts you into an almost professional photographer thanks to the automatic adjustments that happen without you even noticing. Your phone unlocks by just recognizing your face, and this same form of access allows you to access your banking app and make payments. A fingerprint may also serve to identify you. Data of all kinds are collected from our daily activity, being stored and processed on the cloud to build accurate profiles for each of us. All these AI applications are now part of our daily lives in a way that we are not yet able to understand, and yet we cannot comprehend the consequences.

AI has been discussed since the early days of digital computing. In 1950, Alan Turing published 'Computing machinery and intelligence'[1] where he discussed whether a machine can 'think'. In order to explore this question, he proposed what he called the 'Imitation game' (best known now as the 'Turing test'). In this game, a person who is in a separate room asks questions to players X and Y; one of them is human and the other a machine. The questioner poses questions one at a time to X and Y, and they respond with typed answers. The questioner has to determine which one, either X or Y, is a computer and which is a human being. At that time, it was not possible for a machine to pass as a human, but Turing guessed that one day this could

1. Alan M. Turing, *Computing machinery and intelligence*, LIX Mind 433–460 (1950).

be achieved by creating a 'child machine' that could *learn* and finally *compete with humans in all purely intellectual fields*. Different variations of the Turing test have been produced to see whether a program can show human-like behaviour. An example of this is the Computer Game Bot,[2] where judges have to determine in a shooter video game, which players are artificial bots and which are humans. Another Turing test is the CAPTCHA (which stands for *Completely Automated Public Turing test to tell Computers and Humans Apart*). Since 1990, a standard Turing test competition has been held, the Loebner Prize, where judges determine whether an AI program behaves like a real human. It includes deciphering and understanding text, visual, and auditory input. So far no one has won the maximum prize of USD 100,000.

In 1956, only a few years later, John McCarthy organized a summer workshop at Dartmouth College, where various researchers on *thinking machines* met for several weeks and defined the term *Artificial Intelligence*. This new field generated great expectations, and they predicted that it would be possible to create a machine as intelligent as a human being before the end of the century. Shortly after, they began to receive generous funding for this purpose. In the following years, some advances were made, mainly based on what is known as *symbolic reasoning*. The idea is that if a machine can manipulate numbers, it can also manipulate symbols, which could well be considered the essence of human thought. They created programs such as the *General Problem Solver* (GPS),[3] an application capable of finding a solution to a problem that could be specified as a set of well-formed formulas that describe an initial situation, a goal to accomplish, and the means used (operators that can be used to change the state of the system). GPS has been illustrated with some classical case studies in AI such as the *blocks world* (how to move a certain configuration of stacks of blocks to another configuration by using a set of permitted operations) or the *driving to school problem* (how to plan a set of actions to take a child to school in an automobile, taking into account circumstances such as the vehicle breaking down and needing repair). Other reasoning systems were developed to solve problems of algebra or geometry or to plan the actions of a robot to run through a maze avoiding obstacles.

There were also some attempts to make programs with the ability to process natural language, such as the famous *Eliza*,[4] a parody of a psychotherapist built to

---

2. *Computer Game Bot Turing Test*. There are a couple of bots that have passed the Turing test in this context as they were considered even more human than other human players. One of them was basically mimicking opponent reactions, so its success is relative as it was borrowing the human-like nature of other players.
3. Newell Allen, John Shaw & Herbert A. Simon, *Report on a general problem solving program*, in IFIP congress 256–64 (1959).
4. Joseph Weizenbaum, ELIZA – a Computer Program for the Study of Natural Language Communication Between Man and Machine, 9 Communications of ACM, 36–45 (1966).

   An example of conversation with an Eliza chatbot:

   Eliza: I am the psychotherapist. Please, describe your problems.
   User: I am scared of flying.
   Eliza: Why do you say you are scared of flying?
   User: Because I have anxiety attacks when I need to travel by plane.
   Eliza: Is it because you have anxiety attacks when you need to travel by plane that you came to me?

maintain a coherent text conversation with a user. This program was not able to pass the Turing test, but it got a lot of attention and can certainly be considered the precursor of *chatbots*.[5]

Although they represented an advance from an academic point of view, these projects failed when addressing most real-world problems, partly because of the limitations of the hardware and software available at that time, but mainly due to the complexity of the required computation. For instance, GPS and similar searching programs suffered very quickly from a combinatorial explosion, which means that there are so many paths to explore that it becomes unfeasible or too difficult to obtain a solution (a typical case of the combinatorial explosion is a chess program, where the number of combinations of moves is huge). Furthermore, many of the applications quickly required such a vast amount of data (imagine, for instance, a robot trying to identify all of the different objects that can be found when moving around a house or an office) that it was not feasible to gather, store and process it all. Therefore, in the mid-seventies, the initial enthusiasm of investors soured. Research diminished, and an 'AI winter' set in.

Even so, there were some new achievements. *Prolog*,[6] a logic programming language that has been quite popular in the AI community, especially in Europe, was launched in the 1970s. Prolog represented a new programming paradigm. Instead of specifying a set of steps showing what the computer should do (imperative programming), the program is defined as a set of facts and rules that describe a problem domain. The program is able to answer a query (a statement with values to be determined) by finding some values of the parameters in the query that make it possible to build a proof of it (this process is called *resolution*). Prolog is applied to different purposes such as theorem proving, natural language processing, expert systems, querying in databases, or planning.

In the 1980s, Japan developed an ambitious programme, the *Fifth Generation Computer (FGC)*,[7] which reactivated research in AI. Its aim was to create a system that could perform many tasks by reasoning like humans. They created a variant of Prolog called *Kernel Language* that was able to run on parallel computers and was, therefore, expected to offer better performance. However, their efforts to build expensive, highly parallel computer hardware were soon surpassed by commercially available machines and distributed computing. In addition, the concurrent logic programming approach ran into some limitations that were not satisfactorily solved.

User: Yes, I need help because the fear does not allow me to enjoy the journey.
Eliza: Does it bother you that the fear does not allow you to enjoy the journey?
...
User: Bye
Eliza: My secretary will send you a bill.

5. A chatbot, also known as conversational bot or chatterbot, intends to facilitate interaction with an assistance service by means of a text or audio conversation with the user.
6. Alain Colmerauer & Philippe Roussel, *The birth of Prolog*, *in* History of Programming languages – II 331–367 (1996).
7. The first generation of computers were made with vacuum tubes, the second with transistors, the third with integrated circuits, and the fourth with Very Large Scale Integrated (VLSI) circuits. That is the reason why the program was called FGC.

This revival of AI had anyway a positive impact on the development of *Expert Systems*, which were adopted by many companies, as they finally found potential for AI application. Expert systems are programs that can manage knowledge in a specific domain, such as answering questions or finding solutions to problems from that domain. Being specific to a domain, they can cope with some of the problems of general approaches such as the GPS and, consequently, have become useful applications for the real world. The idea was introduced by Edward Feigenbaum in the mid-1960s, with early developments such as Dendral,[8] to identify organic molecules, Mycin,[9] to identify bacteria causing severe infections, and PROSPECTOR[10] for mineral exploration (this was quite complex with more than one thousand rules and a semantic network to describe the knowledge). In the 1980s, expert systems favoured the development of an AI industry with relative success for many applications such as diagnosis of system malfunctions, risk assessment, action planning for autonomous vehicles, real-time process control, space shuttle mission control, medical diagnosis, etc.

Expert systems, however, faced some issues. The first concern was how to acquire and represent the knowledge from human experts or other sources such as texts. This requires a systematic way to gather relevant knowledge and structure and represent it as facts and rules (or another mechanism for representation) in a knowledge base. Furthermore, the knowledge has to be verified (it has to satisfy certain desirable properties, such as completeness, consistency, correctness and redundancy) and validated (i.e., whether it is a good representation of reality)[11] in order to assess the credibility, objectivity and reliability of the expert system. Another issue is the lack of modularity of the techniques for implementing them, which is usually a problem of declarative programming languages such as LISP (LISt Processor)[12] and Prolog, although this has been solved in other programming paradigms. This made expert systems difficult to maintain and update and finally, only in very specific cases are they usable. Again, by the end of the decade, there was a certain disappointment regarding AI, and financial setbacks returned. A great number of AI start-ups shut down or were acquired by big companies. AI entered a new winter.

By then, the AI research community was already well established, and the discipline continued to evolve, this time sustained by relevant changes that paved the way to more reliable results. The most relevant was probably criticism of the dominant position of symbolic approaches. This came mainly from the fields of robotics (also part of AI, but usually more focused on issues such as vision, motion and control) and

8. Robert K. Lindsay et al., *Dendral: A case study of the first expert system for scientific hypothesis formation*, 61 Artificial Intelligence 209–261 (1993).
9. Randall Davis, Bruce Buchanan & Edward Shortliffe, *Production rules as a representation for a knowledge-based consultation program*, 8 Artificial Intelligence 15–45 (1977).
10. P. E. Hart, R. O. Duda & M. T. Einaudi, *Prospector – A computer-based consultation system for mineral exploration*, 10 Mathematical Geology 589–610 (1978).
11. 1. Robert M. O'Keefe & Daniel E. O'Leary, *Expert system verification and validation: a survey and tutorial*, 7 Artif Intell Rev 3–42 (1993).
12. LISP is another programming language, where the main data structure and source code are expressed as lists. It was originally developed by John McCarthy at the Massachusetts Institute of Technology (MIT) in 1958. It has been widely used for the development of many AI programs and some of its variants are still in use.

cybernetics (control and communication). These were more concerned with the understanding of how the physical systems work and interact and not so much with abstract reasoning. In the words of the robotics researcher, Rodney Brooks,[13] symbols are not always necessary since 'the world is its own best model. It is always exactly up to date. It always has every detail there is to be known. The trick is to sense it appropriately and often enough.' This highlights the relevance of the environment and the context in the design of intelligent systems, as well as the importance of sensors and interactions with the environment.

There were also advances in distributed computing and software engineering that led to *software componentization*. This means that software systems have become more modular. They are made of components with specific functionality that can interact and be replaced. This facilitates updating and evolution and supports the construction of more complex and scalable systems by integrating and replacing different parts. In this sense, it is possible to build very specialized AI components that can be integrated into larger systems. This also makes AI somehow *invisible*, as users manipulate devices or applications without being very conscious of what their components are (for instance, when you use your smartphone apps, you know how to use them, but you do not have any idea of what processes are running inside, and which make use of AI or not).

In the 1990s, the combination of these factors led to a new way of designing intelligent systems that was known as *Multi-Agents Systems* (MAS). AI is no longer a monolithic system (as it is usually shown in many science fiction movies) but a distributed one, made of several specialized agents that communicate with each other. Each agent is aware of its environment and can react to a stimulus from it while pursuing specific goals. Agents can collaborate to achieve common goals, like a team, or compete with each other, like in financial markets. Modelling relationships among agents have required inclusion in AI of new theories based on sociology and economy, or biological systems, and a revision of the concept of rationality. Examples of these agents are robots, artificial trading agents, personal assistants such as Cortana, Siri and Alexa, autonomous vehicles, etc.

In the meantime, because 'Artificial intelligence' and 'Expert Systems' were not good terms to attract funding, advances in the field were sold with other names, as technical solutions to specific problems: planning, scheduling, knowledge management (KM), pattern recognition, etc. This proliferation contributed to greater diversification in the field. At the same time, improvements made to computer hardware facilitated the progressive application of intensive mathematical models, with a special relevance of probability and decision theory methods such as Bayesian networks, stochastic modelling, classical optimization, and others such as genetic algorithms and neural networks. They are the basis for a myriad of applications such as automatic translation, voice recognition, recommender systems, colouring black and white movies, autonomous vehicles, text generation, medical diagnosis, game bots, vacuum cleaners, ambient intelligence, robotics, intelligent manufacturing, etc.

13. Rodney A. Brooks, *Elephants don't play chess*, 6 Robotics and Autonomous Systems 3–15 (1990).

Finally, the evolution of these methods and the availability of large amounts of data and processing power has paved the way to *machine learning* techniques that were hardly applicable before. The basic idea behind this is to feed a system with large amounts of data so that an algorithm, usually based on statistical methods, can derive (*learn*) patterns in the data. After identifying these patterns, it is possible to make a prediction or a decision. Examples of these patterns are the user profiles that large companies are building while we browse the web, so it is possible to predict which information should be presented to us.

One of these techniques is *deep learning* (DL). This is a kind of artificial neural network (ANN), whose first computational model was defined by McCulloch & Walter Pitts in 1948.[14] This was the basis for the *Perceptron algorithm* for pattern recognition, by Frank Rosenblatt,[15] which was also implemented as a machine (the *Mark I Perceptron machine*). This approach raised great controversy and was fiercely attacked by some of the mainstream researchers of symbolic AI (this history is a classic example of how official views in a discipline displace those approaches that deviate from dogma[16]). Apart from this, the approach failed mainly because the technology at that time only allowed simple networks and very little data. Today, however, with the availability of huge quantities of data and computing power, this is the dominant paradigm in AI (much more than symbolic reasoning approaches). It has once again sparked interest in the field and is now considered by many as a new revolution in the evolution of humankind.

§1.02 WHAT IS ARTIFICIAL INTELLIGENCE?

The term 'artificial' intelligence implies a distinction from 'natural' intelligence that involving human beings as it is performed by machines. Computers can perform calculations much more quickly and precisely than human beings, but some tasks that are very simple for us humans, such as recognizing a face, understanding a joke or walking on two legs, are way too difficult to be performed by machines. Although there have been relevant advances in the past decade, machines are still far from being able to perform all the tasks that we are able to do. AI has evolved to create machines that can beat the world champion of the games of Chess and Go, but they are not able to do all the other tasks that humans do at the same time on a daily basis.[17] This means that AI can be successful for very specialized goals, but not for all of them at the same time.

14. Warren S. McCulloch & Walter Pitts, *A logical calculus of the ideas immanent in nervous activity*, 5 Bulletin of Mathematical Biophysics 115–133 (1943).
15. Frank Rosenblatt, *The Perceptron – a perceiving and recognizing automaton*. Report 85-460-1, Cornell Aeronautical Laboratory (1957).
16. There is an interesting analysis of this concrete case in: Mikel Olazaran, *A Sociological Study of the Official History of the Perceptrons Controversy*, 26 Social Studies of Science 611–659 (1996).
17. This is known as the *Moravec's paradox*, which can be summarized with this sentence: 'it is comparatively easy to make computers exhibit adult level performance in intelligence tests or playing checkers, and difficult or impossible to give them the skills of a one-year-old when it comes to perception and mobility', in: Hans Moravec, Mind Children, Harvard University Press (1988).

The ability to deal with the real world as human beings do is called Artificial General Intelligence (AGI). We will discuss this later.

There is no clear definition of AI, as the discipline has evolved over time. As we have seen, between the 1990s and 2000s, the term had no good commercial connotations. Nevertheless, the situation changed subtly with the introduction of *smart* things: smartphones, smart cities, smart buildings, smart cars, smart everything. When the term *smart* finally became worn out from overuse, we saw the revival of the term *intelligence*.

One way to find out what AI is lies in comparing it with traditional software. Imagine that you are typing a text with a word processor. When you do this, you first have to command the program to create a new file, then you can start typing the text, and if you want to highlight some words, you again have to command the program to do it, etc. This is how traditional software works by obeying the user's orders. When you browse the web looking for an article, you click on a link to see whether it is interesting; if not, you try another and so on. In this process, you always make the decision to click and look at other pages. An intelligent program makes this kind of decisions for you. It is able to analyse the contents of the pages for you and, after becoming familiar with your profile (your tastes and means) and your current needs, it can directly provide you with the page containing the article you need. This is probably one of the main differences between traditional software and AI software: who decides. Making decisions involves the ability to *reason*, and because AI software makes decisions, it can fail. Therefore, an AI program has to cope not only with success in the completion of actions but also with failure. In order to improve performance, AI programs *learn* from failures and successes. Consequently, we can conclude that reasoning and learning are distinctive features of AI.

In this sense, AI tries to emulate certain human abilities that go beyond the processing of repetitive tasks (e.g., calculations). This usually involves the ability to recognize patterns that describe objects, situations, etc. and how to find the actions towards a *goal* (which can be described as a desired pattern). Pattern recognition is, therefore, a fundamental task of AI, and this can be applied to different purposes such as images, sound, speech, video, text, data mining, physical signals, etc. Recent advances with machine learning (ML) techniques for pattern recognition are largely responsible for the current expectations generated by AI.

In the long term, AI intends to provide computers with more advanced capabilities, such as creativity and social intelligence. Nevertheless, although it is possible to make a machine perform well in one aspect, AI is still very far from emulating the ability of human beings to move around the world, interact in many different ways with different kinds of objects and animals, define new goals, and ask themselves about the meaning of life. In this sense, we usually differentiate between *weak AI* and *strong AI*. We refer to weak AI as the ability to solve specific problems, usually better than humans do. Strong AI, also known as *Artificial General Intelligence* (AGI), means that AI is able to accomplish any goal at least as well as humans do. Most of the advances in different areas of AI have once again sparked the discussion on whether, and when, AGI could be achieved. There are several opinions about whether this will happen and whether or not it is good for humanity, and the possibility to arrive at the next step of evolution, *Life 3.0.*[18]

§1.03 AI METHODS AND TECHNIQUES

There is a great diversity of AI methods and techniques. The classical text of the discipline, by Russell and Norvig,[19] has more than one thousand pages that provide a detailed description of the most relevant. In this section, we provide a quick review of some that we consider illustrative of the present state of the art.

As we have seen in the historical review, there are mainly two basic approaches for AI:

(1) *Knowledge-based AI,* which tries to work with an explicit symbolic representation of knowledge. They acquire knowledge from experts or documents and represent this in some explicit and formal way (ontologies, knowledge-based, conceptual models), which can be processed by an algorithm to reason and infer solutions to problems or queries in a domain of expertise. A typical example is a rule-based expert system.

(2) *Data-driven AI,* most commonly known as *machine learning*, focuses on learning from examples or experience using the system. Observed data represent incomplete information about phenomena, and learning algorithms try to generalize this information in order to make predictions on the phenomena. There is no explicit representation of knowledge. These systems have only become feasible very recently because they require huge amounts of data and computing resources to be effective. The advent of big data is, therefore, very closely related to ML development.

Each approach has its own advantages. ML is quite appropriate in tasks that require identification of patterns, such as perception (vision, speech recognition, robotics, spam filtering, etc.) Knowledge-based AI is still useful for tasks in specific domains where knowledge and reasoning can be well systematized, such as expert problem-solving. The combination of both approaches can be achieved by building systems made of different components by designing intelligent systems as *multi-agent systems*.

18. Max Tegmark, *Life 3.0 Being Human in the Age of Artificial Intelligence* (2018).
19. Stuart J. Russell & Peter Norvig, Artificial Intelligence: A Modern Approach. Third Edition (2016).

[A] Multi-agent Systems (MAS)

A multi-agent system is a well-established model for developing intelligent systems. An *agent*[20] is a software entity that can interact with its environment (*see* Figure 1). Agents receive events through sensors, when they are situated in a physical environment (e.g., a robot), or messages from other entities, which can be other agents. If the environment is the web, they have access to online resources (e.g., web services). Therefore, agents receive inputs from their environment, and they can filter them to consider whether to ignore them or to process them. As a result, agents act on the environment in different ways, such as moving around, using objects, or sending messages to other entities. Some examples of agents are those that trade in stock markets, autonomous vehicles, a team of robots playing soccer in the RoboCup competition, bots in computer games, etc.

Figure 1.1 An Agent as an Entity That Interacts With Its Environment

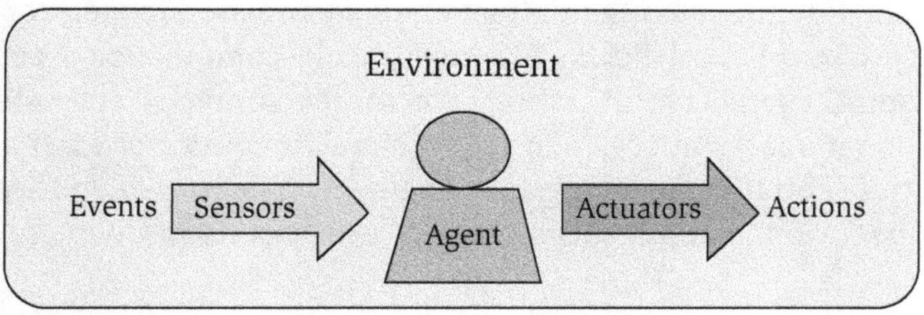

Agents do not need to be commanded by human beings at all times. They are given a goal and decide how to accomplish it, taking into account what they find in the surrounding environment. In this sense, their principal characteristic is that they are *autonomous* entities, so they have the ability to decide what to do. Autonomy is a fundamental property that distinguishes agents from conventional software. Agents follow the *principle of rationality*, as specified by Newell:[21] *If an agent has knowledge that one of its actions will lead to one of its goals, then the agent will select that action.* Note that agents make decisions that they consider right, although they may be wrong. In fact, the rationality of the agents is limited.[22] First, because agents cannot have a complete view of the state of the environment, as this is too complex, and the perception of the agent does not cover all elements and dimensions of said environment. Even if the agent had a complete model of the situation of the environment at a

20. There are many definitions of an agent and the term is usually preceded with some qualification such as artificial, software, autonomous, intelligent, rational, cognitive, etc. Here, we prefer to review some of the main features that identify them, as there are many variations and possible characterizations.
21. Allen Newell, *The knowledge level*, 18 Artificial Intelligence 87–127 (1982).
22. This is what the economist Herbert Simon has defined as bounded rationality: Herbert A. Simon, Models of Man, Social and Rational: Mathematical Essays on Rational Human Behavior in a Social Setting, 59 Journal of Philosophy 177–182 (1962).

given instant, the environment can change in the time needed to process the information. The agent is, therefore, always acting in an *uncertain environment* and can only *try* to perform a correct action, but this is not guaranteed. A rational agent *reasons* about what is the right action, but it will also need to *learn* about which actions work well, and which do not. Learning is then another desirable property for agents, so they can progressively adapt to changes in dynamic environments. An example might be an artificial real estate agent, which will not wait for users to connect to the website but will actively look for sites to place adverts, try to publish them or look for potential customers. This does not guarantee its success, but its actions are an attempt to achieve its goal. In the process, it can learn which customer profiles are more interesting to contact or which sites are better for advertising purposes.

Agents are not alone, and they can collaborate or compete with others in the environment. Collaboration towards the achievement of a common goal benefits from the organization of the multi-agent system, which can follow different strategies such as hierarchies, holarchies, coalitions, teams, congregations, societies, federations, markets, and matrix organizations.[23] Interaction among agents is the cause of emergent behaviours. This has motivated the simulation of agent-based models for the study of complex systems in different fields. For instance, in computational economics, for modelling financial markets,[24] in ecology for the evolution of ecosystems[25] or the management of natural resources,[26] for crowd simulation in cases such as emergency evacuation,[27] transportation and traffic management,[28] etc. As we will see later in this book, agents' behaviour can affect competition as discussed in Chapter 6.

[B] Knowledge Management

Knowledge, information and *data* are concepts that are usually interchanged, as they are closely related, but it is important to understand their difference. *Data* means items that the system can acquire or perceive. For instance, a sensor can produce a series of numerical data such as *22.0, 22.3, 22.8, 21.4, etc. Information* requires the addition of semantics to the data, so it can be contextualized (*what, where, when, how many*), with relevance and purpose. In this example, the information interprets that the data corresponds to a temperature that is measured in degrees celsius at a specific location, and each temperature reading is provided at intervals of one minute. *Knowledge* is obtained by interpreting the information, through learning and experience, and implies

23. Bryan Horling & Victor Lesser, *A Survey of Multi-agent Organizational Paradigms*, 19 Knowl. Eng. Rev. 281–316 (2004).
24. Leigh Tesfatsion & Kenneth L. Judd, Handbook of Computational Economics: Agent-Based Computational Economics (2006).
25. F. Bousquet & C. Le Page, *Multi-agent simulations and ecosystem management: A review*, 176 Ecological Modelling, 2004, at 313–332.
26. A. López-Paredes & C. Hernández, Agent-based modelling in Natural Resource Management (2008).
27. Rafael Pax & Juan Pavón, *Agent architecture for crowd simulation in indoor environments*, 8 J Ambient Intell Human Comput 205–212 (2017).
28. Paul Davidsson et al., *An analysis of agent-based approaches to transport logistics*, 13 Transportation Research Part C: Emerging Technologies 255–271 (2005).

understanding, in order to be able to evaluate and learn new experiences and information. Knowledge is implemented in the form of routines, practices and norms. In the previous example, when the temperature increases above a certain threshold (e.g., 40°C), this is an indicator of system malfunction.

KM involves several tasks: Knowledge acquisition, knowledge representation, and finally, knowledge reasoning.

Knowledge can be represented either in a declarative way, by specifying objects, their properties and relationships, or in a procedural way, by specifying how to do something. An example of declarative knowledge lies in the assertions *Madrid is the capital of Spain*, and *the population of Madrid is 3.2 million inhabitants*. An algorithm to calculate the age of a person is an example of procedural knowledge. In an intelligent system, it is also important to distinguish among:

(a) *Normative knowledge*, which describes general knowledge within a domain, which can be expressed in a declarative way, for instance, as a set of rules such as:
   - IF situation THEN action.
   - IF premises THEN conclusion.

(b) *Factual knowledge*, which refers to the objects of the domain and their characteristics. This is declarative knowledge that is based on observations (i.e., data that is interpreted to have some meaning), or that is derived from reasoning.

(c) *Control knowledge*, which handles factual and normative knowledge in order to deduce new knowledge. This is used to control the deduction of new knowledge, to define strategies of how to organize the search for an objective and deal with exceptions and uncertainties. For instance, if normative knowledge is expressed as a set of rules, control knowledge specifies which of all amongst the possible rules is the best to apply, taking into account the facts in the knowledge base.

Figure 1.2 shows a typical structure of a knowledge management system (KMS). The system provides an interface for the acquisition of the knowledge from experts and has some extra functionality for knowledge engineers in order to be able to verify and validate knowledge supplied by the system. Knowledge is stored in a knowledge base. Users have another interface for querying the system and can include facts or observations.

The inference engine is a collection of algorithms for problem-solving. It implements a cycle of *recognition→action*: First, it determines which rules are applicable, taking into account the facts that describe the current situation. Then, it chooses one of the applicable rules and performs the action that it specifies. It re-evaluates the situation and repeats these steps until it attains the goal (or continues trying forever).

There are two basic mechanisms to *resolve* the rules, i.e., to decide which rules to apply to obtain a solution. One is *forward reasoning*, which takes the available data and uses inference rules to extract more data until the goal is achieved. This is used by *production rule systems* and expert systems. For instance, if it is raining (a fact), I take my umbrella (action), so I do not get wet (the goal). Another is *backward chaining*, which is the basis of Prolog, which starts from the goal and tries to find a demonstration for it. It is, therefore, used in automated theorem provers, inference engines and proof assistants. In this approach, we start from the goal (not to get wet) and *see* whether we take an umbrella (action) if it is raining (fact).

Figure 1.2 General Architecture of a Knowledge Management System

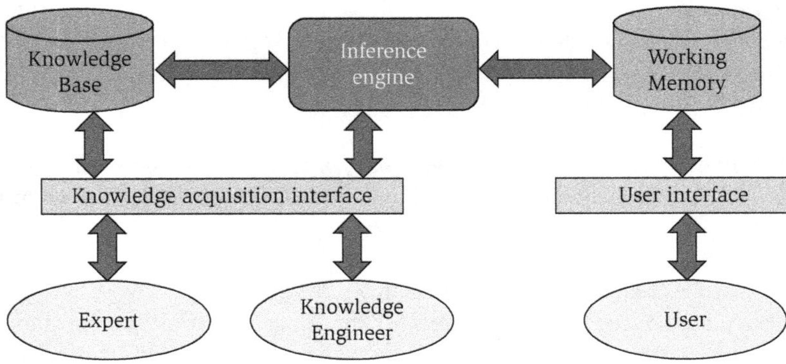

One advantage of this kind of systems is that knowledge can be represented in a way that is independent of a programming language, as a set of facts and rules. This should be more understandable by a human being because we are used to stating facts and applying rules when reasoning. The system can provide an answer of what to do in a certain situation and explain which rules have been applied to obtain the response. This is interesting as it provides a trace of the reasoning process, so it is possible to follow the motivation behind each step, the conditions that were considered, the applicable rules, and the result of the one selected at each step. There are some limitations, however. Essentially because it is not easy, in practice, to have a complete collection of rules, and because the process for pattern recognition (i.e., which rules are applicable at each step) is usually quite inefficient when the number of rules is large. Furthermore, it is difficult to verify the consistency of the knowledge base, i.e., whether there are rules and facts that are not consistent. There are some concrete domains of application where this approach has known to be successful: medical and fault diagnosis, scheduling, legal advice, etc.

[C] Machine Learning

The extensive use of probability and statistical methods has led to a new, more effective and flexible way to perform pattern recognition (i.e., the ability to classify and identify specific elements, shapes or examples in images, texts, sounds, etc.), where programs learn from the analysis of data sets.

Figure 1.3 shows the basic schema of a ML system. There are two main parts: a *learning process* by using data sets that are used as *training data*, and the *prediction process* where the system is used with data that is provided by a user of the system in order to obtain the results.

Figure 1.3 Simplified Process of a Machine Learning System

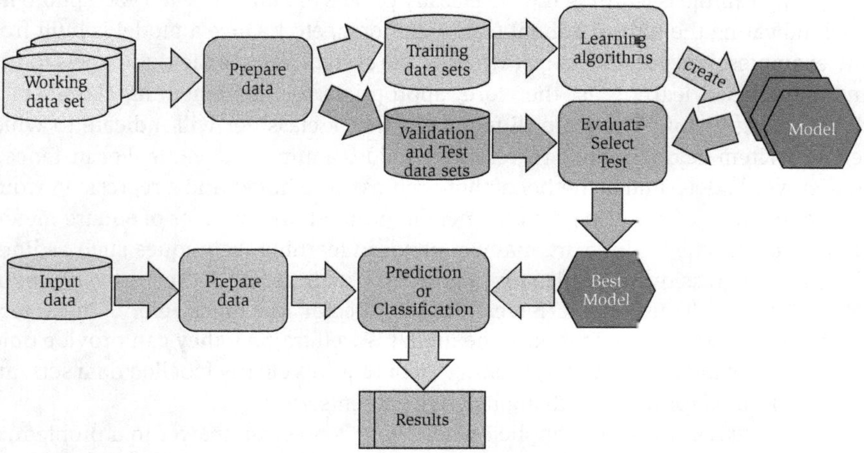

One of the most time-consuming tasks in this process is the acquisition and preparation of data sets.[29] They usually come from different sources, so they have to be integrated, cleaned, filtered and converted into a convenient format (normalized) to be processed by the available ML tools. Some working data sets are used for training the learning algorithms in order to create models. These models must be validated to ensure that they are doing the right pattern matching (*validation*) and that they have certain desirable properties such as coherence, consistency, etc. (*verification*). The best performing model is chosen for production (normally undergoing a prior test session with another data set). This model is finally used to make predictions or classifications based on new input data that users provide when querying the system.

ML normally uses a kind of *inductive reasoning*, which is different from the *deductive reasoning* that is most used in symbolic reasoning. Deductive reasoning infers facts from the general truth (some rules) and is usually supported by a logical system. The typical example is the rule – *All humans are mortal*. If *Socrates is a human*, then it can be deduced that *Socrates is mortal*. With inductive reasoning, the premises are just supplying some evidence for the truth of the conclusion. Therefore, inductive reasoning is not valid or invalid; it is just something *probable*, based on the evidence given. Inductive reasoning allows some general rule to be derived (the *model* in Figure 1.4) from evidence. An example of inductive reasoning is that if we consider that

29. This is confirmed by some studies, such as the survey that is reported in the 2016 Data Science Report by CrowdFlower (http://visit.crowdflower.com/rs/416-ZBE-142/images/CrowdFlower_DataScienceReport_2016.pdf), which indicates that 60% of the time data scientists employ is for cleaning and organizing data, 19% for collecting data sets, and 3% for building training data sets. Only around 15% is dedicated to mining data for patterns and refining algorithms.

Socrates is human and mortal, Plato is human and mortal, and *Aristotle is human and mortal*; then *Probably all humans are mortal.*

Several techniques are used to implement inductive learning, and these are normally categorized as *supervised* or *unsupervised* learning.

Supervised learning implies that training is carried out with a labelled data set. The typical example is learning how to classify photos of animals when each photo has a label indicating the type of animal (cat, dog, horse, etc.). Once a model is built from many examples, it is possible to test whether the system assigns the right labels to new items. Supervised learning is, therefore, appropriate for implementing classifiers as well as for regression. The main difference is that a classifier will indicate to which category an item belongs, while regression provides a numerical value. For instance, a classifier would determine whether a photo represents a house and a regression would estimate the price of a house given the neighbourhood, the number of square meters, and other parameters. There are many supervised learning techniques such as linear and logistic regression, classification algorithms such as the K-Nearest Neighbours (k-NN), Decision Trees, Naive Bayes, Support Vector Machines, etc.[30] These techniques have the advantage that once the model is well trained, they can provide quick answers to new inputs. However, training them requires clearly labelled data sets, and it is difficult to adapt them to changing environments.

Unsupervised learning is applied when there is no clear answer to a problem, so it is not possible or difficult to label a training data set. The system should try to find a structure in the data by extracting and analysing useful features. In this case, the system learns by its own observation, and can more easily adapt to changing environments, although the solutions it finds are not always those desired. They are highly dependent on experience gained during the learning process. The best example in this category is Deep Learning *(DL)*.

There are different ways to structure data when using unsupervised learning. One of them is *clustering*, which consists of creating groups of similar data objects. Another is to *identify anomalous data*, for instance, to detect frauds or cyber-attacks. It is also very useful for recommender systems, by identifying associations or correlations, for instance, recommending a movie because other users with a similar profile have already given it a good mark.

DL is nowadays one of the most relevant techniques. It is based on ANNs. The basic element, an artificial neuron, which is depicted in Figure 1.4, can receive signals (inputs) and these are combined with a function, which takes into account a weight for each one. This function gives a value that triggers the neuron and produces output signals when it is above a specific threshold.

30. Many of these are described in quite a comprehensible way in: Badreesh Shetty, Supervised Machine Learning: Classification Towards Data Science (2018), https://towardsdatascience.com/supervised-machine-learning-classification-5e685fe18a6d (last visited 22 Mar. 2019).

Figure 1.4 An Artificial Neuron

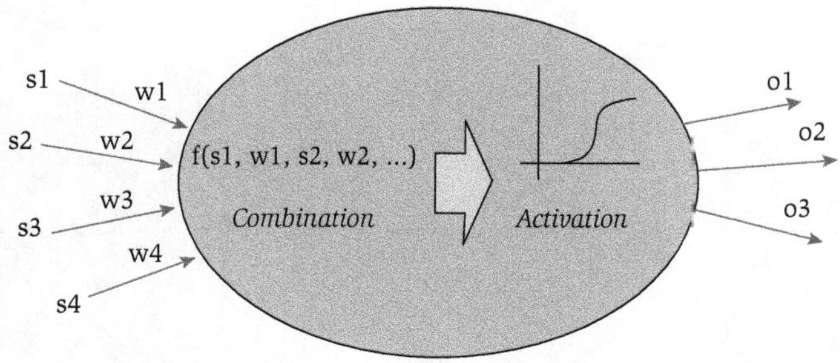

Artificial neurons can be connected in a network. This network is normally structured in several layers, where each layer takes care of a specific task. The data of the problem are the input signals of the first layer of artificial neurons (e.g., a picture), and the last layer provides the solution to the problem (e.g., whether there is a car or signal traffic in the picture). The network has to be trained in order to configure the values of the weights that have to be applied to each signal that is received by a neuron.

Figure 1.5 shows a simplified example of an ANN with several layers. Here, the first layer takes the pixels of the visual input (a photo). Then there is a series of hidden layers, each one with a specific purpose. For instance, the first hidden layer tries to identify edges in the picture. The next one could connect edges into forms, another puts together several forms to obtain parts (a mouth, a nose, a tail, a leg, etc.), and these together allow us to see that there is an animal in the picture that is a cat. Artificial neurons on one layer are connected to those on the other layers. The training of the neural network will assign weights to each input that it receives from a neuron in the previous layer, so it can finally identify specific patterns.

Figure 1.5 An Artificial Neural Network

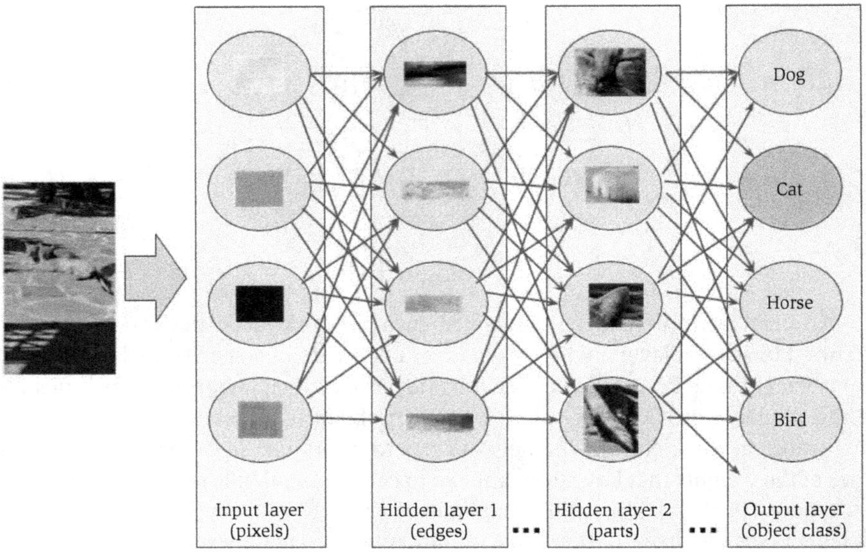

For ANNs to be effective, a large number of artificial neurons are required. For instance, the ImageNet classifier[31] required 60 million parameters and 650,000 neurons. This means that the use of these techniques requires considerable computing power. Methods are currently being studied to make this more scalable, such as the recent sparse evolutionary training.[32] Furthermore, how to design the different layers and their interconnections is not an easy task and methodologies are being developed for this purpose. The main issue, however, is traceability. DL is very much based on trial-and-error, which makes the final result hard to explain without access to the previous iterations.[33]

Semi-supervised learning falls between these two categories; both labelled and unlabelled data can be used for training. This is used when data must be labelled by humans, as this is a time-consuming task. For instance, this can be used to recognize tumours on medical images with methods such as *General Adversarial Networks* (GAN).[34] GAN is derived from DL as it uses two neural networks that compete with each other. For instance, there could be a generating network that creates images of fake cats that look real. The other is the discriminator network, which examines the

31. Alex Krizhevsky, Ilya Sutskever & Geoffrey E. Hinton, *ImageNet Classification with Deep Convolutional Neural Networks*, 60 Commun. ACM 84–90 (2017).
32. Decebal Constantin Mocanu et al., Scalable training of ANNs with adaptive sparse connectivity inspired by network science, 9 Nature Communications 2383 (2018).
33. Vincent Aravantinos, *Traceability of Deep Neural Networks* (2018), https://arxiv.org/abs/1812.06744v1 (last visited Mar 22, 2019).
34. Ian J. Goodfellow et al., *Generative Adversarial Networks*, arXiv:1406.2661 [cs, stat] (2014), http://arxiv.org/abs/1406.2661 (last visited Mar 22, 2019).

pictures and tries to determine whether they are real or fake. This competition between the two networks makes them perform better. They can be used to produce photorealistic images based on others, for instance, to generate a zebra from a horse, to change the way a person looks in a photo, to illustrate video games, or to create talking head animations.[35]

Finally, *reinforced learning* results from interaction with the world. Each action has an impact on the environment, which will provide a reward or punishment that will be used to guide the learning process. This is a very iterative process and quite appropriate when an agent is operating in an unknown environment. This can also lead to change strategies, and it has been used, for instance, in gaming.

[D] Other Approaches

Other areas of AI, such as *evolutive programming* or *genetic algorithms*, allow us to solve certain search and optimization problems by generating solutions with variations, starting from an initial set of potential solutions. A genetic programme consists of a population of artificial genes, where each gene is a series of values that represent a potential solution. The population goes through cycles of reproduction. At each step, some genes are selected to reproduce (normally those whose values approach the desired solution according to a fitness function, but also others), and there can be variations (changes in values of the genes) during reproduction. In this way, the population of genes evolves until the moment when some genes represent a good approach to the desired goal. This technique works for very specific tasks but requires a lot of cooking by the developer in order to determine how to define the genes, the fitness function, the rate of variation, how many are selected at each cycle, etc. They are being used in a variety of applications such as computational creativity, decryption tools, electronic circuit design, hardware and software debugging, trading systems, process optimization, etc.

§1.04 CONCLUSIONS

The availability of very large data sets and the increase in computing power to process them has led to a change of approach in AI. Nowadays, the main trend considers that *intelligence* has to be derived from data, instead of being explicitly coded. There are many tasks, such as information retrieval or automatic translation that, despite requiring some explicit knowledge, base their learning process mainly on data processing. ML has also made considerable progress in perception through its interconnection with different kinds of sensors and a variety of pattern recognition techniques, with applications, such as the face, voice or fingerprint authentication, handwritten text recognition, identification of spam, speech recognition, radar signal analysis, etc.

---

35. Egor Zakharov et al., *Few-Shot Adversarial Learning of Realistic Neural Talking Head Models* (2019), http://arxiv.org/abs/1905.08233 *(last visited May 26, 2019)*.

Although AI is solving new categories of problems with great success, it still faces relevant limitations as it lacks an intrinsically human capacity: common sense reasoning. Although AI systems can manage relationships among the objects they manipulate, they do not have a real understanding of the meaning of what they do. While a machine requires thousands or millions of images of dogs to be trained to recognize one, a child only needs to see three or four to distinguish them from other items, even if there are great variations in shape or colour. This makes it very difficult for machines to react in unexpected situations where a human being would react naturally.

There are also limitations on perception. There are many different kinds of sensors to gather data, which can be interpreted and filtered in specific ways. Obtaining data from different sources, e.g., sound, vision, touch, smell, etc., and interrelating it in real-time is not an easy task. In a typical environment, sensors will perceive many noises, and this should also be taken into account.

AI is becoming more and more integrated into a variety of devices and applications. Thus, there are no single AI machines but AI applications. AI is currently successful in carrying out specific tasks, but we are still very far from reaching the so-called AGI. The main challenge today, as we are more and more dependent on ML approaches, is how to control the decision-making process of intelligent systems since there is no explicit representation of knowledge in these techniques.

CHAPTER 2

AI and the Law: Regulating Artificial Intelligence

Moises Barrio Andres

§2.01 INTRODUCTION

Artificial intelligence (AI) is a *vintage* technology. Its inception began in the wake of the Second World War, as explained in the previous chapter. We are currently witnessing AI's boom due to a significant reduction in hardware costs, the capabilities and availability of big data and the cloud, and 'Artificial Intelligence as a Service' (AIaaS), which allows software developers to use components from, for instance, IBM, Google or Microsoft instead of having to program all aspects of the application from scratch. AI is *gradually* becoming ubiquitous: in our domestic devices of the Internet of Things (IoT),[1] in services and digital platforms, in robots, in the streets of smart cities, in offices, in factories, in hospitals, etc. And finally, albeit very limited for the time being, in law firms and courts.

In the present day, of course, the legal world was not going to be left impervious to this disruptive technology. States are beginning to legislate on the technology, albeit unhurriedly. This chapter summarises the attempts to create legally binding regulations for AI.

§2.02 NATIONAL REGULATORY FRAMEWORKS FOR AI

As Jacob Turner[2] has pointed out, states' public policies regulating AI generally fall into at least one of the following three categories: (i) promoting the growth of a local AI

1. Rolf H. Weber, *Internet of Things* (Springer, 2010). *See also*, Moises Barrio Andres, *Internet de las Cosas* (Reus, 2020), 2nd edition.
2. Jacob Turner, *Robot Rules* (Palgrave Macmillan, 2018), p. 225 *et. seq.*

industry; (ii) ethics and regulation of AI; and (iii) tackling the problem of unemployment caused by AI. These categories may sometimes be in tension and, at other times, can be mutually supportive. This chapter focuses on regulatory initiatives rather than economic or technological ones, which are analysed in other chapters of this book.[3]

The following exposition is merely a brief summary and does not intend to comprehensively examine all laws and government initiatives concerning the regulation of AI. Public policies are clearly developing fast, and any exhaustive study would soon become outdated. Instead, our intention is to capture an array of general regulatory approaches with a view toward establishing the general tendency in various of the foremost jurisdictions involved in the AI industry.

[A] Europe

The European Union (EU) has launched several initiatives aimed at developing a comprehensive AI strategy, including its regulation. The three key documents in this regard are the General Data Protection Regulation[4] (GDPR), the European Parliament's Resolution of February 2017 on Civil Laws for Robotics,[5] and the Ethics guidelines for trustworthy AI produced by the European Commission's High-Level Expert Group (HLEG) on AI[6] (AI HLEG), a final version of which was presented in April 2019.

Although the GDPR was not aimed specifically at AI, its provisions nevertheless appear likely to have fairly drastic effects on the industry even beyond what its drafters might have intended.[7] The GDPR extends the scope of EU data protection law to all foreign companies processing data of EU residents. The GDPR is intertwined with AI for several reasons, including that it requires a certain amount of explanation, which can be challenging with 'black box' AI systems. Article 22 GDPR stipulates that: 'In particular, the controller must allow for a human intervention and the right for individuals to express their point of view, to obtain further information about the decision that has been reached on the basis of this automated processing, and the right to contest this decision.'

The European Parliament's Resolution of February 2017 on Civil Laws for Robotics includes thought-provoking content, but it has not yet created binding law; instead, it was merely a recommendation to the Commission for future action. Specifically, it is the preparatory document for the drafting of a Directive concerning

3. *See also*, Ryan Calo, A. Michael Froomkin, and Ian Kerr (eds.), *Robot Law* (Edward Elgar Publishing, 2016), and Moises Barrio Andres (ed.), *Derecho de los Robots* (Wolters Kluwer, 2018).
4. Regulation (EU) 2016/679 of the European Parliament and of the Council of 27 Apr. 2016 on the protection of natural persons with regard to the processing of personal data and on the free movement of such data, and repealing Directive 95/46/EC (GDPR).
5. European Parliament resolution of 16 Feb. 2017 with recommendations to the Commission on Civil Law Rules on Robotics (2015/2103(INL)), available at http://www.europarl.europa.eu/sides/getDoc.do?pubRef=-//EP//TEXT+TA+P8-TA-2017-0051+0+DOC+XML+V0//EN, accessed 1 Mar. 2019.
6. Available at https://ec.europa.eu/digital-single-market/en/news/draft-ethics-guidelines-trustworthy-ai, accessed 1 Mar. 2019.
7. José López Calvo (ed.), *La adaptación al nuevo marco de protección de datos tras el RGPD y la LOPDGDD* (Wolters Kluwer, 2019).

civil-law rules on robotics. The results and a summary of this consultation were made available in a later report published in October 2017. Meanwhile, the European Parliament voted on the resolution in February 2017 to regulate the development of AI and robotics throughout the EU. The Joint Declaration on the EU's legislative priorities for 2018–2019 also named data protection, digital rights, and ethical standards in AI and robotics as priorities.

Taking up the European Parliament's appeal to create binding legislation, the European Commission issued a call in March 2018 for an HLEG on AI, which, according to the Commission, 'will serve as the steering group for the European AI Alliance's work, interact with other initiatives, help stimulate a multi-stakeholder dialogue, gather participants' views and reflect them in its analysis and reports.'

The work of the AI HLEG includes 'propos[ing] to the Commission AI ethics guidelines, covering issues such as fairness, safety, transparency, the future of work, democracy and more broadly the impact on the application of the Charter of Fundamental Rights, including privacy and personal data protection, dignity, consumer protection and non-discrimination.'[8] An initial version of the guidelines was published on 18 December 2018, and the experts presented their final version[9] to the Commission in April 2019 after extensive consultation throughout the European AI Alliance. Based on fundamental rights and ethical principles, the document lists seven key requirements that relevant systems should meet in order to be trustworthy. Aiming to operationalise these requirements, an assessment list is presented to provide guidance on the requirements' practical implementation. This assessment list will undergo a piloting process to which all interested stakeholders can participate. The objective is to then bring Europe's ethical approach to the global stage. The Commission is opening up cooperation to all non-EU countries that are willing to share the same values.

In April 2018, 25 EU countries signed a joint declaration of cooperation on AI, the terms of which included a commitment to '[e]*xchange views on ethical and legal frameworks related to AI in order to ensure responsible AI deployment*'.[10] Subsequently, on 25 April 2018, the European Commission adopted a Communication on AI for Europe[11] laying down the European approach to take utmost advantage of the opportunities offered by AI and address the new corresponding challenges of AI. In 2019, the Commission developed and made available the Guidance on the interpretation of the Product Liability Directive to prepare its reform in 2020.

Also, on 7 December 2018, the Commission submitted a Communication to the European Parliament, the European Council, the Council, the European Economic and Social Committee and the Committee of the Regions entitled *Coordinated Plan on*

8. European Commission, *Call for a High-Level Expert Group on Artificial Intelligence*, website of the European Commission, https://ec.europa.eu/digital-single-market/en/high-level-expert-group-artificial-intelligence, accessed 1 Mar. 2019.
9. Available at https://ec.europa.eu/newsroom/dae/document.cfm?doc_id=58477, accessed 1 May 2019.
10. *EU Member States Sign Up to Cooperate on Artificial Intelligence*, website of the European Commission, 10 Apr. 2018, https://ec.europa.eu/digital-single-market/en/news/eu-member-States-sign-cooperate-artificial-intelligence, accessed 1 Mar. 2019.
11. COM(2018) 237 final.

Artificial Intelligence,[12] accompanied by the *Coordinated Plan on the Development and Use of Artificial Intelligence Made in Europe – 2018* prepared by Member States (as part of the Group on digitizing European industry and AI), Norway, Switzerland, and the Commission.

Finally, on 19 February 2020, the European Commission published a White Paper[13] aiming to foster a European ecosystem of excellence and trust in AI and a Report on the safety and liability aspects of AI.[14] The White Paper proposes measures that will streamline research, foster collaboration between the Member States and increase investment into AI development and deployment. It also proposes policy options for an imminent EU regulatory framework that would determine the types of legal requirements that would apply to relevant actors, with a particular focus on high-risk applications.

Despite these encouraging signs and laudable intentions, the EU's regulatory agenda remains at a nascent stage.

[B] USA

In its final months, the Obama administration produced a major report on the Future of AI, along with an accompanying strategy document.[15] Although these documents focused primarily on the economic impact of AI, they also briefly covered topics, such as 'AI and Regulation' and 'Fairness, Safety and Governance in AI'.[16] In late 2016, a large group of US universities sponsored by the National Science Foundation (NSF) published *A Roadmap for US Robotics: From Internet to Robotics*, a 109-page document edited by Ryan Calo.[17] The report included calls for further work on AI ethics, safety, and liability.

Although the subsequent Trump administration initially appeared to have abandoned the topic as a major priority, as of the beginning of 2019 stands out to have changed course. In a 31 July 2018 memo from the Executive Office of the President, leadership in AI (along with '*quantum information sciences and strategic computing*') is listed as the second-highest R&D priority for the fiscal year 2020, just after the security of the Americans. And on 7 September 2018, the U.S. Department of Defense

12. COM(2018) 795 final.
13. COM(2020) 65 final.
14. COM(2020) 64 final.
15. *The Administration's Report on the Future of Artificial Intelligence*, website of the Obama White House, 12 Oct. 2016, https://obamawhitehouse.archives.gov/blog/2016/10/12/administrations-report-future-artificial-intelligence, accessed 1 Mar. 2019. For the reports themselves, *see* https://obamawhitehouse.archives.gov/sites/default/files/whitehouse_files/microsites/ostp/NSTC/preparing_for_the_future_of_ai.pdf, and also https://obamawhitehouse.archives.gov/sites/default/files/whitehouse_files/microsites/ostp/NSTC/national_ai_rd_strategic_plan.pdf, accessed 1 Mar. 2019.
16. *Preparing for the Future of Artificial Intelligence*, Executive Office of the President National Science and Technology Council (NSTC) Committee on Technology, 17–18 and 30–32 October 2016, https://obamawhitehouse.archives.gov/sites/default/files/whitehouse_files/microsites/ostp/NSTC/preparing_for_the_future_of_ai.pdf, accessed 1 Mar. 2019.
17. *A Roadmap for US Robotics: From Internet to Robotics*, 31 Oct. 2016, http://jacobsschool.ucsd.edu/contextualrobotics/docs/rm3-final-rs.pdf, accessed 1 Mar. 2018.

(DoD) announced that it would invest up to USD 2 billion over the following five years in the advancement of AI. That amount would be in addition to existing government spending on AI R&D, which totalled more than USD 2 billion in 2017 alone, an amount that includes only unclassified programs and not any amounts under the Pentagon and intelligence agencies' budgets. Existing funding has already propelled more than 20 active programs under the Defense Advanced Research Projects Agency (DARPA) exploring diverse aspects and uses of AI, and dozens of new projects have now been promised.

This funding follows the announcement in August 2018[18] of a National Security Commission on AI that was subsequently made official with President Trump's signing of the *2019 National Defense Authorization Act* (NDAA). The Commission will include fifteen members selected by various government officials in the coming months. The Commission will assess the national-security implications of AI, including the ethical considerations of AI in defence. The DoD also established[19] a Joint AI Center (JAIC) in July 2018 to explore the agency's use of AI, although the contours of the JAIC's mission have yet to be defined. The JAIC will ostensibly work on AI National Mission Initiatives, improve collaboration with the private sector, academia, and military allies; attract AI talent and establish an ethical framework for AI in defence; and aid the National Defense Strategy. The DoD may also soon publish an AI Strategy.

In May 2018, President Trump and the White House held a Summit on AI for American Industry with the participation of key technology companies. The White House also released a Fact Sheet, entitled *Artificial Intelligence for the American People,*[20] highlighting the Trump administration's priorities for AI. Trump declared his intention for the US to be the global leader in AI, pointing out that '[t]o the greatest degree possible, we will allow scientists and technologists to freely develop their next great inventions right here in the United States.' Any attention to job losses, the impact of immigration policies on the technology sector, privacy, cybersecurity, and the impact on vulnerable groups was minimal. Instead, the priorities discussed were funding AI research, removing regulatory barriers to the deployment of AI-powered technologies, training the future American workforce, achieving strategic military advantage, leveraging AI for government services, and working with allies to promote AI R&D. The White House announced plans to help provide US companies with new data sources and to establish a Select Committee on AI to help government agencies contemplate and use the technology, as well as consider partnerships with industry and academia.

What is more, President Trump specifically named AI as an Administration R&D priority in his 2019 Budget Request to Congress. AI was also featured for the first time in the National Security Strategy in relation to its role in helping the US lead in technological innovation, as well as AI's role in information statecraft, weaponization,

18. Available at https://www.executivegov.com/2018/08/fy-2019-ndaa-to-authorize-10m-for-ai-national-security-commission/, accessed 1 Mar. 2019.
19. Available at https://www.fedscoop.com/dod-joint-ai-center-established/, accessed 1 Mar. 2019.
20. Available at https://www.whitehouse.gov/briefings-statements/artificial-intelligence-american-people/, accessed 1 Mar. 2019.

and surveillance. AI also appears for the first time in the National Defense Strategy, where it is described as one of the technologies that will change the character of war and afford increasingly sophisticated capabilities to our adversaries, including non-state actors. Moreover, autonomous systems that include AI and machine learning (ML) are described as one of the primary areas in which modernisation of key capabilities is desirable.

President Trump issued an Executive Order launching *the American AI Initiative*[21] on 11 February 2019. The Executive Order explained that the Federal Government plays an important role not only in facilitating AI R&D, but also in promoting trust, training people for a changing workforce, and protecting national interests, security, and values. And while the Executive Order emphasizes American leadership in AI, it is stressed that this requires enhancing collaboration with foreign partners and allies. The initiative is guided by five principles, which include (in a summarized form) the following: 1. Driving technological breakthroughs, 2. Driving the development of appropriate technical standards, 3. Training workers with the skills to develop and apply AI technologies, 4. Protecting the American values, including civil liberties and privacy and fostering public trust and confidence in AI technologies, and 5. Protecting the US technological advantage in AI while promoting an international environment that supports innovation. The day after the Executive Order was released, the US Department of Defence followed up with the release of an unclassified summary of its own Artificial Intelligence Strategy. The US Air Force released an Annex to this strategy to share its own 2019 Artificial Intelligence Strategy in September 2019.

Numerous bills have also been introduced in Congress that either refer to or focus on AI. There are at least nine bills that relate to autonomous driving, including *The SELF DRIVE Act*, now called *AV START Act*, which passed the House in September 2017.[22] The bill charges the Department of Transportation (DoT) with undertaking research on the best way to inform consumers about the capabilities and limitations of highly automated vehicles. But without a doubt, the most relevant regulatory instrument is the *Algorithmic Accountability Act*[23] presented last April 2019 in the Senate, which, if finally approved, requires companies that apply automated decision-making techniques to audit their machine-learning systems for bias and discrimination and to take corrective action in a timely manner if such issues were identified. It would also require those companies to audit all processes beyond ML involving sensitive data for privacy and security risks. Should it pass, the bill would place regulatory power in the hands of the US Federal Trade Commission (FTC), the agency in charge of consumer protection and antitrust regulation.

Several other AI-related bills are being introduced at state and local levels. For example, in August 2018, the California State Senate passed a resolution in support of

---

21. On 19 Mar. 2019, the US federal government released http://AI.gov to make it easier to access all of the governmental AI initiatives currently underway. The site is the best single resource from which to gain a better understanding of US AI strategy.
22. *See* https://www.congress.gov/bill/115th-congress/house-bill/3388/, accessed 1 Mar. 2019.
23. *See* https://www.wyden.senate.gov/imo/media/doc/Algorithmic%20Accountability%20Act%20of%202019%20Bill%20Text.pdf, accessed 1 May 2019.

the Asilomar AI Principles[24] (a set of twenty-three guidelines for the safe and beneficial development and use of AI). Likewise, the New York City Council passed an algorithmic accountability bill in 2017 that established the New York Algorithm Monitoring Task Force; the group studies how municipal agencies employ algorithms to make decisions that affect the lives of New Yorkers. In December 2017, Supervisor David Canepa introduced a resolution in California's San Mateo County that called on Congress and the United Nations to restrict the development and use of lethal autonomous weapons. Elsewhere in California, San Francisco Supervisor Jane Kim created an initiative in 2017 called the Jobs of the Future Fund to help prepare for the likelihood of job losses due to automation.[25]

At the very least, it appears that the US Federal Government aspires to regain lost ground and has been attempting to position itself among the leading AI nations.

[C] Japan

Industry in Japan has for nearly half a century placed a particular focus on automation and robotics.[26] The Japanese Government has generated various strategy and policy papers with a view toward maintaining this position. For instance, in its 5th Science and Technology Basic Plan (2016–2020), the Japanese Government declared its aim to 'guide and mobilize action in science, technology, and innovation to achieve a prosperous, sustainable, and inclusive future that is, within the context of ever-growing digitalization and connectivity, empowered by the advancement of AI'.[27]

In line with these goals, the Japanese Government's Cabinet Office convened an Advisory Board on AI and Human Society in May 2016 under the initiative of the Minister of State for Science and Technology Policy 'with the aim to assess different societal issues that could possibly be raised by the development and deployment of AI and to discuss its implication for society'. The Advisory Board published a report in March 2017 that recommended further work on issues, such as ethics, law, economics, education, social impact and R&D.[28]

The Japanese Government's proactive approach, driven by its national industrial strategy and aided by a strong public discourse on AI, provides an excellent model for how governments can foster discussion nationally and internationally. The challenge for Japan will be to sustain this early *momentum*, something that will be maintained if other countries follow its approach. Pending the submission of binding legislation, Japan has so far produced only a number of ethical recommendations.

---

24. *See* https://futureoflife.org/ai-principles/, accessed 1 May 2019.
25. *See* https://www.jobsofthefuturefund.com/, accessed 1 May 2019.
26. Fumio Shimpo, 'The Principal Japanese AI and Robot Strategy and Research Toward Establishing Basic Principles', *Journal of Law and Information Systems*, Vol. 3 (May 2018).
27. *Report on Artificial Intelligence and Human Society*, Japan Advisory Board on Artificial Intelligence and Human Society, 24 Mar. 2017, Preface, available at http://www8.cao.go.jp/cstp/tyousakai/ai/summary/AISociety_en.pdf, accessed 1 Mar. 2019.
28. *Report on Artificial Intelligence and Human Society*, Japan Advisory Board on Artificial Intelligence and Human Society, *op. cit.*

[D] China

In July 2017, the AI 2.0 proposal from the China Academy of Engineering triggered the launch of a fifteen-year New Generation AI Development Plan. The plan is focused on a forward-looking blueprint for basic theories and common key technologies, including big-data intelligence, swarm intelligence, cross-media intelligence, hybrid-enhanced intelligence, and autonomous systems, and their applications in manufacturing, urbanization, healthcare, and agriculture, as well as AI hardware and software platforms, policies and regulations, and ethical concerns. Another R&D project related to AI is the *Brain Science and Brain-Inspired Research*, comparable to Europe's Human Brain Project, the BRAIN Initiative in the US, and other State-level projects. It is expected to be approved this year and should run for fifteen years.

Also, in July 2017, China's State Council issued the *Next Generation Artificial Intelligence Development Plan (新一代人工智能发展规划)*.[29] The policy plan outlines China's strategy to build a domestic AI industry worth nearly USD 150 billion over the next few years and to become the leading AI country by 2030. This document officially marked the development of the AI sector as a national priority and was included in President Xi Jinping's 'grand vision' for China. Although this represented the first time that AI had been specifically mentioned in a work report of the Communist Party of China, the sentiment is seen more broadly as a continuation of the 13th Five-Year Plan and the State-driven industrial plan *Made in China 2025*. The Next Generation AI Development Plan was described by two experienced analysts of Chinese digital technology as '[o]ne of the most significant developments in the artificial intelligence (AI) world' that year.

Although its main focus was on fostering economic growth through AI technology, the Plan also provided that '[b]y 2025 China will have seen the initial establishment of AI laws and regulations, ethical norms and policy systems, and the formation of AI security assessment and control capabilities'. As Jeffrey Ding[30] points out, '[n]o further specifics were given, which fits in with what some have called opaque nature of Chinese discussion about the limits of ethical AI research'.

The Ministry of Science and Technology (MOST), as well as a new office, named the AI Plan Promotion Office, are responsible for the implementation and coordination of the emergent AI-related projects, which are driven primarily by government-led subsidies. An AI Strategy Advisory Committee was also established in November 2017 to conduct research on strategic issues related to AI and to make recommendations. Furthermore, an AI Industry Development Alliance was established; the Alliance is co-sponsored by more than 200 enterprises and agencies nationwide and focuses on

29. Available in English translation from the New America Institute: *A Next Generation Artificial Intelligence Development Plan*, China State Council, translated by Rogier Creemers, Leiden Asia Centre; Graham Webster, Yale Law School Paul Tsai China Center; Paul Triolo, Eurasia Group; and Elsa Kania, 20 Jul. 2017, available at https://na-production.s3.amazonaws.com/documents/translation-fulltext-8.1.17.pdf, accessed 1 Mar. 2019.

30. Jeffrey Ding, 'Deciphering China's AI Dream', in *Governance of AI Program*. Future of Humanity Institute (Oxford: Future of Humanity Institute, March 2018), 30, available at https://www.fhi.ox.ac.uk/wp-content/uploads/Deciphering_Chinas_AI-Dream.pdf, accessed 1 Mar. 2019.

building a public-service platform for the development of China's AI industry in order to integrate resources and accelerate growth.

In November 2017, Tencent Research, an institute within one of China's largest technology companies, and the China Academy of Information and Communications Technology (CAICT) produced a book of 482 pages, the title of which roughly translates to *A National Strategic Initiative for Artificial Intelligence*. Topics covered include law, governance, and the morality of machines.

In a paper entitled *Deciphering China's AI Dream,*[31] Ding hypothesises that 'AI may be the first technology domain in which China successfully becomes the international standard setter.' The report points out that the book National Strategic Initiative for AI identified Chinese leadership on AI ethics and safety as a way for China to seize the strategic high ground. Ding notes that the book emphasises that 'China should also actively construct the guidelines of AI ethics, play a leading role in promoting inclusive and beneficial development of AI. In addition, we should actively explore ways to go from being a follower to being a leader in areas such as AI legislation and regulation, education and personnel training, and responding to issues with AI.'[32]

Ding[33] observes further:

> One important indicator of China's ambitions in shaping AI standards is the case of the International Organization for Standardization [...] Joint Technical Committee (JTC), one of the largest and most prolific technical committees in the international standardization, which recently formed a special committee on AI [SC 42]. The chair of this new committee is Wael Diab, a senior director at [Chinese multinational company] Huawei, and the committee's first meeting will be held in April 2018 in Beijing, China - both the chair position and first meeting were hotly contested affairs that ultimately went China's way.

In furtherance of its policies, China established a national AI-standardization group and a national AI expert-advisory group in January 2018.[34] At the launch event for these groups, a division of China's Ministry of Industry and Information Technology released a 98-page White Paper on AI standardization.[35] The White Paper noted that AI raised challenges in terms of legal liability, ethics and safety, stating:

> [...] considering that the current regulations on artificial intelligence management in various countries in the world are not uniform and relevant standards are still in

31. Jeffrey Ding, 'Deciphering China's AI Dream', *op. cit.*
32. *Ibid.*
33. *Ibid.*
34. Paul Triolo and Jimmy Goodrich, 'From Riding a Wave to Full Steam Ahead As China's Government Mobilizes for AI Leadership, Some Challenges Will Be Tougher Than Others', *New America*, 28 Feb. 2018, available at https://www.newamerica.org/cybersecurity-initiative/digichina/blog/riding-wave-full-steam-ahead/, accessed 1 Mar. 2019.
35. *White Paper on Standardization in AI*, National Standardization Management Committee, Second Ministry of Industry, 18 Jan. 2018, available at http://www.sgic.gov.cn/upload/f1ca3511-05f2-43a0-8235-eeb0934db8c7/20180122/5371516606048992.pdf, accessed 1 Mar. 2019. Contributors to the white paper included the China Electronics Standardization Institute, Institute of Automation, the Chinese Academy of Sciences, the Beijing Institute of Technology, the Tsinghua University, the Peking University and the Renmin University, as well as private companies such as Huawei, Tencent, Alibaba, Baidu, Intel (China) and Panasonic (formerly Matsushita Electric) (China) Co., Ltd.

a blank state, participants in the same AI technology may come from different countries which have not signed a shared contract for artificial intelligence. To this end, China should strengthen international cooperation and promote the formulation of a set of universal regulatory principles and standards to ensure the safety of artificial intelligence technology.

China's goal of becoming a leader in the regulation of AI may be one of the motivations behind its call in April 2018 to United Nations Group of Governmental Experts on lethal autonomous weapons systems 'to negotiate and conclude a succinct protocol to ban the use of fully autonomous weapon systems'.[36] In so doing, China, for the first time, adopted a different approach regarding autonomous weapons than that of the US. The Campaign to Stop Killer Robots announced that China had joined twenty-five other nations in calling for such a ban.[37]

Triolo and Goodrich[38] have pointed out that '[a]s in many other areas, Chinese government leadership on AI at least nominally comes from the top. Xi has identified AI and other key technologies as critical to his goal of transforming China from a "large cyber power" to a "strong cyber power" (also translated as "cyber superpower")'. This approach seems to originate from the White Paper.

In May 2019, the Beijing AI Principles were released by a multistakeholder coalition including the Beijing Academy of Artificial Intelligence (BAAI), Peking University, Tsinghua University, Institute of Automation and Institute of Computing Technology in Chinese Academy of Sciences, and an AI industrial league involving firms like Baidu, Alibaba and Tencent. The 15 Principles call for "the construction of a human community with a shared future, and the realization of beneficial AI for humankind and nature."

The Principles are separated into three sections: Research and Development, Use, and Governance. They include focus on benefitting all of humanity and the environment; serving human values such as privacy, dignity, freedom, autonomy, and rights; continuous focus on AI safety and security; inclusivity; openness; supporting international cooperation and avoiding a "malicious AI race"; and long-term planning for more advanced AI systems, among others.

Finally, there are also local government AI policy initiatives throughout China. For example, the Shanghai government issued its own implementation plan for new-generation AI in November 2017; Beijing announced a major new AI-focused industrial park to be constructed in Mentougou District in June 2018; Guangzhou launched an International Institute of AI; and many other districts have committed funds for AI research.

---

36. The original recording of the Chinese delegation's statement is available on the UN Digital Recordings Portal website, available at: https://conf.unog.ch/digitalrecordings/index.html?guid=public/61.0500/E91311E5-E287-4286-92C6-D47864662A2C_10h14&position=1197, accessed 1 Mar. 2019.
37. *Convergence on Retaining Human Control of Weapons Systems*, Campaign to Stop Killer Robots, 13 Apr. 2018, website at https://www.stopkillerrobots.org/2018/04/convergence/, accessed 1 Mar. 2019.
38. 94 Paul Triolo and Jimmy Goodrich, 'From Riding a Wave to Full Steam Ahead As China's Government Mobilizes for AI Leadership, Some Challenges Will Be Tougher Than Others', *op. cit*.

§2.03 CONCLUDING REMARKS

In the absence of an international treaty or mandatory EU or national legislation to regulate AI, private companies have begun to act unilaterally. For instance, in 2016, six major technology companies (Amazon, Apple, Google, Facebook, IBM and Microsoft) formed the Partnership on AI to Benefit People and Society[39] to 'study and formulate best practices on AI technologies, to advance the public's understanding of AI, and to serve as an open platform for discussion and engagement about AI and its influences on people and society'. Similarly, in October 2017, DeepMind, one of the world's leading AI companies acquired by Google in 2014, created a new ethics committee, DeepMind Ethics & Society,[40] 'to help technologists put ethics into practice, and to help society anticipate and address the impact of AI in a way that works for the benefit of all'.

These initiatives are highly positive and valuable but are not sufficient. They lack the legitimacy that the State can provide. In fact, they leave out the myriad small- to medium-sized enterprises that are also developing AI. Nevertheless, it is also imperative that the State ensures compliance with the legal systems and the fundamental principles and rights enshrined in national constitutions and the Charter of Fundamental Rights of the EU.

But why do we need *binding* global legal regulation? In other studies,[41] we have dealt at length with new issues that are not covered by current laws. For example, it is not entirely clear who should be held liable if AI causes damage (e.g., in an accident with an autonomous car or by incorrect application of an algorithm): the original designer, the manufacturer, the owner, the user or even the AI itself.[42] We also discuss whether an autonomous electronic personality should be recognized for the most advanced systems that directly assign them rights and obligations. There are even moral dilemmas about how AI should make specific important decisions even if there would be decisions involved on which it should not have the last word. If we apply solutions on a case-by-case basis, we risk uncertainty and confusion. As Oliver Wendell Holmes[43] said, 'hard cases make bad law', referring to which an extreme case is a poor basis for a general law that would cover a wider range of less extreme cases. Lack of regulation also increases the likelihood of hasty, instinctive, or even anger-fed reactions.

These issues are not merely theoretical concerns to entertain academics. AI systems already have the ability to make difficult decisions that have until now been based on human intuition or the laws and the practice of courts. Those decisions range from questions of life and death, such as the use of autonomous killer robots in the military, to issues of economic and social importance, such as how to avoid algorithmic

39. *See* https://www.partnershiponai.org/, accessed 1 May 2019.
40. *See* https://deepmind.com/applied/deepmind-ethics-society/, accessed 1 May 2019.
41. Moisés Barrio Andres (ed.), *Derecho de los Robots* (Wolters Kluwer, 2019), 2nd edition, p. 101 and Moisés Barrio Andrés, 'Hacia una personalidad electrónica para los robots', in *Revista de Derecho Privado*, N° 2/2018.
42. This is further discussed in chapter 7 of this book.
43. *Northern Securities Co. v. United States*, 193 U.S. 197 (1904).

biases when AI decides, for example, whether to award a scholarship to a student or when to grant parole to an inmate. If a human being were to make these decisions, the human would always be subject to a legal rule and must accompany the decision with a legal motivation, i.e., to explain the *rationale* for the decision under the law. There are at present no such rules for AI.

The regulation of AI is currently presided over by corporate interests and is promoted from an ethical approach; this is not always desirable. A mere glance at the global financial crisis of 2008 illustrates the result of a self-regulated industry careening out of control. While the State has intervened to require banks to hold better assets to back their loans, the global economy continues to suffer the repercussions of a framework that was previously fundamentally self-regulatory.

That is not to say that progress is not being made. DeepMind has hired leading public analysts, including transhumanist philosopher Nick Bostrom and economist Jeffrey Sachs, as members of its ethics committee, and the list of the Partnership on AI members now includes non-profit organizations, such as the American Civil Liberties Union, Human Rights Watch, and United Nations Children's Fund (UNICEF). By early 2020, however, the Partnership on AI only has representatives from thirteen countries.

Nevertheless, ethical frameworks differ notably from legal frameworks given that legal frameworks can only be developed by international or state legislatures. Furthermore, ethical rules are only binding in the internal forum and entail, in cases of non-compliance, sin and potential eternal punishment, while legal rules are binding in the external forum, with their non-compliance entailing liability, sanctions, fines or even prison sentences.

For the time being, all states are still trying to catch up with Silicon Valley regarding AI regulation; the longer they wait, the more difficult it will be to properly manage the future of AI. Earlier we noted that the European Commission had launched a group of experts in June 2018 to examine the challenges posed by the development of AI and its impact on the fundamental rights of the EU (the HLEG on AI, AI HLEG). On 8 April 2019, this group had presented the final version of ethical guidelines for the development and use of AI.

While it is a difficult achievement, it is not an impossible one. At the national level, states already oversee many other complex technologies, including nuclear power and cloning. At the international level, the European Medicines Agency (EMA) sets pharmaceutical standards for twenty-eight countries, and Internet Corporation for Assigned Names and Numbers (ICANN) regulates key parts of the entire Internet.

It is important to have an imperative – yet prudent and thoughtful – body of laws. Self-regulation is insufficient. If standards remain purely voluntary, some technology companies will decide to ignore any rules that do not benefit them, giving some organisations advantages over others. For example, none of the major Chinese AI companies, such as Alibaba, Tencent or Baidu, has announced that they will set up ethics committees or that they intend to join the Partnership on AI. It is not easy for a company to establish an ethics committee. The difficulties faced by Google in this field are very enlightening.

In addition, without a unified framework, too many private ethics committees could also lead to too many sets of rules. It would be chaotic and dangerous for every large company to have its own code for AI, just as it would be if every private citizen could establish his or her own legal statutes. Only the State has the power and the mandate to ensure a fair system that imposes compliance in all areas. That is why all States are sovereign, typically have parliaments and a judiciary. In short, they have the backing of democratic legitimacy.

Therefore, when rules are drafted for AI systems, the voices of companies must remain contributors; yet, while highly relevant, they should not be akin to legislators. Technology companies may be well-positioned to design rules because of their experience in the field, but industry actors are rarely in the best position to adequately assess democratic, moral, ethical, and legal risks.

History shows what can happen if the State withdraws and allows private companies to set their own exclusive regulatory standards. Allowing this to happen in the case of AI would be not only reckless but also exceedingly dangerous. However, States have not yet reached definitive positions on how AI should be governed. We have a unique opportunity to create laws and principles governing AI on a common basis and with an indispensable public-private partnership that should preferably be international in scope with the leadership of the UN or, failing that, at European level led by EU institutions, as they had already achieved in the areas of privacy and data protection.

Reflecting our view, the European Commission drafted a White Paper, the final version of which was published in February 2020, which sets out the key pillars of the forthcoming regulatory framework for AI and actions to facilitate access to data through legally binding legislation in the EU law.

CHAPTER 3

Ethical and Social Issues in Artificial Intelligence

Virginia Dignum

§3.01 INTRODUCTION: RESPONSIBLE AI: WHAT IS IT AND WHY CARE

Recent developments in Artificial Intelligence (AI) have generated much interest from media and the general public. As AI systems (e.g., robots, chatbots, avatars and other intelligent agents) are moving from being perceived as a tool to being perceived as autonomous agents and team-mates, an important focus of research and development is understanding the ethical impact of these systems. What does it mean for an AI system to make a decision? What are the moral, societal and legal consequences of the actions and decisions of such systems? Can an AI system be held accountable for its actions? How can these systems be controlled once their learning capabilities bring them into states that are possibly only remotely linked to their initial, designed, setup? Should such autonomous behaviour in commercial systems even be allowed, and how should use and development be regulated?

The current wave of digital transformation entails the adoption of a range of advanced technologies, such as big data/analytics, Internet of Things, robotics, sensors, which when combined with AI will give people and organisations the capacity for decision-making and learning at a scale that wasn't possible before. Using AI methods, machines can sense, classify, analyse, draw inferences, act, and, most importantly, learn from past data and experience. However, it is very important to realize that the data these systems use is data that people have generated, and which may contain all the good, bad and ugly of human behaviour. AI absorbs and reflects and amplifies all the assumptions and bias that we have in society. AI reflects who we are but at the same time, gives us the opportunity to learn very quickly and can present us with better options for action in the future. That is 'AI gives us an opportunity to consider, and make real decisions about, the kind of digital world we want to live in.'

The way society and our systems will be able to deal with these questions will, for a large part, determine our level of trust, and ultimately, the impact of AI in society, and the existence of AI. However, and contrary to the frightening images of a dystopian future from the media and popular fiction, where AI systems dominate the world and are the cause of increasing violence and warfare, AI is already changing our daily lives, and mostly in ways that improve human health, safety, and productivity. This is the case in domains, such as transportation; service robots; healthcare; education; low-resource communities; public safety and security; employment and workplace; and entertainment.

In order to ensure that AI applications are used for the benefit of humankind and for the improvement of well-being and environmental sustainability, AI systems must be introduced in ways that can be trusted, and that respect human and civil rights. That is, we need to consider the ethical, legal and societal impact of AI applications alongside their economic contribution and technologic innovation.

The need for ethical considerations in the development of intelligent interactive systems is becoming one of the main influential areas of research in the last few years.

In all areas of application where AI is used to make decisions that affect people and society, AI reasoning must be able to take into account societal values, moral and ethical considerations, weigh the respective priorities of values held by different stakeholders and in multiple multicultural contexts, explain its reasoning, and guarantee transparency. As the capabilities for autonomous decision-making grow, perhaps the most important issue to consider is the need to rethink our responsibility with respect to AI systems [Dignum, 2017]. First, it must be clear that whatever their level of autonomy and social awareness and their ability to learn and adapt to a changing environment, AI systems are artefacts constructed by people to achieve some human purpose.

We need to integrate societal, legal and moral values into technological developments in AI, at all stages of development (analysis, design, construction, deployment and evaluation). These frameworks must deal both with the autonomic reasoning of the machine about such issues that we consider to have an ethical impact, but most importantly we need frameworks to guide design choices, to regulate the reaches of AI systems, to ensure proper data stewardship, and to help individuals determine their own involvement.

The above considerations show that ethics and AI are related at several levels:

- **Ethics <u>in</u> Design**: the regulatory and engineering methods that support the analysis and evaluation of the ethical implications of AI systems as these integrate or replace traditional social structures.
- **Ethics <u>by</u> Design**: the technical/algorithmic integration of ethical reasoning capabilities as part of the behaviour of the artificial autonomous system.
- **Ethics <u>for</u> Design**: the codes of conduct, standards and certification processes that ensure the integrity of developers and users as they research, design, construct, employ and manage AI systems.

We will further discuss these three approaches in the next section.

§3.02 THE INTERPLAY BETWEEN AI AND ETHICS

[A] Ethics in Design

Ethics in Design is about the responsible design of AI systems. It concerns the role of all stakeholders as they research, design, construct, use, manage and dismantle AI systems, and the *governance* issues required to prevent misuse of these systems. The focus here is the prioritization of ethical, legal, and policy considerations in the development and management of AI systems to ensure responsible design and operation.

The design, development and use of AI systems should be able to take into account societal values, moral and ethical considerations; weigh the respective priorities of values held by different stakeholders in various multicultural contexts; explain its reasoning; and guarantee transparency. To reflect societal concerns about the ethics of AI, and ensure that AI systems are developed responsibly, incorporating social and ethical values, we propose to complement these properties with the ART principles: Accountability, Responsibility and Transparency [Dignum, 2017].

- **Accountability** refers to the requirement to explain and justify decisions and actions to the interaction partners, i.e., users and others with whom the system interacts. To ensure accountability, decisions must be derivable from and explained by, the decision-making algorithms used. This includes the need for representation of the moral values and societal norms in the context of the operation, which the agent uses for deliberation. Accountability in AI requires both the function of guiding action (by forming beliefs and making decisions) and the function of explanation (by placing decisions in a broader context and by classifying them along with moral values).
- **Responsibility** refers to the role of people themselves, and to the capability of AI systems to answer for decisions and identify errors or unexpected results. As the chain of responsibility grows, means are needed to link the AI systems' decisions to the fair use of data and to the actions of stakeholders involved in the system's decision. Responsibility is not just about making rules to govern intelligent machines – we also need to consider how we regulate the data they create and share. It is time to make up our minds and respond to the novel, data-driven reality with a constructive operational framework that is able to inform sustainable new modes of political thinking. Digital technologies and data science are now used to shape our societies, to constitute the very fabric of our sociality, often circumventing democratic decision-making and scientific facts.
- **Transparency** refers to the capability to describe, inspect and reproduce the mechanisms through which AI systems make decisions and learns to adapt to its environment, and to the governance of the data used or created. Current AI algorithms are basically black boxes. However, regulators and users demand explanation and clarity about the data and algorithms used. Methods are needed to inspect algorithms and their results and to manage data, their

provenance and their dynamics. Transparency requires proper treatment of the learning process along with approaches to remove the so-called algorithmic black box. Trust in the system will improve if we can ensure the openness of affairs in all that is related to the system. Being explicit and open about choices and decisions concerning data sources, development processes, and stakeholders should be required from all models that use human data, affect human beings, or can have other morally significant impacts.[1]

Responsible AI is about human responsibility for the development of intelligent systems along with fundamental human principles and values, to ensure human well-being and that humans flourish in a sustainable world. In fact, Responsible AI is more than the ticking of some ethical 'boxes' in a report, or the development of some add-on features, or switch-off buttons in AI systems. Rather, responsibility is fundamental to autonomy and should be one of the core stances underlying AI research.

Values are dependent on the socio-cultural context and are often only implicit in deliberation processes, which means that methodologies are needed to elicit the values held by all the stakeholders and to make these explicit can lead to better understanding and trust on artificial autonomous systems. Design for Values approaches (also known as Value Sensitive Design) [Friedman et al., 2006, van den Hoven, 2005] provide rational procedures for designing artefacts under the guidance of moral values and are therefore very relevant for the design of AI systems. These frameworks bridge the gap between abstract values and concrete system requirements and implementation choices.

A Design for Values approach to AI models ensures that these principles are analysed and reported at all stages of system development. A Design for Values process ensures that the link between values and their concrete interpretations in the design and engineering of systems can be traced and evaluated. During the development of AI systems, taking a Design for Values approach means that the process needs to include activities for (i) the identification of societal values, (ii) deciding on a moral deliberation approach (e.g., through algorithms, user control or regulation), and (iii) link values to formal system requirements and concrete functionalities [Aldewereld et al., 2014].

A responsible approach to the design of AI systems requires continuous evaluation and openness about choices and decisions. Moreover, given the dynamic and adaptable manner of AI systems, system evaluation cannot wait until development is concluded because these are continuously evolving. Responsible use of AI reduces risks and burdens and ensures that societal and ethical values are central to development. It is, however, not always easy for organisations and developers to determine how best to approach Responsible AI in their development processes. We have proposed a novel responsible development life cycle for AI systems (ReLAI) that supports ethical and societal requirements and ensures that the resulting systems are

1. *See* further https://medium.com/@virginiadignum/on-bias-black-boxes-and-the-quest-for-transparency-in-artificial-intelligence-bcde64f59f5b.

aligned with the ART principles [Dignum, 2019]. Figure 1 depicts this process, highlighting the main issues to be considered at each of the main steps of development.

Figure 3.1 The Responsible Development Life-Cycle for AI systems (ReLAI)

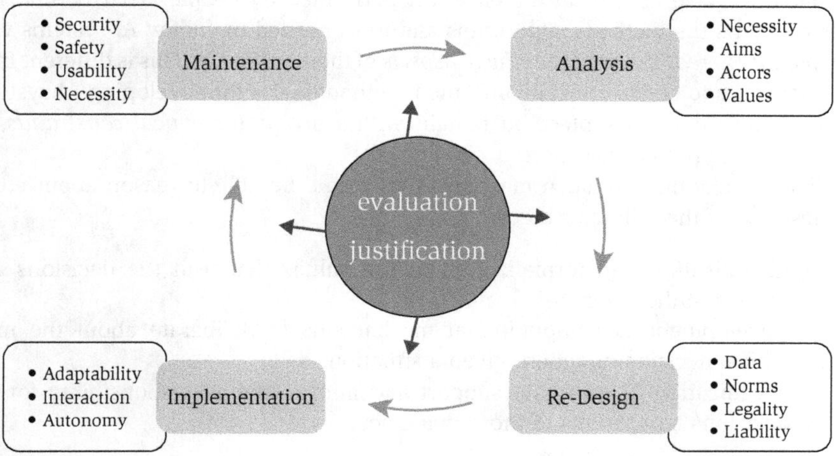

The development life cycle described in Figure 1 is a novel proposal to adapt current development methodologies to ensure a responsible approach to the design of AI systems. This approach supports the requirements put forward in this chapter and ensures that the resulting systems are aligned with the ART principles. The ReLAI framework is an initial proposal to support organizations but can also be used by AI developers to test applications. It requires continuous evaluation and openness about choices and decisions. Moreover, it gives evaluation a central place in design. Given the dynamic and adaptable manner of AI systems, evaluation cannot wait until development is concluded because these are continuously evolving.

[B] Ethics by Design

Ethics by Design, or Machine Ethics, is about understanding, developing and evaluating ethical agency and reasoning abilities as part of the behaviour of artificial autonomous systems (such as artificial agents and robots). Even though AI systems are increasingly able to make decisions and perform actions that have a moral impact, it should be clear that AI systems are artefacts and therefore, are neither ethically nor legally responsible for their actions and decisions, and the consequences thereof. Individual humans or human corporations should remain the moral (and legal) agent. We can delegate control to synthetic intelligent systems but cannot delegate responsibility or liability for them.

The term *machine ethics* refers to different issues, from the engineering of machines that can follow ethical principles and are capable of reasoning about these principles [Allen, Wallach, 2009], to philosophical and pragmatic discussions of what qualifies as 'artificial moral agents' [Anderson, Anderson, 2006], and the desirability of such [Bryson, 2018]. A recent paper by Cave et al. discusses these issues extensively [Cave et al., 2019].

In general, Ethics by Design refers to the behaviour of machines that would be considered to have an ethical dimension if performed by people. That is, machine ethics concerns the methods, algorithms and tools needed to endow AI systems with the *capability to reason about the ethical aspects* of their decisions. This is different from the endeavours to create ethically informed methodologies for developing AI systems whose behaviour is guaranteed to remain within *acceptable ethical constraints,* as discussed in the previous section.

The development of such machines that would be able to reason about ethics includes at least the following steps:

- Identification and formalization of the values that lead the decisions and actions of the machine.
- Development of computational mechanisms to deliberate about the most ethical decision or action, given a situation.
- Specification of means to support and inform human responsibility for the decisions and actions of those machines.

Each of these steps is complex and requires extensive research going way beyond current practices. First, concerning values, one of the main challenges is to determine which moral values to aim for and which ethical principles to adhere to in a given circumstance. Each individual and socio-cultural environment prioritizes different moral and societal values. Which groups and individuals are consulted, the way values are elicited, and the methods chosen to aggregate different values, interpretations and priorities, all affect the values that ultimately the AI system will consider. Even though there are studies showing that ethical values are consistent across cultures, it is also clear that different cultures and individuals prioritize these values differently [Schwartz, 2006, Hofstede & Hofstede, 2010]. The ambition to develop machines that will be able to deal in a uniform way with this complex network of values, interpretation and priorities, may prove to be impossible.

Several authors have proposed approaches to elicit values and ethical decisions by learning from the environment. Malle states that in order to build a morally competent robot, we need to equip them with a mechanism that allows for '... constant learning and improvement ...' [Malle, 2015, p. 11]. His thesis is that robots need to learn norms and morality, like little children do, in order to become morally competent. Similarly, [Cointe, et al., 2016] drafted a model in which an agent can judge the ethical aspects of his own behaviour and that of other agents in a multi-agent system. For this, they need to be able to assess the appropriateness of agents' behaviour with respect to moral convictions and ethical principles. This implies that an agent needs to be aware of other agents' ethical behaviour and adjust its own behaviour according to this.

The risk associated with such data-based, or statistical, approaches to ethics, or 'ethics by crowd-sourcing' is that the system will learn what is socially accepted but not necessarily to what is ethically acceptable or even legally allowed [Verdiesen et al., 2018]. It is well known that sometimes propositions that are de facto accepted are unacceptable by independent (moral and epistemic) standards and the available evidence and that other propositions are de facto not accepted by a society or group, but they are perfectly acceptable from a moral point of view. It is, therefore, important to acknowledge that different groups, societies and application contexts may have different needs and expectations concerning human values and ethical principles. Besides aligning ethics and identifying shared moral bounds and legal rules, in multi-cultural societies, there is also the need to ensure awareness of the different value priorities and interpretations that different members of the society may have.

Nevertheless, even if an appropriate set of values can be identified to guide the machine's decisions, it is still necessary to apply those values to the concrete situations it encounters. Philosophical, ethical theories provide different mechanisms to reason about the ethics of a situation. However, these theories will lead to different decisions, and there is not a clear way to determine which is the 'right' or 'wrong' way of doing things. E.g., consider the well-known moral dilemma of the runway trolley that needs to decide whether to keep its course and kill five people or swerve and kill one. Even though these types of dilemmas are mostly meant for discussion and awareness purposes, they are currently often mentioned with respect to autonomous vehicles (cf. [Bonnefon et al., 2016]). Without discussing the correctness of such an application, we will use the trolley problem here merely to illustrate the differences resulting from the application of different ethical theories. So, if the trolley's reasoning is informed by a Utilitarian or Consequentialist approach, it will mostly consider the quality of the result of its actions, and therefore, its decision would be to save the largest amount of lives. A trolley informed by a Deontological or Kantian theory would consider the quality of its actions, rather than that of the results. Such trolley could then possibly decide not to swerve from the given course, given that it would not be acceptable to actively take an action of which it knew that would lead to harm. Other ethical theories would support the decision to save pedestrians over passengers, or not to consider the number of victims in the decision, given that the number of lives cannot be a consideration as its life is worth in itself. From this simple example, it can be seen that, as in the case of determining the values that should lead machine ethics, determining how to reason about the ethics of a situation is also a simple design choice.

It should be understood that all approaches at Ethics in and by Design presuppose both adherence to the law first and feasibility of action, in which case, it can support differentiation along with ethical evaluation and choice (e.g., fair trade, organic food are the 'better' choice, under the understanding that all available food meets some minimum legal quality). As such, these approaches can best be seen as *soft ethics*, existing only over and above existing regulation [Floridi, 2018].

Ethics by Design approach is currently used for very specific values and interpretations, through 'design-based' regulatory approaches aimed at 'hard-wiring' values into socio-technical systems [Yeung, 2017]. These may include (but are not limited to) Compliance, Security, Data Protection, or Privacy by Design, and are concerned with the implementation of specific regulatory principles, allocating rights, distributing liability, and managing legal identity (including profile transparency in the case of machine learning applications). Previous experiences have shown that law and privacy cannot be fully hardcoded [Koops, Leenes, 2014], and may produce 'legal by design' (LbD) [Katz et al. 2015], which as the risk of overruling human agency, rather than the more desirable 'legal protection by design' (LPbD) [Hildebrandt 2015, 2017]. LPbD requires bringing together legal theorists and AI developers to prevent unwarranted implementation of legal decision systems that force people into compliance, and highlights the need to build transparency and contestability into AI infrastructures, as required, for instance by the new EU General Data Protection Regulation (GDPR).[2]

A further important aspect of Ethics by Design is the issue of *Explanation* – that is the right of a user to receive an informed justification of the reasoning that leads to a given decision by a machine. This is required by EU data protection laws. Explanation should be grounded in moral and social concepts, including values, social norms and relationships, commitments, habits, motives and goals [Miller, 2018]. That is, every AI system must operate within a moral and social framework, in verifiable and justified ways. This extends the obvious demand that AI systems always operate within the bounds of the law, including, for example, the legal requirements associated with the handling of the user data acquired and collected to improve predictions, suggestions and response times. The urgency of this question is increasingly acknowledged by researchers and policymakers alike as shown from the recent reports on the Ethically Aligned Design (EAD) of Autonomous Systems, 100 years AI, the White House report, or the Partnership on AI. In fact, AI Ethics and AI Safety are a growing area of scientific research [Amodei, 2016, Conitzer et al. 2017]. Moreover, implementing ethical actions in machines will help us better understand ethics overall [Bryson & Kime 2011].

AI explanation is necessary to ensure trust and is often brought in connection to algorithmic transparency [Lyons, 2013, Theodorou et al., 2017]. By transparency, we mean that the different factors that influence the decisions made by algorithms should be visible, or transparent, to the people who use, regulate, and are impacted by systems that employ those algorithms, i.e., the understandability of a specific model [Lepri et al., 2018]. Transparency is also seen as and is often taken as a requisite for algorithmic accountability [Bryson and Winfield, 2017]. However, decisions made by machine learning (ML) algorithms can be opaque due to many factors, which may not always be possible or even desirable to eliminate. These include issues not only of technical nature (the algorithm may not lend itself to easy explanation) but also economic (the cost of providing transparency may be excessive, and may include the compromise of intellectual capital aspects) and social (revealing input may violate privacy expectations)[3] [Ananny and Crawford, 2018]. Since human decisions can also be quite opaque, as are the decisions made by corporations and organizations, mechanisms, such as audits, contracts, and monitoring are in place to regulate and ensure attribution of accountability.

2. *See* http://www.eugdpr.org/.
3. Cf. The statement on transparency by the world's largest educational and scientific computing society, Association for Computing Machinery (ACM): http://www.acm.org/binaries/content/assets/public-policy/2017usacmstatementalgorithms.pdf.

Nevertheless, diminishing the opacity of ML algorithms remains an important area of research. Opacity in ML, the so-called *black-box* effect, is often mentioned as one of the main impediments for trust in AI. Currently, ML algorithms are developed with the main goal of improving functional performance. This leads to complex functions that are optimized to provide the best possible answer to the question at hand (e.g., recognize pictures, analyse x-ray images, or classify text) but they do it by fine-tuning outputs to the specific inputs by approximating a function's structure without giving any insights on the structure of the function being approximated. As long as the main goal of algorithm design is to improve functional performance, algorithms will surely remain black boxes. Demanding a focus on the observance ethical principles and putting human values at the core of system design, calls for a mind-shift of researchers and developers towards the goal of improving transparency rather than performance, which will lead to a new generation of algorithms. We discuss the role of designers and developers in the next sub-section.

[C] Ethics for Design(ers)

Currently, several initiatives around the ethical development and use of AI have developed, proposing sets of ethical principles for AI to reflect societal concerns about the ethics of AI, and ensure that AI systems are developed responsibly, incorporating social and ethical values [Floridi et al., 2018]. In particular, national governments and international organizations, such as the European Union (EU), the United Nations, or the Organization for Economic Co-operation and Development (OECD), have developed, or are currently developing, strategies and guidelines concerning AI and its impact in society. At the same time and following Canada's release and implementation of a strategy to promote the use and development of AI in 2017, many governments have released strategies related to the future of AI. The comprehensive report by Tim Dutton lists and compares strategies to date [Dutton, 2018].

At the same time, corporations and individual researchers and developers are also engaged in discussing and adopting codes of conduct and self-regulatory systems to guide their activities. These have resulted in international initiatives, such as IEEE's Initiative for Ethical Considerations in the Design of Autonomous Systems[4], the Partnership on AI[5], the Foundation for Responsible Robotics[6], or more recently the ALLAI alliance in the Netherlands[7]. Together, these initiatives can make a significant impact in promoting Responsibility in AI, through the evaluation of ethical effects, public discussion with stakeholders, and citizen engagement in a multi-disciplinary fashion involving the traditional sciences, social sciences and humanities.

It is also important to consider the role, responsibility and rights of AI researchers, developers and users, and how their own implicit biases and moral principles may inform the AI systems they develop. Calls for codes of conduct and certification and

4. https://ethicsinaction.ieee.org/ by the Institute of Electrical and Electronics Engineers
5. https://www.partnershiponai.org/
6. https://responsiblerobotics.org/
7. http://allai.nl/

auditing mechanisms are increasingly being heard from the part of AI developers themselves as well as from the society, in general. Also, tech giants like Google or Amazon are asking for a clear regulation of the reach and methods used in AI, and request guidance or legislation for e.g., the use of automated facial recognition. Microsoft has gone further, calling for federal legislation on facial recognition, including a requirement for 'conspicuous notice' where it is in use. The recent EU project, AI4EU, is developing a methodological framework within which developers can understand and anticipate the possible ethical issues that their research and innovations might raise, and provides guidelines about what is, and is not, regarded as ethical behaviour.

§3.03 IMPACT: MORE THAN LEGAL

In order to design AI systems that are sensitive to moral principles and human values, methods for Responsible AI rest in three pillars of equal importance. First, society must be prepared to take responsibility for AI impact. This means that researchers and developers should be trained to be aware of their own responsibility where it concerns the development of AI systems with direct impact in society. This requires efforts in education and training and the development of codes of conduct. This requires methods and tools to integrate moral, societal and legal values with technological developments in AI. Moreover, Responsible AI is an issue of regulation and legislation. It is up to governments and citizens to determine how issues of liability should be regulated. For example, who will be to blame if a self-driving car harms a pedestrian? The builder of the hardware (e.g., of the sensors used by the car to perceive the environment)? The builder of the software that enables the car to decide on a path? The authorities that allow the car in the road? The owner that personalized the car decision-making settings to meet her preferences? The car itself because its behaviour is based on its own learning? All these, and more, questions must be informing the regulations that societies put in place towards responsible use of AI systems.

Second, responsible AI implies the need for mechanisms that enable AI systems to act according to ethics and human values. Whether we design them in that way or not, AI systems will and are already making decisions which we would consider having an ethical flavour if they are made by people. Being aware of this is what responsible AI is all about. How do we design systems that take implicit 'ethical' decisions? Or how do we design the system to ensure that it is always clear who is taking responsibility for decisions and actions? And where is the border between decisions that are ethical and those that are not? This requires models and algorithms to represent and reason about, and take decisions based on human values, and to justify these decisions according to their effect on those values. Current (deep learning) mechanisms are unable to meaningfully link decisions to inputs and therefore, cannot explain their acts in ways that we can understand.

Third, participation. It is necessary to understand how different people work and live with AI technologies across cultures in order to develop frameworks for responsible AI. In fact, AI does not stand in itself but must be understood as part of socio-technical relations. Here again, education plays an important role, both to ensure that knowledge of the potential AI is widespread, as well as to make people aware that they can participate in shaping societal development. A new and more ambitious form of governance is one of the most pressing needs in order to ensure that inevitable AI advances will serve societal good.

§3.04 ROADMAP AND CONCLUSIONS

The responsible design, development and use of AI systems are of utmost relevance to AI applications, such as self-driving vehicles, companion and healthcare robots, electronic health records (EHR), and ranking and profiling algorithms, which are already affecting society. In all these applications, AI reasoning should be able to take into account societal values, moral and ethical considerations, weigh the respective priorities of values held by different stakeholders in different multicultural contexts, explain its reasoning and guarantee transparency. In fact, Responsible AI is more than the ticking of some ethical 'boxes' in a report, or the development of some add-on features, or switch-off buttons in AI systems. Rather, responsibility is fundamental to autonomy and should be one of the core stances underlying AI research. For example, advances in computer vision and classification must go hand in hand with the ethical considerations on their use as autonomous 'decision makers' in target identification. In short,

Responsible AI is about human responsibility for the development of intelligent systems along with fundamental human principles and values, to ensure human flourishing and well-being in a sustainable world.

Responsible AI must be understood as part of complex socio-technical systems. As such an empirical/experimental ethics approach that can shape responsible (or good) AI not only from the outside but also from within AI practices, is needed. Responsible AI means that AI systems should be designed and implemented in ways that recognise and are sensitive to human interaction contexts without infringing on core values and human rights. Even though AI in itself does not absolve individuals from responsibility for their actions and decisions, the increasing complexity of AI systems renders attribution of responsibilities more difficult. Therefore, methods are needed that clarify responsibilities and make explicit which are the design choices, data and knowledge provenance, process and stakeholders.

Ensuring that systems are designed responsibly contributes to our trust on their behaviour, and requires both accountability, i.e., being able to explain and justify decisions, and transparency, i.e., understand the ways systems make decisions and to the data being used.

As AI systems grow autonomously with the capability to learn, their development must consider accountability, responsibility and transparency principles in an explicit and systematic manner. The development of AI algorithms has so far been led by the goal of improving performance, leading to opaque black boxes. Putting human values at the core of AI systems calls for a shift of mindset of researchers and developers towards the goal of improving transparency rather than performance, and this will lead to novel and exciting techniques and applications.

Advances in AI are of consequence to the whole society. Labour, education, healthcare, well-being are all impacted by AI. To ensure that this transition will lead to a better future, it is now the time to decide. AI brings in itself the enormous potential to improve the lives of many and to ensure human rights for all. However, how this will be realized depends on us.

CHAPTER 4

AI and Labour and Employment

Caroline Chetrit & María Jesús González-Espejo

§4.01 INTRODUCTION

One of the most discussed issues in AI is its impact on the employment market, and we will reflect on this in the current chapter. As we shall see, we do not yet have any concrete data on this. The forecasts made by different institutions and academics are very varied. It is still very difficult to make predictions given that we are still at a very early stage in the development of many of the technologies that are likely to have the greatest impact on the labour market, such as robots that will offer care services to the sick and elderly, or AI that will carry out functions that are performed today by professionals, such as lawyers or judges but that are more than likely to be performed in whole or in part by machines in the future.

Additionally, we will talk about how AI is supporting those responsible for managing people since this family of technologies has already found its way into talent management field and its use has a legal impact that needs to be reflected upon.

Finally, we will dedicate some time to the impact that AI is having on public bodies responsible for the control and management of the labour market, as well as the effect that it is having and could have on lawyers specialising in labour law.

§4.02 IMPACT ON EMPLOYMENT AND THE LABOUR MARKET

[A] Introduction

Are we heading into the era of mass unemployment? This concern is probably the most common one when thinking about the presence of Artificial Intelligence (AI) applications in our society. Over the centuries, most people have rejected or feared novelty, as well as decisive technological advances. The reason for this is simple: they are sources of progress, but also of instability. These technological leaps are synonymous with the disappearance of certain professions, and the creation of others that require different profiles. This remains valid whether one refers to the invention of the wheel, the steam engine, electricity, the Internet or AI. Nothing changes. In each era, the Cassandras foresee the end of one world, while others imagine the advent of another universe. No one can deny that some professions vanish with technological advances and that this will continue to happen. In the fifteenth century, the invention of printing by Gutenberg prompted the end of the profession of the copyist, despite the fierce struggle led by the master writers and illuminators. But Guttenberg's invention led to the creation of the typographer. With the emergence of the automobiles, the farriers vanished since horses were no longer a 'productive tool'!

Here is where Schumpeter's 'gale of destruction' must be recalled. He wrote that the 'process of industrial mutation that incessantly revolutionises the economic structure from within, incessantly destroying the old one, incessantly creating a new one.[1]' When reflecting on the impact of AI and the employment market, we could ask ourselves does this process of 'creative destruction', announced by Schumpeter, apply as well.

[B] Impact of AI on the Job Market: Destruction or Not?

In an exhaustive comparative analysis on the existing reports and forecasts related to the future of Jobs in the area of AI & Robotics, the tech researcher, Olivier Ezratty, reminds that *in 1933 John Maynard Keynes was already talking about the potential job losses related to automation, even before computers were invented.*[2] The attraction and curiosity that robots generate in humans generally, quickly transforms into an opposing movement due to the fear of being outpaced by technology and of being condemned to unemployment. Ned Ludd, by breaking two stocking frames in 1790, initiated the Luddites acts against the introduction of technology in the textile industry! High-powered computers, autonomous robots and AI are major drivers of economic and societal progress. But they are also a threat to jobs. In addition to the historical or cultural determinants, we can now add a new more empirical cause to the fear of robots. Since AI is impacting all economic sectors, no one doubts that the rise of AI, machine learning (ML), robotics, nanotechnology, 3-D printing, biotechnology and genetics, (coined as 'the Fourth Industrial Revolution' 4th Industrial Revolution (4IR)) will transform the job market. How can we succeed in making digital and human beings live together?

In a very interesting book titled *My Colleague is a Robot,*[3] Valery Bonneau, draws up an inventory of robots from several domains of applications and pinpoints how robots are steadily starting to replace humans in sectors no one would have imagined

1. Joseph Schumpeter, *Capitalism, Socialism and Democracy*, 1942.
2. Olivier Ezratty, *Les fumeuses prévisions sur le futur de l'emploi et l'IA*, 31 Oct. 2018. https://www.oezratty.net/wordpress/2018/fumeuses-previsions-futur-emploi-et-ia/.
3. Bonneau V., « *Mon collègue est un robot* », Alternatives, Gallimard, Paris, 2016.

before. To mention but a few: Motoman SDA 10 (cooking chef),[4] Google Car[5] (a self-driving car that could replace taxis), Rocky or Roxxxy True Companion (prostitution or sex companion),[6] Baxter and Kiva's (store handler), ASIMO (personal assistant),[7] or Airbus Aircobot[8] (Aircraft inspections), and Wall-Ye V.I.N. robot (winemaker).[9] Although not all these robots are yet to be found at daily use, they appear to be a potential threat to workers in the workplace, especially since '*each day brings a new idea, a new job in the hands of the robots*.'[10]

The forecasts on the destruction and job creation linked to the deployment of AI in the economy are varied since 2013. According to Olivier Ezratty, who has analysed numerous reports on the matter, '[t]he net destruction of jobs related to AI by 2023-2025 is between 6% and 47% according to studies, with forecasts that follow a downward trend, the main forecast of 47% dating from 2013 and those of 6% to 7% dating from 2016. More recently, studies have even predicted a positive employment balance within a dozen years! That gives us a lot of room for error and manoeuvre!'[11]

When looking at the different studies, the one published in September 2013 by Carl Benedikt Frey and Michael Osborne, two Oxford University researchers, entitled *The Future of Employment: How Susceptible Are Jobs to Computerization?* threw a paving stone in the techno-optimist pond. Their verdict: 47% of American jobs were threatened by automation by AI technologies.[12]

About one year later, in August 2014, the Pew Research Center published a qualitative study that listed the opinions of various specialists, some of whom estimated that half of all jobs would be at risk by 2025.[13]

The IMF followed in the footsteps,[14] then Deloitte,[15] which anticipated the displacement of 35% of jobs in the UK by robots in twenty years. Regarding the UK, in November 2015, the very serious Bank of England conducted its own study to estimate that 15 million jobs were directly threatened by robotization in the UK.

4. https://www.yaskawa-global.com/.
5. Now called Waymo https://waymo.com/.
6. Kleeman, Jenny, '*The race to build the world's first sex robot*'. Guardian (27 Apr. 2017). https://www.theguardian.com/technology/2017/apr/27/race-to-build-world-first-sex-robot.
7. https://asimo.honda.com/asimo-specs/.
8. a collaborative robot for aircraft inspections. https://www.youtube.com/watch?v = YLikbi48yEg.
9. Winemaker even accompanied by a colleague wine taster, able to identify the most visible defects of the beverages which are submitted to him. http://wall-ye.com/.
10. *See Supra* note 5 V. Bonneau.
11. *See Supra* note 4 Olivier Ezratty.
12. Carl Benedikt Frey And Michael A. Osborne, *the future of employment: how susceptible are jobs to computerization?* University of Oxford, 17 Sep. 2013, https://www.oxfordmartin.ox.ac.uk/downloads/academic/The_Future_of_Employment.pdf, last accessed 28/01/2020.
13. Pew Research Center: *AI, Robotics, and the Future of Jobs*, 2014 https://www.pewresearch.org/internet/2014/08/06/future-of-jobs/, last accessed 28/01/2020, last accessed 28/01/2020.
14. IMF and James Bessen, *Toil and Technology*, March 2015 https://www.imf.org/external/pubs/ft/fandd/2015/03/bessen.htm, last accessed 28/01/2020.
15. Deloitte, *From brawn to brains, the impact of technology on jobs in the UK*, December 2014. https://www2.deloitte.com/content/dam/Deloitte/uk/Documents/Growth/deloitte-uk-insights-from-brawns-to-brain.pdf, last accessed 28/01/2020.

But the most alarmist predictions were made by the global institute of the American consulting firm McKinsey. The report, updated in January 2017, covers forty-six countries and 80% of the world's existing jobs, estimates that 78% of predictable physical work could be replaced in the next 50 years.[16] Studies continue to pour in.

The pessimistic trend started to shift with the 2016 OECD[17] study, putting the above percentages into perspective. It foresees that 9% of jobs are automatable in OECD countries but only 6% in South Korea and 12% in Austria, being France in the average at 9%. The OECD relies on the famous Frey/Osborne study of 2013 but adjusts it by correcting the approach of the latter by analysing the automation of tasks rather than jobs, thus reducing job destruction. Six years after the publication of the Frey/Osborne study, the announced job destruction has not yet happened. On the contrary, by comparing the number of jobs by occupation in the United States between 2013 and 2016: overall, the number of jobs in certain professions has increased by 4.4% in 3 years. Out of 172 different professions, 57% have seen their numbers increase.

Additionally, several reports and surveys are countering the alarmist tone, positioning technology, and particularly automation and AI, as generally creating jobs rather than mass unemployment. Some jobs will indeed be lost or transformed, but others will be created. The most significant case being that of the Forrester Institute,[18] which in June 2016 estimated that *16% of jobs in the USA will be automated by 2025 whether by AI, robots or traditional automation, but that this will be compensated by the creation of 9% new jobs (8.9 million), generating a net loss of 7% of jobs.*

Despite the alarmists and other prophets of doom, many recent studies reveal that less than 10% of jobs are in real danger of disappearing: according to a recent study by the McKinsey consultancy[19] firm, less than 5% of jobs could be fully automated, and nearly 60% of jobs could be partially automated, up to 30% of the tasks that make up the jobs.[20] McKinsey calculated that for every 300,000 jobs eliminated or 'transformed' each year by automation, 320,000 new jobs were created, including jobs as digital marketers or big data analysts.

Of all studies, the one that seems to be more realistic due to the data on which it is based is the one titled *What jobs are affected by AI*, published by The Brookings

16. Mckinsey Global Institute (MGI), A future that works automation, employment, and productivity, January 2017. https://www.mckinsey.com/~/media/mckinsey/featured%20insights/Digital%20Disruption/Harnessing%20automation%20for%20a%20future%20that%20works/MGI-A-future-that-works-Executive-summary.ashx, last accessed on 28/01/2020.
17. OECD *Employment Outlook 2019: Act now to build a future that works for all #thefutureofwork* http://www.oecd.org/employment/outlook/, last accessed on 28/01/2020.
18. Forrester, *The Future of Organizations*, June 2016. https://go.forrester.com/future-of-organizations/?utm_source=forrester_pros&utm_medium=web&utm_campaign=capstone_org&utm_content=button, last accessed on 28/01/2020.
19. McKinsey Global Institute, *Jobs lost, jobs gained: workforce transitions in a time of automation*, December 2017.
20. *Four fundamentals of workplace automation*, McKinsey Quarterly, 2015.

Institution.[21] This study made its calculations of job exposure by comparing the most recent 16,400 patents for AI technology. It figured out what jobs will AI do by looking for patent phrases describing what it will accomplish and comparing those accomplishments with the U.S. Department of Labour's list of job descriptions. The study is based on a novel research technique developed by the Stanford PhD student in economics Michael Webb, who built his own algorithm to compare language from 16,400 AI patents with the specific words used to describe 769 different jobs in the government's official occupational database, known as O*NET. Some key conclusions of this research are that:

(1) 25 million workers in the US or 15% of that nation's labour force will be affected by AI.
(2) Jobs, where AI is expected to make the furthest inroads in the foreseeable future, are sales managers, computer programmers, and personal financial advisers.
(3) Employees with bachelor's degrees are seven times more exposed to AI than those with just a high school diploma.
(4) Asian-American and white workers look to be far more subject to the changes brought by AI than are Hispanics or African Americans.

As we have seen, most forecasts also have an unfortunate tendency to focus on the situation in the USA and do not take a global approach to the problem. Also, they do not consider the civil servants who are often the last to be robotized because they are protected by the slow pace of innovation in administrations and the lack of political courage. Also, most of the reports conclude that although short-term disruptions due to automation may be lower in developing countries than in rich countries, developing countries will face more difficult challenges in the long term when the costs of these technologies fall significantly.

[C] A Polarization of the Work Market Will Come with the 4IR Opportunities and Challenges

It is not so much the disappearance of work that is at the centre of concern as its degradation of the jobs. According to two surveys of executives (and managers) and workers, conducted both by the international firm Boston Consulting Group (BCG) in collaboration with other institutions[22] or firms[23] the majority of executives view AI positively (performance, speed and reliability of decision-making, organization and

---

21. *See* report at: https://www.brookings.edu/wp-content/uploads/2019/11/2019.11.20_BrookingsMetro_What-jobs-are-affected-by-AI_Report_Muro-Whiton-Maxim.pdf, last accessed on 28/01/2020.
22. S. Ransbotham, S. Khodabandeh, R. Fehling, B. LaFountain, and D. Kiron, 'Winning With AI,' MIT Sloan Management Review and Boston Consulting Group, October 2019. https://sloanreview.mit.edu/projects/winning-with-ai/.
23. 'IA et Capital Humain' Malakoff Médéric and Boston Consulting Group, March 2018. https://media-publications.bcg.com/Intelligence-artificielle-et-capital-humain.pdf.

way of working, functioning, steering and corporate governance). However, over 50% of the workers fear, a dehumanization of work, loss of social ties, as well as ethical problems (i.e., respect for privacy, protection of personal data, non-discrimination) and a failure to improve managerial practices, and almost half fear increased reporting and control. The McKinsey report points out that between 75 million and 375 million people around the world may need to change occupational categories and acquire new skills by the year 2030.[24]

Many robots provide an economic gain and help to provide an enhanced service, but in addition, improve the working conditions of employees. We should be pleased with robots doing some work, such as the impressive Skypod.[25] This small robot, created by Exotech, navigates warehouses at full speed. The robots in the automotive industry with their fine and delicate gestures, seem so human. The robots do the tiring or tedious tasks. They allow humans to focus on their strongest skills, the 'soft skills', such as creativity and personal interaction.

While there is no discussion on AI's capacity to create new jobs, it is also clear that in comparison to its capacity to destroy present jobs, the generated value in employment terms will be negative and therefore, Schumpeter's theory seems not to be valid in this case.[26] A 2015s article in the Atlantic magazine[27] compared AT&T, a leader in telecommunications fifty years ago, with Google. In 1964, AT&T had 758.611 employees and was valued USD 267 billion. Google has around 80.000 employees and is valued more than USD 1 trillion, which is around 4 times AT&T's. In other words, for every dollar of stock market value, AT&T employed 35 times more people yesterday than Google today.

Another relevant point is that the range of jobs affected by the robotization movement today is far greater than in past industrial revolutions. At the time Schumpeter presented his concept of creative destruction, innovations were certainly made in *clusters*, but appeared successively and in specific sectors (e.g., grooms and farriers were replaced by the automobile manufacturers following the invention of the internal combustion engine). Today, innovations are appearing simultaneously and in all sectors of the economy. From industry to education, through human services, agriculture, banking, commerce, health, transport or defence, most sectors are affected in the same period. The transition is, therefore, on a completely different scale and, consequently, much more difficult to manage.

Today's weak AI can certainly consider millions of data entries in a second, an impossible task for a human brain. However, AI cannot so far predict the future, nor *think differently*. For example, when used for recruitment, even though it can make clever connections of data, that humans would never have thought of, it can also encourage discrimination (when there is bias in the algorithm or data, for example) and even discourage recruitment 'outside the box'. In fact, human resources specialists are

24. McKinsey Global Institute, *Jobs lost, jobs gained: workforce transitions in a time of automation*, December 2017.
25. https://www.exotec.com/.
26. *Supra* note 3 Schumpeter.
27. Derek Thompson, *A World Without Work*, The Atlantic, 2015. https://www.theatlantic.com/magazine/archive/2015/07/world-without-work/395294/.

not really concerned about the number of jobs that would be created;[28] they are more concerned about other issues, such as reskilling of the least qualified or the new social class divisions that could emerge because of AI success.

The potential replacement of humans by AI and robots could be seen as an opportunity. Humans, formerly slaves to their work, would be freed by the latter and could engage in other activities, such as community or family life, or even forms of work that call on purely human qualities, such as creativity, inventiveness or management, as opposed to the boring work of yesteryear. Nonetheless, let's not neglect the structuring role of work in the lives of individuals. Work is at the origin of many social interactions; it gives individuals the feeling that they are useful to society and that they are paid for the service they provide, and it gives everyone a structured timetable.

The right approach when considering the impact of the AI on employment should not be in terms of competition but in terms of complementarity. Anyhow, for the moment, we can talk more about hybridization of the activities between AI and humans since AI can automate some tasks, but not an entire profession. This is the case of an oncologist or ophthalmologist who are already able to benefit from the contribution of imaging systems using artificial vision, but who still have a role as an integrator of sources of information on the patient, treatments and keep the relationship with the patient over time. As we pointed out in the first chapter, we are rather at *weak AI momentum* rather than at the *strong AI* one.[29] For the moment, AI technologies are essentially reinforcing human skills and capabilities.

Hence, as AI becomes more and more present in the work environment, two scenarios emerge. The first where AI completely replaces the human being and the second where technology increases its capabilities to make it a 'super collaborator'. We will go from jobs to 'Superjobs'.[30] The foreseen disruption of the professions won't be as fast as the media or some experts are now claiming. The technology is not ready. Anyone who uses Alexa, the Amazon personal assistant, which was launched with such a noise, knows that all its answers are rather basic. Who has not struggled with a service chatbot when dealing with a bank or any another service company, and has ended up in a dead-end dreaming of being helped by a real human being?

This is also raising major concerns regarding inequality. With AI, there will be, as we have already seen, an increase of employment in high-skilled cognitive jobs, but the low or middle-skilled service occupations are the ones mainly affected and under the disappearance threat. This will lead to a polarised labour market.

The future job market will probably consist more of jobs that require humans to monitor, repair, reskill, and educate machines, rather than doing the work itself. New professions will emerge, such as designer, trainer, manager, educator, evaluator of the functioning of AI and robots. In fact, many robots are designed to complement

28. Vid *supra* fn 24.
29. The distinction between *weak AI* and *strong AI* (or *Artificial General Intelligence*) is explained in chapter 7.
30. Deloitte, *2019 Deloitte Global Human Capital Trends*. https://www2.deloitte.com/content/dam/Deloitte/cz/Documents/human-capital/cz-hc-trends-reinvent-with-human-focus.pdf.

humans. For instance, the famous Robocop of Dubai,[31] which is expected to represent a quarter of the local police force by 2030, but it is designed to inform police officers, not to replace them when it comes to making arrests. In fact, there is a growing consensus that jobs requiring empathy, adaptability and creativity will remain the preserve of humans, while dangerous jobs or those with repetitive tasks are destined to be taken over by machines. In other words, to paraphrase Michel Serres, we are *all condemned to become intelligent*.[32]

§4.03 AI IMPACT ON THE EMPLOYEE'S LIFE: WORK RELATIONSHIPS, PEOPLE MANAGEMENT

[A] Are We Heading to an 'Augmented' Human Resources Department?

Although still emerging in the professional world, AI applications are also being developed and used for the management of work relationships. Will and/or should AI technologies take over the entire process from recruitment to job termination? Several legal and ethical problems emerge from this question.

Due to AI's features, some major issues are to be considered.

(1) AI could be biased, and therefore, reproduce social discriminations or inequalities existing in today's world (e.g., racial or gender bias in the selection of CVs or for a promotion) or even create new ones.
(2) AI consists of high-level mathematical algorithms that make some results difficult to be explained. Transparency and explainability become relevant.
(3) Privacy is also a major concern as AI requires the collection of large amounts of data. Moreover, this data could enable the personalization of offers at the individual level, which may lead to questioning certain 'democratic' social codes (e.g., individual pricing in health care, etc.). Finally, other questions raise from AI that makes autonomous decisions in complex situations.

AI applications are already being used by some companies to filter CVs, search for the right candidates, identify the reasons for job abandoning, conduct better job interviews, for training or to fire employees. They even make it possible to anticipate departures!

Let us see more in detail how AI is helping the Human Resources Department (HRD). AI can be of great help to provide additional information about the candidates. With the advances in AI and a higher need for skilled talent, HRDs will increase their efficiency by broadening their pool of candidates and by speeding up CV pre-screening, boosting candidate engagement and much more. AI can also be used to model typical candidate profiles for a specific position. But also, to compare them to a pool of internal

31. Joana Oliveira, *Un 'robocop' español se une a la policía de Dubái*, El País, May 2017. https://elpais.com/tecnologia/2017/05/25/actualidad/1495704315_118401.html.
32. Michel Serres, *Petite Poucette*, Ed Manifestes, 2012.

or external candidates. Recruitment and the decision-making process are being optimized and accelerated with AI.

AI can also help companies to analyse the productivity of its employees. This is what Amazon, for instance, did but had to stop doing. According to a document revealed by the specialized site, The Verge,[33] Amazon has used AI to analyse the productivity of its employees, sanction them and even dismiss them. This document, a letter published after a former employee's complaint following his dismissal, describes the functioning of an automated management system. 'Amazon's system tracks each employee's productivity rate and automatically generates warnings or dismissals based on quality or productivity, without the supervisor's input,' wrote a company lawyer.

Some AI applications could even predict a decision the employee himself has not yet made, such as determining if the employee is looking for a job or might be quitting in the near future. Two professors from Georgetown University and Warwick business school, have developed an algorithm that assigns employees a departure probability rate, which increases when the employee is probably considering an external offer.[34] At BBVA bank, an AI-based solution has been developed to identify the reasons for high rotation and has helped to identify patterns and reasons that lead to job abandonment.

But AI can also help the other side, the job seekers to find a better match. MY-ROCKET,[35] for example, offers the chatbot 'Hippolyte', the first personal assistant for any worker looking for a job, internship or work-study. The social dimension of this HR innovation is to streamline the labour market by facilitating the matching of job supply and demand.

When we were writing the last pages of this book, the government of Andalusia (Spain) tendered the acquisition of an AI-based development to support public employment service professionals in their work. The profiling tool aims to provide better resources to the technical staff dedicated to employment orientation of unemployees, so as to facilitate greater personalization of job demands and offers and the individualized treatment of job profiles. Through predictive methods, the tool will serve to anticipate the needs of employers and relate the knowledge and experience of job seekers to those needs with a higher level of disaggregation.[36]

33. Collin Lecher, *How Amazon automatically tracks and fires warehouse workers for 'productivity'*, The Verge, 25 Apr. 2019. https://www.theverge.com/2019/4/25/18516004/amazon-warehouse-fulfillment-centers-productivity-firing-terminations.
34. Brook Holtom and David Allen, *Better Ways to Predict Who's Going to Quit*, Harvard Business Review, August 2019. https://hbr.org/2019/08/better-ways-to-predict-whos-going-to-quit?ab=hero-subleft-1.
35. https://www.my-rocket.fr/.
36. RRHHPress.com: https://www.rrhhpress.com/zona-tech/48503-andalucia-licitara-un-sistema-estadistico-de-intermediacion-laboral-basado-en-inteligencia-artificial-y-big-data, last accessed 15 Feb. 2020.

[B] What Should Be the Role of the Human Resources Departments (HRD)?

AI could enable the HRD to free itself from repetitive and time-consuming tasks to focus on its core business: talent management and team support. The rise of AI in companies is therefore not part of a logic of replacing man by machine but, on the contrary, of enhancing specifically human qualities. Many HR experts consider that using AI tools to manage the relationship with the employees is a fantastic opportunity to reposition the HRD within companies. As stated by Carlos Pelegrín Fernández,[37] former HR manager in companies such as Iberia, Orange, Telefónica, '[f]ar from being a threat, this is an opportunity for HRD to regain strategic space to anticipate problems... Now there is going to be a war for talent.... HRD must respond to the demand and bring in the best profiles in the most efficient way.'

In our view, HRD should play a key role in the deployment of AI. In companies with less knowledge of AI, HRD needs to establish a framework of trust. In companies more skilled in terms of AI acquisition and use, HRD can progressively structure their support through the consolidation of a data approach and the integration of AI into all the usual HR mechanisms: skills management plan, redefinition of hybrid professions, dissemination of an 'AI culture' within the organization, support for managers, etc. But moreover, we believe that HRD might have an essential role as supervisors on the compliance of AI with the company's social or workers ethical policy.

The Malakoff Médéric[38] report proposes fifteen actions that the HRD of the future should launch to become strategic in AI projects for their companies. These actions can be summarized into five main roles as:

(i) Partner of business development to create the framework for AI deployment (as support).
(ii) Warrant of skills (in charge).
(iii) Strategist (support).
(iv) Facilitator of the social and societal relationship (in charge).
(v) Head of the HR function (in charge).

HR directors are therefore called upon to be on the move to disseminate a data culture, develop a learning policy for these new intelligent tools and, above all, to rethink the organization of work, the division of tasks between humans and AI.

§4.04 THE IMPACT OF AI IN LABOUR LAW AND PRACTICE

We are only at the beginning of an unparalleled transformation not only of the labour market and employment but also of the employment relationship. The undergoing shift to the 'digital economy' is increasing the de-standardization of employment patterns,

37. Capital Humano, Inteligencia Artificial, una tecnología que transforma y multiplica las capacidades de las personas, https://institutodeinnovacionlegal.com/wp-content/uploads/2019/04/COLOQUIO-IA.pdf (last accessed 6 Jan. 2020.
38. *Supra* note 25 Malakoff Médéric.

involving greater flexibility in working time, evolving work arrangements, and a break with the traditional linear life-course career path. The automation due to AI technologies is expected to accelerate these trends. When we talk about labour relations, we talk about labour law. However, labour law should be able to serve as a tool to accompany the obvious transformations generated by the presence of AI in companies.

As the World Bank points out, Labour Legislation is geared for working methods during the industrial era and as such robotization, and AI could have a significant impact on labour Law. What exactly is the impact of AI on labour law and labour relations? Should labour law apply to robots? Should robots be entitled to paid holidays or sick leave for overheating? Should they have Working hours? The answer is no, of course. Robots operate without time constraints or breaks. Robots do not need maternity or parental leaves, guarantees of respect for its privacy (no search or breath test will ever be performed on a robot, and there is no need to check its email inbox). Consequently, it makes no sense to apply labour law to robots, despite their eventual humanoid appearance.

Although labour law cannot govern the work of robots, it has to give an answer to the obvious transformations generated by the presence of AI in companies. In other words, labour law will have to evolve into a new framework in order to anticipate and integrate the obvious mutation derived from the impact of AI in the world of employment.

We must contemplate ways of adapting labour law in order to anticipate and enable a smooth transition to the new world by considering the three phases of the life of the employment contract: hire/execution of the employment contract/termination of the employment contract. This also raises a more general question on how AI will impact a worker's life, from recruitment to execution and termination of the labour relationship.

[A] Recruitment

In the new AI-dominated professional world, people will have to demonstrate more than ever their added value and usefulness if they want to remain 'employable'. In order to fight against the inescapable fear of machine control of man, man must reaffirm his free will and assert the very human qualities that make him and will always make him superior to the robot, however sophisticated it may be.

While individuals do have an obligation to adapt to the demands of this new employment market, society should be liable for demanding a non-discriminatory use of AI.

Although all developed economies are built upon a non-discrimination legal principle, it seems that it is not so easy to develop AI for recruitment that does not discriminate as showed the experiment developed by researchers from Carnegie Mellon University and the International Computer Science Institute. They built a tool called AdFisher to probe the targeting of ads served up by Google on third-party websites. What they found was that Google's advertising targeting algorithms are more likely to offer women lower-paid job offers.[39] In fact, it happens often: algorithms simply reproduce the discrimination already present in the data on which they are built. However, as Mr Villani wrote in his report to the French government,[40] *AI cannot be a new exclusionary machine.*

The European Economic and Social Committee (EESC), a consultative body that assists the European Parliament, the Council and the European Commission, wonders in particular about AI that make it possible to assess the productivity of employees and those that facilitate recruitment, and states that their use must be made in 'the protection of rights and freedoms with regard to the processing of workers' data (and) in compliance with the principles of non-discrimination'.[41] Particularly, the EESC look into AI that can be used to assess the productivity of the employee and those that facilitate recruitment and states that their use must be in *the protection of rights and freedoms with regard to the worker's data processing and in compliance with the principles of non-discrimination*. In the face of these real risks, which are recognized by all stakeholders, it seems essential to integrate ethics into AI.

[B] Employment Execution

As said before, the development of digital technologies has profoundly transformed the organization of workspace/time – teleworking, co-working, etc. – and work relationships. There is a trend towards individualization, flexibility and 'informalization' that characterize new forms of work, such as 'cloud working'. The number of non-standard workers with non-standards contracts has increased. With the likely decline of certain forms of work and of some professions, we can expect even a more flexible exercise of professional activity in a more collaborative model. (i) These will be new, less pyramidal work organizations. The Manager will become more of a coordinator than a supervisor. (ii) Humans tend to have more confidence in the solution given by a machine. The danger could consist of a transfer of decision-making to the machine, although, as we know, AI & robots are not perfect.

Nonetheless, most of the current existing labour legal frameworks, are not adapted to the advent of AI in the daily life of the companies and their employees as we have already seen with the so-called collaborative platforms such as Uber.[42] In this new world of work, and while awaiting the necessary updating of regulatory codes, the formal place of employer-employee relationships may be weakened. However, some countries have moved to address this new issue, as also the right to disconnect for the

39. https://tgsus.com/diversity/google-shows-men-ads-for-better-jobs/ and https://www.technologyreview.com/s/539021/probing-the-dark-side-of-googles-ad-targeting-system/ (last accessed 29/01/2020).
40. Rapport Villani, '*Donner un sens à l'intelligence Artificielle – Pour une stratégie nationale et européenne,*' March 2018.
41. European Economic and Social Committee, *Artificial intelligence: anticipating its impact on jobs to ensure a fair transition (own-initiative opinion),* 19 Sep. 2018, INT/845-EESC-2018. https://eur-lex.europa.eu/legal-content/EN/TXT/?uri=OJ%3AC%3A2018%3A440%3ATOC.
42. Isabelle Daugareilh, Christophe Degryse and Philippe Pochet, *The platform economy and social law: Key issues in comparative perspective,* 2019.

employees, admitted recently by France. But it seems that a set of new risks and new situations, linked to the development of digital technologies in the company, are hardly considered to date. Probably the framework of working conditions is unsuited to the new working arrangements, while not considering the specific new risks.

The labour regulation will have to be correspondingly modified or adapted and address those risks:

(i) Reduction of wages and limited ability to save or to invest in pensions. In the prospect of the scarcity of work and a prospective higher unemployment, there are growing voices in favour of a Universal Living Wage[43] - also called Basic Income - or the structure of the wages might have to change or evolve. The idea is to combat job insecurity and dependency through a primary sharing of the wealth produced by society. This is undoubtedly an attractive idea, but it might not be sustainable and a satisfactory solution to the announced automation movement. It can indeed be criticized on two levels: the financing of such universal wage and its questionable philosophy. Somehow this will be a recognition of the inability of the current system to reach full employment in an AI era.

(ii) Working time. Increase in the number of hours worked since AI applications and robots are not subject to timetables themselves.

(iii) Intrusions on other rights such as discrimination or privacy violations.

(iv) Isolation: having to comply with the instructions of a machine and not being able to interact with other individuals might create this feeling.

Reskilling is probably the most important worker's necessity if they want to be part of the AI area. To our knowledge, only France has implemented a legal tool to enable the necessary continuous training of the employee by the employer, called *Gestion prévisionnelle des emplois et des compétences* (GPEC) or Job and Competency Planning solution based on the employer's legal obligation to provide skill development of the employees.[44]

---

43. President Barack Obama himself, in an interview on 24 Aug. 2016 with the director of the MIT Media Lab, Joi Ito, said: 'Whether a universal income is the right model - is it gonna be accepted by a broad base of people? - that's a debate that we'll be having over the next 10 or 20 years'. - However, the European Parliament did not take up the idea of universal income in its resolution to the Commission of 16 Feb. 2017 (European Parliament, Resolution with recommendations to the Commission on Civil Law Rules on Robotics, (2015/2103(INL)), 16 Feb. 2017) whereas the idea was suggested by the initial report of the Legal Affairs Committee (Draft Report with recommendations to the Commission on Civil Law Rules on Robotics, (2015/2103(INL)), European Parliament, Committee on Legal Affairs, 31 May 2016, speaker: Mady Delvaux, point 23).

44. Article L. 6321-1 of the French Labour Code sets that an employer must offer training as part of the skills development plan, which aims at ensuring that employees adapt to their workplace and maintain their ability to retain their jobs, particularly considering technological developments.

[C] Employment Termination

Since one of the main threats of AI is job cuts, an issue that will arise more and more often is if companies will able to invoke technological changes to justify them. The case has already been judged in Spain. In September 2019, a court declared the termination of an administrative employee who was replaced by a robot to be unjustified.[45]

This pronouncement is important due to the topicality of the issue. The case related to the automation of a task. The plaintiff was part of the administrative staff of a Hotel for thirteen years, working in accounting and debt collection. Four months before she was fired a bot, doing mostly the same, was installed, and unlike her, it did not need to stop for lunch or on weekends. The company decided to fire her (and a co-worker) when they realized that this task was carried more efficiently by Jidoka, an RPA (robotic process automation) for collection management.

The company claimed that what the (human) worker took minutes to do what the machine did it in seconds and could do it twenty-hours hours a day without breaks. To justify the dismissal, they alleged technical, organizational and productivity causes both in the termination letter and in the judicial procedure. The most substantial point of the judgment relates to the distinction between technological cause stated by the judge, and the conflict between freedom of entrepreneurship and the right to work. The ruling summarizes it in the following terms: *automation – as a technical cause of objective dismissal – implies an opposition between the Social Rights achieved by the workers that are seen as an obstacle or impediment to achieving a more optimal business performance, as opposed to the possibility that an instrument of production can carry out that same work without a time limit, without salary or social contributions. The automation by means of bots or robots, with the only justification of reducing costs to increase competitiveness, means the same as reducing the Right to Work to increase the Freedom of Enterprise. Therefore, a termination in these terms cannot be considered appropriate, given the interpretation that must be given to objective termination for technical reasons.*

This judgment is not creating a firewall against the replacement of workers by machines. It is only making it more expensive for the employer to fire someone and replace him with a bot.

When it comes to justifying job cuts, there are legal systems such as the French, in which companies can invoke technological changes - acquisition of new tools leading to new working methods, computerization – as a reason for dismissal. According to Article L.1233-3 of the French Labour Code, a redundancy (or dismissal due to business reasons) is *a dismissal decided by the employer for one or more reasons that are not related to the employee, which result from the elimination or transformation of a position, or a modification, refused by the employee, of an essential element of the employment contract, notably due to economic difficulties or technological changes.*

Such transformations constitute an autonomous ground for dismissal: the elimination or transformation of employment or the modification of the employment

45. Juzgado de lo Social N°. 10 de Las Palmas de Gran Canaria, Judgment from 23 Sept. 2019, Proc. 470/2019.

contract does not have to be linked to economic difficulties. Viable companies would, therefore, be likely to justify workforce reductions solely by investing in robotics and AI. Nonetheless, the French Labour law also sets some safeguards - not to prevent job losses due to technological change, but to limit them.

Therefore, and as we have seen in the Spanish judgment, it will be in the judge's hands, to be vigilant about the efforts made by the companies to adapt employees when they have to rule on the merits of dismissals justified by technological change. Especially in a context of job cuts linked to the introduction of a new AI-related work tool. An obligation could be created to try to adapt the employee to a new position before any dismissal measure is taken.

Continuous reskilling is a key issue in this technical revolution. The challenge is there: adapting today's workers to tomorrow's jobs. The public service employment in Europe has a crucial role to play, as a role model. According to the most recent Deloitte's report,[46] 86% of the surveyed believe they must reinvent their ability to learn when facing the relentless acceleration of AI, cognitive technologies, and automation.

[D] AI Impact on Labour Law Advice

The labour lawyer is specialized in Labour and Social Security Law. His work consists of advising individuals and companies on all kinds of issues related to this area of law. His advice covers all the legal issues that may arise during the different phases of the employment relationship: selection, hiring and dismissal and the representation in a court of the client, as well as mediation and negotiation roles. To carry out their work, they need to research, reflect and write reports, lawsuits, letters, opinions, collective agreements, etc.

For the lawyer who defends his clients in litigation, probability tools can be very useful in defining procedural strategy, as can tools that support the work of writing legal texts, providing arguments, applicable rules, etc. based on natural language.

At the procedural level, the labour lawyer will have to understand the fundamental elements of AI because the expansion of its use will sometimes make it play a relevant role in the substance of the issues to be resolved.

AI can also be useful for the labour lawyer in his task of identifying certain patterns in the analysis of documentation in Due Diligence processes.

Other tools that may be useful are those that allow the automatic classification of documentation and those that facilitate its search.

As a concrete use case of AI applied to the labour field, it is interesting to analyse the project called Lynx Legal Knowledge Graph and its application to Compliance Assurance Services in Labour Law. The project is led by Universidad Politécnica de Madrid and deploy with the support of Cuatrecasas.[47] The goal is to provide access to the aggregate and interlinked relevant legal information in the law labour sector across

46. Deloitte, *2019 Deloitte Global Human Capital Trends*. https://www2.deloitte.com/content/dam/Deloitte/cz/Documents/human-capital/cz-hc-trends-reinvent-with-human-focus.pdf.
47. http://lynx-project.eu/, last accessed 7/2/2020.

multiple legal orders, jurisdictions, and languages. This *solution will leverage multilingual linked data enabling the integration of disparate legislation, administrative acts, case law, and doctrine. This proposed solution will be realized by (i) enriching the LKG with legal sources from different legal orders, countries or languages in the domain of labour law; (ii) creating extensive links (see Semantic Annotation, Extraction and Linking Services) between legal provisions, case law, administrative resolutions and expert literature even across different jurisdictions; (iii) offering a tailored service for lawyers that effectively identify the relevant documents that may affect the case they are handling in a more efficient way (see Recommender and Alert Service) and (iv) creating alerts, through the life cycle of the case, of news and relevant changes to any of the legal provisions or documents that the lawyer working the case has identified as applicable or of interest for the case. The pilot will cover the different jurisdictions (EU, DE, AT, IT, ES)*. The prototype will let the firm do a complete identification of all the relevant legal provisions in terms of employment in order to give informed advice to the client on the viability of the country and favour a better-informed strategy definition for the internationalisation of companies.

§4.05 CHALLENGES FOR THE WELFARE SYSTEM AND SOCIAL PARTNERS

The nature of work is being increasingly altered by the technological changes in addition to other factors, such as declining birth rates, rising life expectancy, a new type of works, higher cross-border mobility. More and more voices are rising to say that Social Security systems financed by payroll taxes created for times of stable employment are becoming fiscally and socially unsustainable. At the same time, policymakers need still to address the old challenges of providing adequate yet affordable support to workers and strengthening incentives for individuals to save more, invest continuously in their skills, and look for work. The current welfare systems, as the organization of work, seem to be outdated.

The big challenge for the social protection institutions as well as the Unions or any social partner is to keep up with the pace of change.

Many countries have prepared and published strategies for the development of AI (e.g., Canada, China, Denmark, France, Finland, India, Italy, Japan, Mexico, Singapore, Sweden, South Korea, Taiwan, USA, etc.). They all want to lead the AI global race. Some of the initiatives are international such as in the European Union (EU)[48] or the Nordic-Baltic Regions.[49]

Those reports have considered the use of AI in companies. By doing so, they became aware that this had a major impact on the labour market, and some include

48. In April 2018, the European Commission presented a coordinated plan prepared with Member States to foster the development and use of AI in Europe.
49. The Nordic-Baltic Region released in May 2018 a declaration for the collaboration on artificial intelligence, called 'AI in the Nordic-Baltic Region'. https://www.regeringen.se/49a602/globalassets/regeringen/dokument/naringsdepartementet/20180514_nmr_deklaration-slutlig-webb.pdf.

regulatory recommendations to their governments, some of them focused on labour law.

The EU has issued several studies. We will focus on two of them, the one from May 2019 requested by the European Commission to Michel Servoz,[50] Senior Adviser on AI, Robotics and the Future of Labour, and the report of the European Parliaments led by Mady Delvaux-Stehres, a Luxembourgish MP.[51]

[A] The Impact on Social Security Systems

[1] Sustainability of the Funding of the Social Security System and Social Protection of the New Workers

We have seen that one of the impacts of this 4IR is, among others, a shift from traditional full-time employment to various non-traditional forms of work, and to self-employment. This exacerbates funding challenges, but also creates the need to extend legal coverage to new categories of worker. Furthermore, the growing number of workers in non-standard employment, which is often associated with gaps in social protection coverage, has been identified as one of the main challenges for social protection systems for the future. Some National social protection institutions are taking decisions to consider new work relationships. For example, the Swiss National Accident Insurance Fund issued a decision classifying an Uber driver as an employee and Uber should pay social security contributions for them.[52]

The European Commission, (2018), ILO[53] and OECD,[54] agree that the social protection systems of the future will need to be based on a set of broad policy principles that can ensure universal and adequate coverage, and sufficient adaptability to new requirements. Some broad principles have been established to guide policymakers in strengthening social protection systems: (1) Universality of protection and accessibility, (2) adequacy, (3) transferability, (4) transparency, (5) gender equality, (6) good governance.

As the International Labour Organization (ILO) states in a recent report *[s]ocial protection is a defining feature of contemporary economies and societies and an important part of their social fabric, acting as a key means to achieve equity and social justice.*[55] The changes brought by AI and automation will impact the funding of all the

---

50. European Commission *'The future of work? Work of the future!'* May 2019.
51. *See Supra* note 43.
52. *See Supra* note 42.
53. International Labour Office (ILO), 2018a. Innovative approaches for ensuring universal social protection for the future of work, Issue Brief No. 12, prepared for the 2nd Meeting of the Global Commission on the Future of Work, Geneva, 15–17 Feb.
54. OECD, 2018. Promoting adequate social protection and social security coverage for all workers, including those in non-standard forms of employment, paper prepared for the EWG meeting, Buenos Aires, 20–21 Feb.
55. ILO: Issue Brief #12 Prepared for the 2nd Meeting of the Global Commission on the Future of Work 15–17 Feb. 2018, cluster 6, Innovative approaches for ensuring universal social protection for the future of work. https://www.ilo.org/wcmsp5/groups/public/---dgreports/---cabinet/documents/publication/wcms_618176.pdf.

social system. If robots and other AI technologies will replace specific jobs and will generate certain unemployment, the social security systems will find difficulties for its financing. Who will be paying for managing the transitions workers will need to undergo, and the necessary accompanying social protection measures?

The EU has established that the share of labour income is declining as, in parallel, the share of capital is increasing[56] everywhere. Increasing the pressure on the employer does not seem the right or only approach to face the funding of the welfare state in the future. Under these conditions, it is difficult to reconcile rising costs with a shrinking funding base. It seems clear that in the medium term if not the near term, other funding sources need to be found.

One possibility would be to continue funding the social protection; the tax revenues might need to come increasingly from capital rather than from labour. The other solution will be having the robot pay social taxes. This idea is similar to the 'Robot Tax' promoted by the founder of Microsoft, Bill Gates.[57] Gates argued that if human workers' income is taxed today, and then a robot is deployed to do the same work, it seems logical to think that we should tax the robot at a similar level to the human. This solution is broadly endorsed by the European Deputy from Luxembourg, Mady Delvaux,[58] among others.

[2] AI Applications Used by Social Security Systems

On October 2019, the International Social Security Association (ISSA) issued a landmark report[59] showing that social security institutions around the world are innovating to adapt to the digital economy and new forms of work and that Social security administrations are no less impacted by digitalization than other providers of public services. The social security institutions are already taking advantage of the opportunities for service improvement offered by advanced technologies such as AI.

AI techniques enable the implementation of fully automated systems based on ML and similar techniques to deliver more proactive social security services, such as for the moment the implementation of chatbots. An example is Argentina's social institution (Superintendencia de Riesgos del Trabajo – SRT), which has implemented a chatbot to respond to questions related to work injury benefits.

Some of these chatbots are for the moment only at an experimental use (e.g., Belgium, Finland, Saudi Arabia). Some are already a step further, such as Belgium's Auxiliary Unemployment Benefits Fund (CAPAC) is exploring how to apply AI and deep learning systems to assist staff in supporting decision-making on benefit claims. Finland seems to be leading this transformation, where the Social Insurance Institution

56. European Commission: Employment and Social Developments in Europe 2018. https://ec.europa.eu/social/main.jsp?catId = 738&langId = en&pubId = 8110.
57. R. Waters, *Bill Gates calls for income tax on robots*, FT February 2017. https://www.ft.com/content/d04a89c2-f6c8-11e6-9516-2d969e0d3b65.
58. *See supra* note 43.
59. ISSA Report: 10 Global challenges for social security – October 2019. https://www.issa.int/en/details?uuid = edf9c9ac-0952-4aad-89c0-c01cd689bbd3.

(KELA) is currently conducting a strategic transformation of its platform and business model by adopting AI.[60]

The ISSA underlines that ensuring the inclusiveness of any system is key and avoid the emergence of a digital divide.

[B] Role of the Labour Unions as AI Emerges

The previously mentioned, eighteenth-century United Kingdom's Luddites wrecking of stocking frames, at the dawn of the Industrialization, illustrates that trade unions do not have any ability to prevent the implementation of automation or change the trend of technology adoption, and this also applies to the AI.

New organizational models and shorter workdays are two viable solutions to address the struggles of encroaching automation, but neither addresses the heart of the problem that AI exposes. In addition to the natural mandate of the Trade Unions (e.g., prevent job loss, ensuring that work conditions are acceptable and continuously improving, gaining fair wages, etc.), we can imagine that their role will be to foresee and secure how the disruption caused by AI will be managed in the job market and pointing out in addition to the social issues, ethical ones.

Unions can have a positive impact on many areas in the future AI-empowered environment (e.g., Protecting Workers' Privacy and Productivity, Transparency of the data management Responding to the Myth of Neutrality, reskilling and upskilling the employees etc.). The European Trade Union, UNI Europa ICTS has published in November 2019, a position paper on AI that highlights how unions should engage in the debate on AI, especially with regards to collective bargaining.[61]

UNI Global Union, based in Nyon, Switzerland, represents more than 20 million workers from over 150 countries in the fastest growing sectors in the world – skills and services. The Future World of Work has been one of UNI Global Union's key priorities in recent years. The *Top 10 principles for ethical artificial intelligence*[62] are a set of principles aimed to be included in collective agreements, industrial policies and Global Framework Agreements. The document provides unions, shop stewards and workers with a set of concrete demands to the transparency, and application of AI. It will inform AI designers and management of the importance of worker inclusion.

These are the ten principles:

(1) Demand That AI Systems Must Be Transparent.
(2) Equip AI Systems With an 'Ethical Black Box.'
(3) Make AI Serve People and Planet.

---

60. Ministry of Economic Affairs and employment of Finland, Leading the way into the age of artificial intelligence Final report of Finland's Artificial Intelligence Programme 2019. http://julkaisut.valtioneuvosto.fi/bitstream/handle/10024/161688/41_19_Leading%20the%20way%20into%20the%20age%20of%20artificial%20intelligence.pdf.
61. UNI Europa ICTS *Position on Artificial Intelligence*, November 2019. http://www.uni-europa.org/wp-content/uploads/2019/12/AIUniEuropaWeb_en.pdf.
62. http://www.thefutureworldofwork.org/media/35420/uni_ethical_ai.pdf (last accessed 6/1/2020).

(4) Adopt a Human-In-Command Approach.
(5) Ensure a Genderless Unbiased AI.
(6) Share the Benefits of AI Systems.
(7) Secure a Just Transition and Ensuring Support for Fundamental Freedoms and Rights.
(8) Establish a Global Governance Mechanism.
(9) Ban the Attribution of Responsibility to Robots.
(10) Ban AI Arms Race.

Regarding ethical issues, let us recap two major reputational crises Google has suffered in the last two years. The first one took place between April and May 2018, when the news was spread that 3,100 of its employees had sent a letter to the top of the company asking the company to abandon the so-called Maven project, hired by the US Ministry of Defence. Before this news was known, a group of employees, belonging to the *Algorithmic Warfare Cross-Function Team*, had decided not to work on the project.[63] The reasons that led Google employees to resign from their positions and sign the charter have to do with ethics and the possibility that their company's dedication to certain AI projects could end up damaging their customers' trust. The second crisis was experienced in April of this year when Google was forced to communicate the dissolution of its recently created ethical council, ATEAC (Advanced Technology External Advisory Council), composed of experts, whose role was to advise Google on the application of ethics to its AI. On this occasion, employees again questioned the suitability of some of those elected to the board.[64]

The facts described lead us to an important conclusion: the relevant role that employees and trade unions have and will have in the future, in controlling the respect by their companies of the ethical principles of AI. Reality shows us something perhaps less obvious: it is one thing to state principles, but quite another to make them a reality. By now, almost all the major corporations behind the most important developments in AI already have their declarations of ethical principles for AI, but not the policies and actions that can help them turn the declarations from words into deeds. Companies that develop and/or use AI at any stage of their value chain will have to work on the design of clear strategies and tactics to make respect for ethics a reality at three levels. First, that which refers to respect for ethics in design or, what is the same, the development of methods and standards that allow the analysis and evaluation of the ethical implications of AI systems insofar as these integrate or replace traditional social

63. Maven is a program used by the US armed forces, which takes advantage of AI to improve the orientation of drones. Its purpose, among others, is to develop and integrate artificial vision algorithms, necessary to help military and civilian analysts with the total volume of moving video data collected every day, in support of counterinsurgency and counterterrorism operations. Daisuke Wakabayashi and Scott Shane, Google Will Not Renew Pentagon Contract That Upset Employees, New York Times, 1 Jun. 2018. https://www.nytimes.com/2018/06/01/technology/google-pentagon-project-maven.html.
64. Kelsey Piper, *Google cancels AI ethics board in response to outcry*, vox, April 2019. https://www.vox.com/future-perfect/2019/4/4/18295933/google-cancels-ai-ethics-board.

structures. In the second place, the one that pursues the technical-algorithmic integration of the ethical reasoning capacities as part of the behaviour of the autonomous artificial system, this is the so-called, Ethics by design (*see* chapter §03). And finally, the one that pursues that the developers and users respect ethical principles in the research, design, construction, use and management of the systems, this is the so-called Ethics for design, which demands the creation of codes of conduct, norms and certification processes.

In practice, the intertwining of ethics in AI is being carried out in companies through the development of various types of actions, among others, some formative; others aimed at the development of software; others consultative and informative and others organisational, such as the creation of councils and committees of independent experts. What is indisputable at this point is that trade unions must actively participate in the development of these actions, and not only because it will be necessary to design policies for training and to relocate employees who will lose their jobs when replaced by robots, as the OECD recently pointed out in its recommendations on the proper use of AI, but also because employees may need their support in some cases, as has already happened in the case of Google, to defend the responsible use of AI in employment.

§4.06 CONCLUSION

It is undeniable that AI is going to replace humans in many areas, starting with those that are automatable tasks. There's no point in trying to compete: AI will always do better than humans due to the striking amount of data it can manage, and AI doesn't sleep, never gets sick, has no privacy requirements. This is a competitive advantage that brings specific risks in the business world.

Nevertheless, it might not be as fast as some are predicting as Richard Freeman, an economics professor at Harvard University who studies the impact of technology on work, said at a seminar held in July 2019 at the Oxford University.[65] The problem is that we do not really know much about the future. Many forecasts focus on the situation in the USA and do not take a global approach to the problem; they only look at the impact of AI in the private sector forgetting its potential impact in the public one. Most reports also look only to the impact in the developed countries, forgetting that as Fukuyama said[66] *the world is flat.*

If companies, government and workers themselves work together to address the skills challenge, then probably the technological advances will continue to benefit net job creation. Conversely, trying to curb them or to foster fears is the best way to miss opportunities and create unemployment.

In the end, the main question is if AI will be a 'tool' to serve employees and assist labour relations or AI will instead lead and subdue them? No doubt, the answer to this question will depend on the choice made by the Community of Human Beings. Both

65. Richard Freeman, '*I think the disruptions are going to be slower than people are claiming*'. R. Wright, *Workplace automation: how AI is coming for your job,* Financial Times Sept 2019. https://www.ft.com/content/c4bf787a-d4a0-11e9-a0bd-ab8ec6435630.
66. Francis Fukuyama, The world is flat, Penguin 2007, 3rd edition.

options are possible. It is up to man to make a choice. In the end, we come back to the philosophical question: are Human beings masters of their destiny or is destiny mastering human beings?

CHAPTER 5

AI and Taxation

María Jesús González-Espejo & Javier Martín Fernández

§5.01 INTRODUCTION

The inclusion of a chapter dedicated to taxation is essentially justified for three reasons. First, the real and potential use of Artificial Intelligence (AI)-based tools by Tax Administrations for various purposes, such as planning, tax investigation or the improvement of processes. Second, the need to reflect on the impact that AI is having and will have on the economy and employment and, consequently, on tax collection. And third, the use of AI by tax advisers to support their work. This same conclusion was reached by the German Research Centre for Artificial Intelligence, Deutsche Forschungszentrum für Künstliche Intelligenz (DFKI) and The International Tax Consulting Firm WTS Global in their joint study.[1] Ultimately, 'it is necessary to understand the impact of this technology in the different types of taxes; identify specific application scenarios for AI technologies, such as machine learning (ML), process

1. https://www.researchgate.net/publication/328996170_Getting_Ready_for_the_Future_of_the_Tax_Function_-_Global_Survey_on_Digital_Tax_Maturity_and_AI_Readiness.
 This study investigates the specific use of AI technologies in the field of taxation. It is the basis for a systematic assessment of the current status of digitalization (the 'digital maturity') of companies regarding their tax function. It reports the results of an empirical study among experts from WTS Global on the digital maturity of tax departments. The result is a comprehensive overview of digital maturity in the tax function, taking into account various country-specific characteristics as well as the opportunities and challenges of digitalization from the perspective of the experts. Based on these results, a tax-specific Maturity Model is developed, which can be used to assess and develop the digitalization maturity of tax departments. The Tax Digital Maturity Model represents an approach for the systematic evaluation of as-is situations and enables the consistent development of capabilities to leverage the potentials of digitalization and AI, thus providing guidance on future developments.

mining, information extraction, knowledge management, speech processing and multimodal systems for various control applications and develop the first software prototypes.'

According to Chávez Castillo,[2] AI may have an impact in four different fields: tax experience; tax employee experience; tax operations and tax innovation. This expert has also proposed a list of the possible benefits of AI applied by tax authorities and taxpayers that can be classified into two groups:

(a) Benefits for the tax authorities:
  - Improve services to taxpayers using cognitive services: chatbots with text and/or voice.
  - Improve collaboration amongst tax inspectors through productivity applications on mobile for managing cases in field audits.
  - Improved transparency through the explainability of the algorithms applied for different purposes.
  - Reduction in IT overheads through the use of AI public cloud solutions.

(b) Benefits for taxpayers:
  - Improve their experience as taxpayers through the use of AI-based applications across multiple devices.
  - More data and reports availability that will enable companies to make better decisions.
  - Automatic fiscal auditing, by using data analytics.

There are increasingly more tax advisers who help businesses that work in highly competitive multinational environments and that need to implement compliance policies. For these and other such tasks that require the management of a lot of data and the extraction of information in complex environments, AI offers very interesting solutions. Additionally, with an Administration which is well resourced in terms of data and information, advisers, in turn, need to be equipped with tools that allow them to defend the interests of their clients in a way that is at least as effective.

Additionally, tax enforcement bodies (management, inspection and collection) can rely on using AI-based technologies to better carry out their work (we will *see* that they are already doing so). We are facing an intensive area of data-management, much of it numerical, so AI and big data are the perfect tools for storage and processing purposes and for extracting conclusions as efficiently as possible.

Finally, experts are already warning of a risk whose consequences we are still unable to identify. The use of AI to carry out a certain type of tasks will have, as a direct consequence, the elimination of a large number of jobs, with a corresponding reduction of income for the public treasury. The solutions that have been proposed are the call for a minimum income or the taxing of robots.

2. Artificial Intelligence: Building Smart Digital Tax, https://www.iota-tax.org/sites/default/files/event_presentation_documents/ac_2018_session15_presentation_erica_chavez_castillo.pdf.

In summary, this chapter is centred around analysing how AI is a support tool for the Administration, tax advisers and taxpayers, as well as reflecting on the different options that politicians and legislators should begin to consider in order to handle the consequences that AI will have on employment and tax collection.[3]

§5.02 AI AS A SUPPORT TOOL FOR TAX ADVISERS

As affirmed in the joint DFKI and WTS study: 'wage tax and VAT, customs and transfer pricing are highly suitable for the use of AI technologies when complex routine tasks are performed, and large amounts of information are evaluated. Examples of such areas of AI application include the correct tax assessment of benefits-in-kind and VAT (Value-added tax) based audits. This includes software detection, which demonstrates the recognition of unknown errors and anomalies in mass data, such as transactions in the field of customs duties. Another prototype is Q&A. This innovative assistance system helps its users to quickly and easily access relevant control information and execute. Q&A is an example of a further trend in the field of taxation: the complexity of tax legislation will be reduced by AI. For instance, the question-and-answer system makes it possible for people who are not tax professionals to obtain decision-making support for tax issues from an AI solution. The software is also being used to develop horizontal networking with other company departments. This aspect is becoming increasingly important for tax departments'.

The study also points out the challenges that corporate tax departments face in the field of taxation, such as 'increasing compliance requirements in tax-relevant processes, stricter standards for the implementation of internal control systems and new obligations stipulating the electronic filing of tax returns', and identifies digitalization and the application of AI through intelligent automation of routine activities and cognitive support for intellectual tasks, as the solution to these challenges.

Additionally, some of the biggest players in the taxation field,[4] such as Deloitte, have already publicly declared they are investing heavily in innovation to bring new technology-powered solutions in which taxpayers, tax experts and tax authorities can benefit from AI.[5] As pointed out by this company, 'The current tax environment is characterized by tax authorities requiring increased transparency across jurisdictions, sharing information with each other and applying determined approaches to tax management and collection process, but with a lack of consistency across borders. This is expanding the compliance workload for businesses, while they are exposed to increased tax risk and uncertainty about the sustainability of current business models and group structures...To manage this changing landscape, alongside the increased use of analytics, tax authorities and tax advisors are starting to explore the possibilities

3. In relation to the impact of AI in the future of employment, we also recommend viewing this video, which analyses the risks derived from the educational system and its lack of adjustment to the needs of a society and economy where AI will be intensively used: https://www.youtube.com/watch?v=htAnVeMtrr8.
4. AI is still an expensive technology.
5. As, for instance, Deloitte (https://www2.deloitte.com/global/en/pages/tax/articles/artificial-intelligence-in-tax.html).

for deploying sophisticated data analytics and AI in tax to facilitate compliance and assist professionals and their clients with commonly encountered questions.'

Despite these declarations, as one searches around for AI taxation focused solutions, the conclusion is that there are not so many. The reason being that the business cases where these kinds of solutions would make sense, demand handling huge amounts of data, often of different sources, and this is both a complex task (particularly when bias needs to be avoided) and very time-consuming one. Thus, identifying a business case that can generate enough gains becomes essential, and it is not so easy to find this kind of use case.

§5.03 AI AS A SUPPORT TOOL FOR TAX CONTROL

The new generation of information technologies is creating new exchange possibilities between economic agents, as well as the transformation of the management models of organizations.[6] This has a significant impact on the way in which Public Administrators, specifically tax administrations, interact with citizens to promote efficiency in response to their needs, as well as guaranteeing greater transparency, information and inclusion in all their operations. A good example of this is the use and development of electronic invoicing, introduced with various aims.[7]

The first goal is to fight against tax evasion. A good example of what is happening in this area is Portugal, as well as some Latin American countries (Brazil and Mexico) and Asia. At the most advanced level of development, suppliers and buyers have to send their Tax Administrations invoice data, or at least electronic reports, for real-time online validation. In general, electronic invoicing is compulsory and is eliminating the use of paper (more than half of electronic invoices processed globally were in Latin America).

The efficiency of the internal invoicing process of businesses and the electronic collaboration between suppliers and buyers are still not fully optimized, but VAT or other tax returns can be done easily and more efficiently.

The second of the aims is the simplification of tax obligations. A good example of this is Chile and, in Europe, Austria, Belgium, France, Germany, the Netherlands, the Scandinavian countries and Switzerland. Chile, the precursor of the electronic invoice (a compulsory process that began in 2014), evidences an advanced tax awareness. The characteristics of the Chilean model are very favourable, due to the existence of electronic invoices and the electronic register for the assignment of receivables, all controlled by an Internal Tax System.

The majority of Tax Administrations are applying big data to their tax application procedures. Big data is understood to mean, according to Gartner, 'data containing a

6. J. Martín Fernández y F. Anaya Martín, 'El marco conceptual del Suministro Inmediato de Información en el Impuesto sobre el Valor Añadido', Guía práctica del SII, Tirant lo Blanch, Valencia, 2018, pp. 29–46.

7. Cfr. 'Impacto en la Evasión por la Introducción de la Factura Electrónica', Investigador-Coordinador Hugo Javier Fuentes Castro (núm. IA-006E00002-E37-2016), Instituto Tecnológico y de Estudios Superiores de Monterrey (Mexico).

large variety that is increasing in volume and at a higher speed'. These are known as 'the three Vs' (volume, velocity and variety). In other words, large and more complicated groups of data are involved, especially those coming from new sources. These groups are so large that simple, conventional processing software cannot manage them. However, they can be used to tackle business problems that it would previously not have been possible to solve.[8]

In May 2016, the Organisation for Economic Co-operation and Development OECD published '*Advanced analytics for Better Tax Administration*',[9] a report that highlights the key opportunities and challenges in establishing, operating, or improving advanced analytics functions in tax administrations. The report provides practical examples of how administrations are currently utilizing advanced analytics and discusses key topics, including organizational arrangements, governance, management and data. The report also discusses how administrations are using analytics to improve their operations and deliver better outcomes to taxpayers. Finally, it sets out conclusions, recommendations, and next steps.

As stated in this report, while tax administrations have been using analytics for more than fifteen years, much of this use has focused narrowly on case selection, but the emergence of advanced analytics allows the introduction of other kinds of approaches to data, such as pattern recognition, outlier detection, cluster analysis, experimental design, network analysis, and text mining. Chapter 5 of this report includes a benchmarking of best practices in the use of data analytics.

In '*Technologies for better tax administration: A Practical Guide for Revenue Bodies*,'[10] the OECD points out the need to foster cooperation amongst tax administrations to collaborate in the exchange of best practices in the collection, management and use of data. The report looks at effective e-service provision by tax administrations, summarizing eight critical areas, and explores big data management and portals in detail. It highlights key opportunities in these areas, looking at how these emerging technologies can be best used by tax administrations. It also provides practical examples of how tax administrations have begun to utilize these technologies and deliver a maturity matrix for the two areas to assist strategic and operational decision making by tax administrations.

Taking the Spanish case, for instance, the Spanish National Tax Administration, Agencia Estatal de Administración Tributaria (AEAT, as per its Spanish acronym), one of the most technologically advanced Tax Administrations in the world,[11] launched a big data project in Spain, choosing the most appropriate technologies from within the group of tools from the ecosystem called Hadoop, a common reference in the

8. Oracle: Qué es el Big Data: https://www.oracle.com/es/big-data/guide/what-is-big-data.html.
9. https://www.oecd.org/publications/advanced-analytics-for-better-tax-administration-9789264256453-en.htm.
10. https://www.oecd.org/publications/technologies-for-better-tax-administration-9789264256439-en.htm.
11. Award to the Spanish Tax Agency in the 22nd General Assembly of the IOTA (Intra-European Organisation of Tax Authorities) for its digital support tools for VAT.

processing of massive volumes of information.[12] This ecosystem currently contains, based on the Impala analysis, 40 billion records (4*10^10) corresponding to the data from the last 4 years.

Together with the Hadoop ecosystem, other tools that have been used are:

(a) Spark-GraphX (Pregel Algorithm), is a system that allows the user to determine the corporate wealth of an individual, that is to say, people who have stocks and shares in companies that in turn have stakes in other companies.
(b) Lucene is a text search system (with approximately 10 million indexed documents), and it has been verified that it scales appropriately when adding nodes to the cluster. Many of the documents used by the system come from those submitted by the taxpayer, of which an OCR (Optical Character Recognition) scan is made (45 million pages completed).

Even though the use of Hadoop ecosystem tools has demonstrated its versatility, the AEAT has spent many years investing in the creation of a corporative Data Warehouse, known as Zújar, which, with more than a thousand sources of data, represents the very analytical heart of the institution. This Data Warehouse allows the AEAT to quickly and easily have at its disposal all information necessary to carry out its work.

Zújar supports an interactive function for searching and viewing data, sorting, filtering, grouping, adding or comparing them. This system compares information allowing it to identify inconsistencies between data sources (for instance, VAT that a business states to have incurred, versus that which others declare they have charged it). This tool offers quick response times for the free processing of large volumes of data, but this lapse is worse when the number of sources exceeds 1,000 million records. For these and larger sources, Hadoop-Impala is used, but with the same user interface as Zújar.

This relies on more than 10,000 different users (around 40% of the AEAT employees and other external authorized users), and it is used extensively, not only for the selection and analysis of taxpayers in the fight against fraud but also to carry out statistical analysis and monitoring of the organization's activity at all levels.

Each user can only access the information that is truly relevant for his or her job, whether this be from a functional or territorial point of view or even depending on the features of data to which they wish to have access. This allows control to be maintained over what can or cannot be done independently by users and the variety of the data.

In order to make it useful, an arduous task of modelling the information has been carried out that allows each user to understand the data he/she is seeing and search those which are of interest. All this information with the assurance that it has the right quality is poured into a metadata dictionary and becomes the heart of the system.

12. A. Castro: 'El valor de los datos de las AAPP y su valor como herramienta para las mejoras de los servicios públicos', Boletín, núm. 81, 2017 (https://www.astic.es/sites/default/files/articulosboletic/boletic_81-monografico9-alfonso_castro.pdf).

This is complemented by a standardized report generator (called Genius), that allows predefined complex analyses. This is especially useful when the desired diagnosis is clear and highly effective, for example, in the selection of taxpayers to be checked, where an additional level of objectivity is provided.

This, despite the difficulties encountered (lack of market specialists and very high tool ecosystem), increases the effectiveness of the AEAT to allow it to do more with less, dedicating human resources, which are always finite, to more important issues, increasing productivity and enhancing the figures in the fight against fraud.

A large part of this huge amount of information is supplied mainly by third parties.[13] Articles 29.2.f) and 93 of Act 58/2003, of 17 December, General on Taxation, establish that persons, be they natural or legal, public or private, as well as entities without legal personality, are obliged to provide the Administration with any type of tax-related data, reports, background or supporting information, related to compliance with the Administration's obligations or inferred from their economic, professional or financial relationships with other persons. In the words of the Spanish Constitutional Court Ruling 76/1990, of 26 April, 'the duty to communicate tax-related data thus becomes a necessary tool not only for a fair contribution to general expenses (Article 31.1. Spanish Constitution) but also for effective tax management.'

Being an obligation that, as we can see, links to compliance with the duty to contribute, the data for which there is an obligation to provide information and supply are only those with 'tax relevance.' This requirement, although vague, implies making administrative powers subject to a specific purpose so that actions to acquire information will only be lawful to the extent that the data to be supplied lead, directly or indirectly, to the application of the taxes. The problem is – how to determine when this circumstance concurs?

We can establish that the 'tax relevance' of data is defined by two basic characteristics. First, the data must be specific, and it must be specified in the regulations or in the requirement addressed to the citizen. This excludes generic requests that refer, for example, to all economic data referred to an individual. Second, there must be a link between the said data and the tax consequences arising therefrom. However, they do not have to refer immediately to previously ignored taxable cases, in whole or in part (direct usefulness), but also includes requests for other data that, in so far as they indicate that such cases might concur, will serve to commence a verification procedure against specific persons (indirect usefulness).

Finally, the data that must be provided are those which are deduced from 'economic, professional or financial relationships' with other persons. Therefore, data that have come to be known as a result of relationships other than those listed above, such as strictly personal data, remain outside the sphere of this obligation.

Data that the Tax Administration can obtain from other sources of information is another issue where the use of said data may violate the right to privacy. This is applicable not only to the Tax Administration but also to private enterprises. This is the

13. J. Martín Fernández: Tratado práctico de Derecho Tributario General Español, Tirant Lo Blanc, Valencia, 2017, p.p. 317–330.

case for the Web Crawler[14] or Web Spider program used to explore web pages methodically and automatically. It allows one to track and cross economic data from more than 200,000 domains that are incorporated into its database.[15]

§5.04 A CASE IN POINT: AVIVA, THE SPANISH NATIONAL TAX AGENCY'S VAT CHATBOT

In 2018, the AEAT put in place a system called Immediate Information Supply System (SII, as per its Spanish acronym) aimed at managing VAT through the almost immediate supply of invoicing records via the Electronic Office the AEAT (SE, as per its Spanish acronym). The setting up of this system forms part of the actions to control and prevent fraud, both in VAT and its related obligations (example: Corporation Tax) since it enables the acquisition of enough information of high enough quality as quickly as possible.

Since its introduction, the SII has raised numerous queries among those employers who, either obligatorily or voluntarily, record their invoices through the SE in order to keep VAT registry books. With the aim of maintaining the quality of the information provided and a satisfactory response time ratio, the AEAT decided to resolve those most simple issues automatically, using AI under the name 'Virtual SII Assistant'. This virtual assistant is able to respond to non-predefined questions and uses AI to learn to understand and continually improve the service. The system has been expanded, going from being an SII assistant to a general VAT assistant, now known as AVIVA (Asistente Virtual de IVA).

This is composed of predetermined conversations whose design has been carried out by SII specialists, starting with decision trees. The aim is to analyse all the factors that must be taken into account when it comes to offering an appropriate response to the specific case raised by the user. For this and faced with the formulated question, AVIVA asks a series of questions.

In this way, the conversation that a user sees on the computer or phone screen is translated through AVIVA's decision tree technology, where the arrows indicate nodes or options chosen from the answers offered by the consultant.

The tool incorporates almost 400 different responses that resolve the main issues related to the following topics: who applies SII, deadlines for the submission of records and settlement period, type of invoices, type of operation, errors in invoices or records, special schemes, annual records and information, consultation of recorded invoices and other matters.

The aim of AVIVA is to offer 'comprehensive information', and to do this the responses are accompanied by links to frequently asked questions and any other informational content from the SII banner relevant to the topic, as well as the corresponding SE procedures. In this way, AVIVA not only offers a response to the

---

14. A web crawler is a program that visits a list of URLs, identifies the links in these pages and adds them to the list of URLs to visit frequently and according to search parameters that are designed.
15. Vid., https://www.elmundo.es/economia/2015/03/12/5500ae2022601d20498b4574.html y http://www.expansion.com/economia/2018/12/26/5c235d3246163fe4a68b458c.html.

question made but also acts as a search engine making available to the user the contents of the AEAT website that may be of interest.

To access AVIVA, an email address is required. Once the system is accessed, the user needs to choose the thematic block on which the consultation is to be carried out and then ask as many questions as he/she wishes, also about topics different to the one initially chosen.

Each thematic block presents the most frequently asked questions or trending topics. If the user cannot find his/her query among these, he/she may ask AVIVA using plain language. At this point, it is important to point out that, for the tool to work correctly, it is necessary to formulate a complete question and not use single words as one would with a search engine, as this hinders AVIVA's understanding of the query. The user asking the question must maintain a conversation with AVIVA in such cases where it is necessary to obtain the most appropriate response to the query made.

Once the answer has been secured, the tool allows the user to evaluate it, indicating its usefulness. If the answer is negative, the user gets access to a form where it is required to insert the query to be sent to the group of specialists is possible, who will send the answer to the email initially indicated when AVIVA was accessed. If the user answers positively, the tool allows the latter to print and save the response.

The user's evaluation is taken into account to improve the service through a constant audit of the conversations, in order to incorporate into the virtual assistant's knowledge of the issues that were not resolved at first instance.

Since its launch in July 2017, the results obtained with AVIVA have been quite satisfactory, managing to reduce the number of queries received via email by more than 75% and reaching a number of 1,500 weekly accesses, a figure that almost doubles the number of queries sent to the queries mailbox before its appearance. An advantage of AVIVA is that the user receives an immediate response, 24 hours a day, 365 days a year that may be printed and saved, contributing to greater tax certainty.

These advantages show the AEAT commitment to this type of cognitive technology, making it the first public administration to open a new communication channel with citizens based on AI. In fact, the Tax Control Plan for 2019 of the AEAT foresaw generalizing it for all VAT taxpayers, and its completion is expected in the short term.

An additional service is offered to taxpayers who request an appointment regarding a VAT information request. They will be offered AVIVA to ask the question so that after getting the answer, they can decide whether to continue with the request for an appointment or not.

§5.05 TAXATION CHALLENGES REGARDING ROBOTIZATION

None of the studies that have been done, which are not few in number, doubt the significant impact that robots will have on jobs, and they highlight the need to seek methods to compensate for the consequences that the loss of these incomes will have for countries.[16] If robots do all or part of the work previously done by taxpayers and social security contributors, the system will be deprived of part of its revenue and the negative impact on the public treasury is indisputable. Consequently, the lower the incomes, the lower the taxes and the lower the capacity to maintain infrastructures, pay pensions or health expenses.

Holden indicates that there are 'two main factors that set the AI revolution apart: the different capabilities of the technology and the unfamiliar economic trends that have been created by the technology. The AI revolution may lead to a transition of labour into another sector, but numerous factors indicate that there could be some permanent technological unemployment.'

In addition, it has already been pointed out by various Universities, Think Tanks and consultants that the social class that will suffer the greatest impact as a result of AI is the middle class, a fundamental pillar of modern democracies, economies and welfare systems. Although we still cannot know the real impact it will have on employment, according to McKenzie,[17] 'the scale of shifts in the labour force over many decades that automation technologies can unleash is not without precedent. It is of a similar order of magnitude to the long-term technology-enabled shifts away from agriculture in developed countries' workforces in the 20th Century.' Data provided by the OECD indicate that '1 in 6 current middle-income jobs are at high risk of automation'. In addition, it has also been pointed out that training is the solution to readapt people to the new professional profiles that will be required in an economy where AI will play an essential role, and that it will also need to be paid for.

Against the imposition of taxes on robots, it is argued, on the one hand, that the loss of jobs should not be attributed to their existence, as there are many other factors that may be influencing it. Examples of these are countries such as Germany or Japan, which are highly automated and yet have full employment. On the other hand, this imposition is an obstacle to innovation, as it could discourage it.

It is thanks to Bill Gates that the subject of taxing robots has been brought to the table in an interview with the economic information portal 'Quartz'. Following Xavier Oberson,[18] this can be achieved by increasing Corporation Tax for companies with a high degree of robotization, a tax on the salary assigned to robots with tax withholding at source, as well as on their contribution to Social Security, making them pay VAT, the creation of a tax on the ownership of these machines or taxes for their registration and control.

Before considering any of these measures, we must bear in mind that the digital economy and robotization are, from a tax point of view, different phenomena. The former can lead to a diversion of profits versus innovation and legitimate cost savings.

In relation to the latter, it can be thought that robots differ from machines in that the incorporation of AI means that they can replace human beings, but this is not the

16. E. Holden: Taxes for robots: Automation and the Future of the Labor Market, https://digital.usfsp.edu/cgi/viewcontent.cgi?article=1190&context=honorstheses.
17. A future that Works: automation, employment and productivity: https://www.mckinsey.com/featured-insights/digital-disruption/harnessing-automation-for-a-future-that-works.
18. 'Taxing Robots? From the Emergence of an Electronic Ability to Pay to a Tax on Robots or the Use of Robots', World Tax Journal, May 2017.

case at all. At this moment and from an economic point of view, they are a means of production, of capital. Therefore, taxing could clearly mean a penalty for innovation. In short, companies' loss of competitiveness translates into unemployment. Nor must we forget that all developed countries credit innovation with tax incentives.

The question then is who should bear the cost of robotization? In our opinion, society as a whole, to the extent of its economic capacity and by means of the application of a progressive tax system. Examples include the elimination of favourable tax treatment for income from capital, the increase in the capacity to collect Corporation Tax, the pruning of tax benefits, the reform of Wealth and Inheritance Taxes, the revision of reduced VAT rates, environmental taxation or the financing of Social Security by taxes.

However, it is possible that, in the future, robots will have economic autonomy comparable to that of human beings: they will receive a salary, provide services as businesspersons or professionals, consumer goods and services and will own assets. In this case, they will have a legal personality for civil and tax purposes, as proposed by the European Parliament,[19] and they will be taxed as such.

§5.06 CONCLUSIONS

AI is also transforming tax practices. It helps administrations detect tax fraud, predict market patterns, optimize the tax structure, and improve collection capacity. It also improves the relationship between taxpayers and tax administrations, through intelligent virtual assistants capable of resolving any doubt through natural language and with the aim of collaborating in the compliance of the obligations of the former, reducing or eliminating errors, while the virtual assistants learn on each individual situation. The Spanish example is quite significant in this respect, as AVIVA has turned the AEAT into the first public administration to open a new channel of communication with citizens based on AI.

This, therefore, allows Tax Administrations to focus their efforts on the taxpayers who present cases of greater complexity or live outside the law.

An issue for discussion is taxation on robots, which can be achieved by increasing Corporation Tax for companies with a high degree of robotization; a tax on the salary assigned to robots with tax withholding at source, as well as on their contribution to the Social Security, making them pay VAT or; by creating a tax on the ownership of these machines or taxes for their registration and control. However, taxing them would be a penalty on innovation. In short, it would entail a loss of competitiveness for businesses, translating into unemployment. Nor must we forget that, meanwhile, all developed countries provide tax credits for innovation.

Regarding who should bear the cost of robotization, as we have already exposed, the best solution would be society as a whole, applying the principles of economic capacity and progressivity, increasing the collection of Corporate Tax, removing

19. European Parliament resolution of 16 Feb. 2017 with recommendations to the Commission on Civil Law Rules on Robotics (2015/2103(INL)).

favourable treatment for capital income, cutting tax benefits, in particular, reduced VAT rates, and reviewing the taxation on Wealth, Inheritance and Environment, and contributions to health services and pensions.

Logically, the foregoing would be only appropriate insofar as robots attain a financial autonomy comparable to that of human beings: receiving a salary, providing services as businesspersons or professionals, consuming goods and services and owning assets. If this occurs, the attribution of legal personality for tax and civil liability purposes will probably be an appropriate solution.

CHAPTER 6
AI and Competition

*Bárbara Román & Julia Suderow**

We're not yet dealing with an algorithm quite as smart as [Hitchiker's Guide to the Galaxy's] Deep Thought. But we do have computers that are more powerful than many of us could have imagined a few years ago. And clever algorithms put that power – quite literally – in our hands.

M. Vestager[1]

§6.01 INTRODUCTION

Artificial Intelligence (AI), and Machine Learning (ML), in particular, are already supplanting human decisions in real marketplaces. This affects not only digital markets but also *brick and mortar* markets. For the reasons that we will discuss below, this new situation has provoked an intense debate in the Competition Law community.[2]

Free competition is achieved when each player in the market determines its strategy autonomously. Uncertainty is a critical element of a free market. Agrawal, Gans and Goldfarb conclude that as AI advances, we will use prediction machines to

* This article has been written in the framework of the project RTI 2018-094201-b-c22, el impacto de la economia digital en el derecho de la competencia y la distribución:
1. M. Vestager, 16 Mar. 2017, Algorithms and competition available at: https://ec.europa.eu/commission/commissioners/2014-2019/vestager/announcements/bundeskartellamt-18th-conference-competition-berlin-16-march-2017_en (last access: 23 Mar. 2019).
2. *See* for instance, Ezrachi, A. and Stucke, M. E. (2016), 'Virtual Competition: The Promise and Perils of the Algorithm-Driven Economy', Harvard University Press, United States. Harrington Jr, Joseph E., Developing Competition Law for Collusion by Autonomous Price-Setting Agents (22 Aug. 2017). Available at SSRN: https://ssrn.com/abstract=3037818 or http://dx.doi.org/10.2139/ssrn.3037818.

reduce risks more broadly.[3] First of all, we need to define how uncertainty is reduced and if this reduction is contrary to competition law or if, as might be the case, it results in innovation with positive effects for consumers. All these new circumstances involve difficult legal questions that need to be analysed. Authorities and regulators expect developers and companies to design each new tool or product in compliance with the applicable legal framework. Taking into account the potential consequences of anti-competitive conducts, our view is that the compliance of legal practitioners will be required from the very start in order to avoid any future pitfalls and sanctions.[4]

Digital markets are under the scrutiny of Competition Authorities. Practitioners and Scholars are discussing a potential new Antitrust Regime for Digital Markets that consider the specific features of these markets such as platforms, free products based on the data for data principle and data power.[5] The debate is mainly focused on whether the automatic ultra-fast and autonomous decisions adopted by price agents in digital markets can generate anticompetitive effects and if data giants have, through data concentration, too much data power, they may be blocking innovation when they refuse access to data. We understand AI as the ability of a computational entity to make choices through an evaluating process.[6] AI is already part of our daily life. Every time we use a search engine, the search engine uses us to improve its decision-making process.

Competition laws worldwide promote healthy competition with different rules that need to be known and respected by each player that acts in a specific market. Competition laws prohibit mainly anticompetitive agreements, such as price-fixing or market-sharing and the abuse of the dominant market position, or in some countries, the abuse of superior bargaining power or economic dependence. These rules also allow agencies, at international levels, such as the European Commission, or at the national levels, such as the German Bundeskartellamt or the Spanish Comisión Nacional de los Mercados y la Competencia, to control mergers between businesses when the result of the merger might be anticompetitive.

We will briefly introduce the reader to competition law and its objectives and then present the main concerns discussed by scholars, agencies and regulators. Due to the introductory goal of this book, we have limited the content of this chapter to the analysis of the main areas in which a developer or a company should think when

3. A. Agrawal, J. Gans, A. Goldfarb, Prediction machines, the simple economics of Artificial Intelligence, Harvard, 2018, p.165.
4. *See*, for instance, the antitrust proceedings of the European Commission against Google: The European Commission has sanctioned Google three times in three years for an abuse of its dominant position in relation to different products, such as android, google search and AdSense. *See*: http://europa.eu/rapid/press-release_IP-19-1770_en.htm (last access, 30 Mar 2019).
5. *See* about the current status of the debate: Sokol, D. Daniel and Comerford, Roisin E., Antitrust and Regulating Big Data (4 Sep. 2016). 23 George Mason Law Review 119 (2016); University of Florida Levin College of Law Research Paper No. 16-40. Available at SSRN: https://ssrn.com/abstract=2834611. C. Herrero Suarez, Big data y Derecho de la Competencia, C. 31 in Sociedad Digital y Derecho, Dirs. Tomás de la Quadra-Salcedo y Fernández del Castillo, 2018, p. 633–654. H. Schweitzer, J. Haucap, W. Kerber, R. Welker, Modernising the law on abuse of market power Report for the Federal Ministry for Economic Affairs and Energy (Germany), 4.9.2018 (last access 24 Mar. 2019).
6. J. Turner, Robot rules, regulating artificial intelligence, London, 2019, p. 16.

designing or purchasing AI as a price-setting tool. In fact, as of today and due to the lack of enough case law and expertise, competition agencies are much more active in advocating for more competition or antitrust by design than in investigating and imposing fines on companies that have breached competition law through such mechanisms. Notwithstanding this, there are already some precedents where agencies are dealing with existing business cases and have even imposed fines or initiated sanctions.

As we know, enforcement agencies can impose substantial penalties for infringements and offenders can be fined, disqualified from being a director and in some jurisdictions, sent to prison. Additionally, companies will have to compensate any victim for the damage caused by the anticompetitive conduct. Our goal is to explore how to provide legal support during the development phase of AI in order to reduce future risks.

§6.02 AI AND MULTILATERAL ANTICOMPETITIVE CONDUCT

The emergence of AI and independent decision-making algorithms can generate new potential problems for companies. They may breach competition law.[7] Until now, agencies have sanctioned companies for implementing software to intentionally limit price competition in digital markets, but Agencies and scholars are also concerned about unintentional price collusion or uncontrolled exchange of sensitive information that can be used for tacit collusion.[8] Deep Learning and other AI technologies generate a black box phase that escapes the control of the programmer.[9] As of today and depending on technical details, it is not always feasible to look at the algorithm used for the decision and identify what causes what.[10] First of all, we need to go through the basic prohibitions of Competition Law to see how automatic price-setting tools could adopt anticompetitive decision-making. Competition rules, such as Article 101 Treaty of Functioning of the European Union (TFEU) prohibit anticompetitive agreements

7. Calvano, Emilio and Calzolari, Giacomo and Denicolo, Vincenzo and Pastorello, Sergio, Artificial Intelligence, Algorithmic Pricing and Collusion (20 Dec. 2018). Available at SSRN: https://ssrn.com/abstract=3304991 or http://dx.doi.org/10.2139/ssrn.3304991, p. 2. U. Salaschek, M. Serafimova, Preissetzungsalgorithmen im Lichte von Art. 102 AEUV, in Wirtschaft und Wettbewerb 2019, pp. 118–123.
8. Ezrachi, A. and Stucke, M. E. (2016), 'Virtual Competition: The Promise and Perils of the Algorithm-Driven Economy', Harvard University Press, United States.
   Harrington, J. E., Jr. (2012), 'A Theory of Tacit Collusion', Economic Working Paper, The John Hopkins University, http://www.tse-fr.eu/sites/default/files/medias/stories/SEMIN_11_12/ECONOMIC_THEORY/harrington.pdf.
   Mehra, S. K. (2015), 'Antitrust and the Robo-Seller: Competition in the Time of Algorithms', Minnesota. Law Review, Vol. 100, www.minnesotalawreview.org/wp-content/uploads/2016/04/Mehra_ONLINEPDF1.pdf.
9. OECD, Algorithms and Collusion: Competition Policy in the Digital Age, 2017. www.oecd.org/competition/algorithms-collusion-competition-policy-in-the-digital-age.htm (last access, 23 Mar. 2019). About the unique features of AI *see*: J. Turner, Robot Rules, Regulating Artificial Intelligence, London, 2019, p. 64.
10. Agrawal, A.; Gans, J., Goldfarb, A. Prediction machines, the simple economics of Artificial Intelligence, Harvard, 2018, p.197.

between businesses. These rules prohibit the following conduct between two or more companies:

- Agree to fix prices or terms of trade.
- Agree to limit production to reduce competition.
- Carve up markets or customers.
- Discriminate between customers, for example, charging different prices or imposing different terms where there is no difference in the circumstances of supply.

Any other type of agreement that prevents, restricts or distorts competition is covered (not just the kinds of agreements listed above). An agreement could be formal (such as legally binding contracts) or informal (such as unwritten 'gentlemen's agreements'). This rule mainly applies to agreements between businesses with a significant combined market share. But even the smallest companies need to avoid getting involved in anticompetitive agreements, such as cartels.

Several authors consider that AI assumes critical business decisions, such as pricing and operation without human intervention. The use of AI for pricing or other business decisions could have implications for Competition Law and particularly facilitate cartels or other illegal practices, such as concerted practices or illegal exchange of information. It is well known that digital markets have unique features that are generating new challenges for law and business ethics.

These concerns are also shared by agencies and regulators that have published several studies in recent years about algorithms and 'robocartelists' that may distort the market in an inadvertent manner.[11] Additionally, competition authorities and courts have confirmed the first sanctioning decisions against companies that used algorithms to collude as we will summarize below.

The European Commission's E-commerce Sector Inquiry (2017) found that of the online retailers surveyed who actively monitored competitor prices, 67% use automatic software programs to track and report on competitors' prices. Most of those businesses subsequently adjusted their prices manually. However, a significant number also relied on software to implement automatic adjustments.[12] Monitoring prices is not forbidden by competition rules, but, it can raise specific competition concerns under determined conditions, and it clearly shows that these type of tools are used in order to determine the commercial strategy of several market players.

The OECD in the year 2017 established four different types of algorithms that could be used to implement collusion:

11. *See* Mehra, S. K. (2015), 'Antitrust and the Robo-Seller: Competition in the Time of Algorithms', Minnesota. Law Review, Vol. 100, www.minnesotalawreview.org/wp-content/uploads/2016/04/Mehra_ONLINEPDF1.pdf Autorité de la concurrence and Bundeskartellamt (2016), 'Competition Law and Data', p.15, <http://www.autoritedelaconcurrence.fr/doc/reportcompetitionlawanddatafinal.pdf>.
12. European Commission (2017), 'Final Report on E-Commerce Sector Inquiry', 10 May 2017, COM (2017) 229 final, http://ec.europa.eu/competition/antitrust/sector_inquiry_final_report_en.pdf.

Table 6.1 Summary of the Roles of Algorithms in Implementing Collusion

Monitoring algorithms	Collect and process information from competitors and eventually punish deviations.
Parallel algorithms	Coordinate parallel behaviour, for instance, by programming prices to follow a leader; sharing pricing algorithms; or using the same third-party algorithm.
Signalling algorithms	Disclose and disseminate information in order to announce an intention to collude and negotiate the common policy.
Self-learning algorithms	Maximise profits while recognising mutual interdependency and readapting behaviour to the actions of other market players.

Source: OECD (2017), Algorithms and Collusion: Competition Policy in the Digital Age.[13]

As of today, the first two types (monitoring and parallel algorithms) have been already detected and sanctioned by competition authorities in the cases known as TOPKINS, TROD and E-TURAS.[14] In the WEBTAXI case in Luxembourg, the competition authority considered that the automatic price determination between taxi drivers and through a common algorithm has pro-competitive effects that are shared with the consumers.[15] The first two cases, TOPKINS and TROD, relate to online sellers that programmed an algorithm to determine their prices in Amazon's marketplace. The third one, E-TURAS, represents a new version of the traditional 'hub & spoke' agreement, where a travel booking system sent a notice to the competing travel agencies about a new technical restriction to cap discount rates. The European Court of Justice confirmed that actual knowledge of the administrator's message was required for an infringement to exist, but knowledge could be inferred from 'objective and consistent' indicia.[16]

In all three cases that ended in sanction, the algorithm is used as a mere tool for the collusive agreement agreed by competing companies and their directors. The humans behind the algorithms knew that they were colluding, or knowledge could be inferred from objective and consistent indicia. This type of case does not present any challenge for enforcement agencies apart from designing a fast detection system and evidence gathering in digital markets. In fact, both detection and obtaining pieces of

13. Available at: www.oecd.org/competition/algorithms-collusion-competition-policy-in-the-digital-age.htm (last access, 23 Mar 2019).
14. Department of justice, 30 Apr. 2015, plea agreement No. CR 15-00201 WHO available at https://www.justice.gov/atr/case-document/file/628891/download (last access, 31 Feb. 2019) Competition and markets authority, Online sales of posters an frames, 12 Aug. 2016, Case 50223, available at: https://assets.publishing.service.gov.uk/media/57ee7c2740f0b606dc000018/case-50223-final-non-confidential-infringement-decision.pdf, (last access 31 Feb. 2019) ECJ, 16 Jan. 2016, E- Turas C 74/14, paragraph 51.
15. Conseil de la Concurrence, 7.6.2018, decisiòn 2018-FO, 01 available at https://concurrence.public.lu/dam-assets/fr/decisions/ententes/2018/decision-n-2018-fo-01-du-7-juin-2018-version-non-confidentielle.pdf (last access, 31 Jan. 2019).
16. ECJ, 16.1.2016, E- Turas C 74/14, paragraph 51. *See* about the debate Robles Martín-Laborda, Antonio, Cuando el cartelista es un robot. Colusión en mercados digitales mediante algoritmos de precios (When the Cartelist Is a Robot. Pricing Algorithms and Collusion in Digital Markets) (27 Apr. 2018). Actas de Derecho Industrial, Vol. 38, 2018.

evidence could also be achieved through monitoring algorithms programmed by the authorities and market studies like the e-commerce sector inquiry of the European Commission.

By comparison, signalling and self-learning algorithms that are a self-learning machine or AI are raising more significant questions since they do not mechanically follow the instructions of the programmer. Thanks to AI, machines can develop *pricing strategies from scratch, engaging in active experimentation and adapting to the evolving environment.*[17]

As pointed out by the OECD, powerful automated mechanisms that monitor prices, implement common policies, send market signals or optimize joint profits with deep learning techniques might enable firms to achieve the same outcomes of traditional hardcore cartels through tacit collusion. This discussion is not new. Tacit collusion is a classical problem of oligopolistic markets with high transparency and a reduced number of competitors with relevant market power.[18] There is not a clear definition and uniform treatment of tacit collusion that applies to all jurisdictions, but it refers to situations where competitors can maintain prices by recognizing their mutual interdependence. They do not agree, but they watch each other, and without communicating, they can align their prices by simple observation of the market. Price-monitoring is not prohibited per se, but if the monitoring is completed with additional communication and dependent actions, the authorities may consider that there is a *meeting of minds* supported by additional evidence that proves that the companies have not acted independently of each other.[19]

A recent paper published by Calvano, Calzolari, Denicolo and Pastorello (2018)[20] provides evidence about anticompetitive strategies adopted by AI in an experimental environment. The analysis carried out by the authors shows that algorithms learn to collude. The algorithms learned how to collude without prior knowledge of the environment in which they operate. They did not produce any evidence about a meeting of minds since they did not communicate with one another.[21] Previous literature and studies of competition authorities considered this as a hypothetical

17. Calvano, Emilio and Calzolari, Giacomo and Denicolo, Vincenzo and Pastorello, Sergio, Artificial Intelligence, Algorithmic Pricing and Collusion (20 Dec. 2018). Available at SSRN: https://ssrn.com/abstract=3304991 or http://dx.doi.org/10.2139/ssrn.3304991, p. 2.
18. About collusion, *see*: R. Marshall, L. Marx, The economics of collusion, cartels and bidding rings, 2012, Massachusetts.
19. *See* OECD (2017), 'Algorithms and Collusion – Competition policy in the digital age', <http://www.oecd.org/daf/competition/Algorithms-andcolllusion-competition-policy-in-the-digital-age.pdf, p. 21. Autorité de la concurrence and Bundeskartellamt (2016), 'Competition Law and Data', p.15, <http://www.autoritedelaconcurrence.fr/doc/reportcompetitionlawanddatafinal.pdf>.
20. Calvano, Emilio and Calzolari, Giacomo and Denicolo, Vincenzo and Pastorello, Sergio, Artificial Intelligence, Algorithmic Pricing and Collusion (20 Dec. 2018). Available at SSRN: https://ssrn.com/abstract=3304991 or http://dx.doi.org/10.2139/ssrn.3304991, p. 3.
21. Calvano, Emilio and Calzolari, Giacomo and Denicolo, Vincenzo and Pastorello, Sergio, Artificial Intelligence, Algorithmic Pricing and Collusion (20 Dec. 2018). Available at SSRN: https://ssrn.com/abstract=3304991 or http://dx.doi.org/10.2139/ssrn.3304991, p. 39.

problem far from reality, but we need to review this position in light of Calvano, Calzolari, Denicolo and Pastorello.[22]

Additionally, in the past, agencies solved the problem of the meeting of minds doctrine with evidence of communications between competitors. We believed that humans are unable to coordinate without explicit communication. If tacit collusion becomes widespread in digital markets generating anticompetitive outcomes, regulators and enforcers will need to adjust their policies about tacit collusion in digital markets.

The answer of agencies and regulators to all these questions even in the case of tacit collusion until now has been based on the liability of the programmer. In 2016, M. Vestager noted:

> What businesses can – *and must* – do is to ensure antitrust compliance by design. That means pricing algorithms need to be built in a way that doesn't allow them to collude. Like a more honorable version of the computer HAL in the film 2001, they need to respond to an offer of collusion by saying 'I'm sorry, I'm afraid I can't do that.'[23]

The message is crystal clear: You should know what you build, and you are responsible for it. In order to reduce risks, companies need to control and design in a compliant manner from the beginning. Competition law compliance by design will become more relevant in the future. Businesses must limit the possibilities of rogue AI and restrict its freedom by design.

How can we roll out compliance measures for algorithms? Increasing awareness from the very beginning of the design process is usually a practical measure that does not limit innovation. Programmers need the necessary knowledge about competition law, and lawyers need more specialized knowledge about AI to determine the relevant moments in the decision-making process where they need to intervene by blocking decisions that may have an anticompetitive outcome. Notwithstanding this, fear may hamper innovation when companies prefer to stop using AI if doubts are raised. Therefore, balanced awareness and compliance become essential to avoid unwanted burdens that limit innovation and healthy competition.

From the above, we can conclude that several competition law issues can arise if we use AI in digital markets, so the innovative legal analysis is needed from the beginning of each project. Legal professionals can support their programming teams and clients with proactive solutions in which designers and lawyers scrutinize and audit the AI system before it is released into the market.

To prevent a competition law concerns, if you discover an unintentional anticompetitive behavior in your AI system, you will need to stop it and correct it.

---

22. *See* for instance, Ezrachi, A. and Stucke, M. E. (2016), 'Virtual Competition: The Promise and Perils of the Algorithm-Driven Economy', Harvard University Press, United States, p. 71.
23. Margaret Vestager 'Competition: the mother of invention', European Competition and Consumer Day, Amsterdam, The Netherlands, 18 Apr. 2016. Available at https://ec.europa.eu/commission/commissioners/2014-2019/vestager/announcements/competition-mother-invention_en (last access 24 Mar. 2019).

In our view, the preventive work should start with an audit of the proposed tool. It is crucial to map the decision process of the algorithm and analyse each step from a competition law perspective. First, we need to ask ourselves if innovation and a better product are the real objectives of AI. This will give an important clue as to the real intention of the company. Second, the origin of the input and training data are also essential. How does the company obtain this data? Is this data accessible for third parties or only for specific players in the market?

The three types of data used by AI are input, training and feedback. They all have potential competition law risks. The first two may be related to the origin of the data if the data has been generated or provided by a competitor. The feedback data might also be used by other players in adjacent markets, and this may also raise data power concerns that need to be assessed.

Another way of reducing potential risks or anticompetitive outcomes consists of testing with different input data and comparing the results before release.

§6.03 AI AND UNILATERAL CONDUCTS

Collusion is not the only digital problem for Competition law. There is an increasing concern about the leading AI companies getting too big to compete. Google, Facebook, Apple, Microsoft and Amazon as well as Baidu, Tencent and Alibaba have been accumulating data for many years. The accuracy of their tools achieves unique results, and each use makes the tools even better. This situation may be hampering the entry of new players in the market and therefore, limiting competition in digital markets. Several scholars are concerned about the difficulties of smaller players and consumers and are raising concerns about the power developed by such data giants.[24]

Competition laws, such as Article 102 TFEU prohibit abuse of a dominant market position. This rule applies mainly to companies that have a large market share, usually 40% or more. To determine whether a company is dominant or not, other factors are taken into consideration in determining whether a company is dominant, which include the number and size of competitors and customers and whether new businesses can easily set up in competition. Data power can also be considered a domination factor. The type of practices that could indicate abuse include charging unfair prices or imposing other unfair trading conditions on customers, limiting production, or refusing to supply an existing customer without an objective reason. The refusal to grant access to data can be considered abusive and prohibitive if it is exercised by a company with a dominant position in the relevant market.

AI needs data to exist and work. As mentioned above, it needs three types of data: training, input and feedback data. Feedback data can be generated by the machine itself, but for the training and input, you may need massive amounts of data that are held by data giants. Economies of scale play a decisive role in AI and algorithms require access to a variety of data collected from multiple sources. Small entrepreneurs may not have the necessary complementary assets, or those who are not simultaneously

24. *See*, for instance, T. Wu, The Curse of Bigness, Antitrust in the new gilded age, New York 2018.

present in numerous markets might face barriers to entry, preventing them from developing algorithms that can effectively exert competitive pressure.[25] Data power can create barriers to entry as pointed out by Furman et al.[26]

The discussion is still open.[27] First, it is still unclear if the prohibition of the abuse of dominance is the right tool to fight data power abuses. Scholars and lobbyists request access to data sets to train AI tools. In this debate, we cannot ignore that the traditional essential facilities doctrine is not suitable for all Big Data related cases. This theory was developed for networks or facilities that are not replicable, and data is easily replicable and available.[28]

Notwithstanding this, the refusal to supply data over which a firm has exclusive control, and which is essential for engaging in a given activity in an adjacent market could already qualify as abusive under European competition law.[29] This situation can easily arise in the context of the Internet of Things (IoT), where a particular company holds exclusive data sets that are not otherwise available. It remains, however, whether other types of big data such as position data of persons that can easily be obtained through several digital tools are under the exclusive control of one company. As recently stated by Schweitzer, Haucap, Kerber and Welker (2019),[30] it will be a meaningful discussion, and the structure of any data sharing duty in legal terms is still a completely open issue. One of the potential solutions consists of granting access to data through the competition authority that can analyse in each case whether the access is necessary and proportionate to achieve its aims.[31]

Although the debate remains completely open, we must acknowledge that data power and all related questions will also play a vital role in the development of AI. Again, lawyers have to understand the reasons for access and the technical specifications related to it. Programmers also need to know that they cannot always refuse

25. Available at: www.oecd.org/competition/algorithms-collusion-competition-policy-in-the-digital-age.htm (last access, 23 Mar. 2019), p. 45.
26. J. Furman, Diane Coyle, Amelia Fletcher, Derek Mc Auley, Philip Marsden, *Unlocking Digital Competition, Report of the Digital Competition Expert Panel*, March 2019, (Last access 24 Mar. 2019).
27. *See*, for instance, the opposite view; D. Kaben, Die Bedeutung von Daten für den Wettbewerb zwischen Suchmaschinen, in T. Körber, U. Immenga, Daten und Wettbewerb in der digitalen Ökonomie. Baden-Baden, 2016, pp. 123–152. He considers that data are not the new oil but solar energy.
28. H. Schweitzer, J. Haucap, W. Kerber, R. Welker, *Modernising the law on abuse of market power Report for the Federal Ministry for Economic Affairs and Energy* (Germany), 2018 (last access 24 Mar. 2019), p. 143.
29. *See* about the current status of the debate: C. Herrero Suarez, Big data y Derecho de la Competencia, C. 31 in Sociedad Digital y Derecho, Dirs. Tomás de la Quadra-Salcedo y Fernández del Castillo, 2018, p. 633–654. H. Schweitzer, J. Haucap, W. Kerber, R. Welker, *Modernising the law on abuse of market power Report for the Federal Ministry for Economic Affairs and Energy* (Germany), 2018 (last access 24 Mar. 2019), p. 132.
30. H. Schweitzer, J. Haucap, W. Kerber, R. Welker, *Modernising the law on abuse of market power Report for the Federal Ministry for Economic Affairs and Energy* (Germany), 2018 (last access 24 Mar 2019), p. 172.
31. J. Furman, Diane Coyle, Amelia Fletcher, Derek Mc Auley, Philip Marsden, Unlocking Digital Competition, Report of the Digital Competition Expert Panel, March 2019, (Last access 24 Mar. 2019).

access per se and that the data sharing duties will depend on the exclusivity of the data and the genuine necessity.

Last but not least, AI benefits from big companies, but we still need to determine if the economies of big companies will lead to monopolies or not. Breaking up a monopoly reduces abuse and scale, but scale makes AI better as pointed out by Agrawal, Gans; Goldfarb (2018).[32]

The report Cremer, Montjoye, Schweitzer prepared for the European Commission has recently concluded that the Tech Giants like Apple, Facebook, Amazon and Google are characterized by following main features:

(1) extreme returns to scale;
(2) network externalities/network effects; and
(3) the role of data as a key input for new products and services.[33]

It is important to highlight that data is not always indispensable to compete and that the relevance of data for the development of new AI tools will depend on a case by case assessment. These experts propose the following paths in cases where the access to data is necessary to establish competition in a market:

- Data interoperability and full data portability going beyond the current General Data Protection Regulation (GDPR) framework in order to guarantee multi-homing.
- Pro-Competitive Data sharing and data pooling agreements.
- Data access when it is essential to compete in a broader ecosystem.

Since it is extremely difficult to measure harm in digital markets, each potential remedy should be carefully assessed in order to avoid any undesired outcomes. This problem will certainly monopolize the debate and enforcement priorities of competition authorities in the coming years. From all the potential questions that may arise in this area, we have limited our comments to introduce the reader to the so-called data power debate and possible abuse of a dominant position exercised by the data giants.

§6.04 ANTITRUST BY DESIGN AND AWARENESS

From the above, we can easily conclude that we need to prepare ourselves for a new legal scenario. The outcome is still open. Notwithstanding this, we have already noted the existing concerns and enforcement agencies are reacting to the concerns detected. New authorities for digital markets and new rules or enforcement powers will be introduced in the next years. Thus, preventive legal assessment becomes crucial for sustainable innovation, and competition law aspects can play an important role in the

32. A. Agrawal, J. Gans, A. Goldfarb, Prediction Machines, The Simple Economics of Artificial Intelligence, Harvard, 2018, p. 217.
33. J. Cremer, Y Montjoye, Schweitzer, Competition Policy for the digital era, Final report, European Commission, 2019, (last access, 09 Jun. 2019: http://ec.europa.eu/competition/publications/reports/kd0419345enn.pdf).

definition of the AI strategy of a company. In our view, AI may shift the emphasis from defence to more preventive work for lawyers. In order to carry out this preventive work, lawyers will need to understand AI, the decision-making process of deep learning and to work hand in hand with the trainers, data scientists and programming engineers.

In the design of AI systems, we need to weigh competition factors that used to play a more visible role in the reactive side of the legal work. In the digital economy, competition law risks may not become apparent until the sanction is imposed. Thus, anticipating risks and ensuring proper risk management from the beginning can help to reduce unwanted pitfalls and develop sustainable innovation for the business and (last but not least) remain competitive through compliance by design.

Notwithstanding the above, awareness of businesses about their rights to compete will help in cases where new players encounter hurdles to compete for the market or unjustified entry barriers. In these cases, the new tools, like access to data, will help to re-establish the level playing field allowing innovation by new players. Therefore, Competition Law will become more relevant since, in many cases, it will be the key to convince the gatekeeper.

CHAPTER 7

AI and Intellectual Property

Caroline Chetrit

§7.01 INTRODUCTION

Artificial Intelligence (AI) generally refers to the ability to do things that typically require human intelligence without humans playing a role. The European Parliament has already expressed that '... there is a possibility that in the long-term, AI could surpass human intellectual capacity'.[1] There are two basic types of AI:[2] weak (or narrow) AIs and strong[3] (or general) AIs. Weak AIs handle a particular task within a specific program; while strong AIs are able to analyse large amounts of digital data and learn and adapt to situations through a combination of Machine Learning (ML) or Deep Learning and Big Data and can, therefore, be 'autonomous.' Indeed, AI's differ from one another based on their level of autonomy.

There are now AI applications in virtually every field, from AI book authoring to hotels with robots as receptionists,[4] to AI doctors,[5] legal AI[6] and financial clerks. AI is

1. European Parliament Legislative Initiative (INL) 2015/2013, 'Resolution of 16 February 2017 with recommendations to the Commission on Civil Law Rules on Robotics,'.
2. Bringsjord, Selmer and Govindarajulu, Naveen Sundar, 'Artificial Intelligence', *The Stanford Encyclopedia of Philosophy*, Fall 2018 Edition. https://stanford.library.sydney.edu.au/archives/fall2018/entries/artificial-intelligence/.
3. Jack Copeland, *What is Artificial Intelligence?* May 2000 http://www.alanturing.net/turing_archive/pages/Reference%20Articles/What%20is%20AI.html.
4. In Japan's Henn na Hotel opened in 2015 with a staff of robots, although since then it has cut its robotic workforce after the experience failed to reduce costs or workload for its employees. Esther Hertzfeld, 'Japan's Henn na Hotel Fires Half Its Robotic Workforce,' https://www.hotelmanagement.net/tech/japan-s-henn-na-hotel-fires-half-its-robot-workforce.
5. J Jolene Creighton, 'AI Saves Woman's Life by Identifying Her Disease When Other Methods (humans) Failed,' 5 Aug. 2016, https://futurism.com/ai-saves-womans-life-by-identifying-her-disease-when-other-methods-humans-failed.
6. Jessica Chasmar, Stanford Student's Robot Lawyer Has Beaten 160,000 Parking Tickets, WASH. TIMES (29 Jun. 2016), This Robot Lawyer Could Help You Get Your Parking Ticket Dismissed,

composing music, and even social policymaking or engaging in espionage. Those who consider AI just another new 'buzzword' should look at the World Intellectual Property (IP) Organization's (WIPO)'s 2019 *Technology Trends Report* on AI.[7] The report sheds some light on the developments of patents within AI since the 1950s and points to AI as one of technology's new frontiers. The term AI may have been coined more than sixty years ago, but AI-related patents only took off after 2013, with over 340,000 AI-related inventions patented since that year. We are indeed in what Google AI Chief John Giannandrea calls an 'AI spring'.[8] In WIPO Director General Francis Gurry's words, 'the surge in patenting is striking.'[9]. . .

The *WIPO Technology Trends 2019* report is an empirical study that shows that the number of 'patents in AI increased by an average of 28% per year between 2012 and 2017'. In 2017 alone, a total of 55,660 patents were filed worldwide, the vast majority by privately held companies, but also by a few public research organizations. Digital players are racing frantically to develop ever more efficient algorithms and evermore 'human' AI. Another critical point from the WIPO report states that AI-related patent applications represent only 0.6% of all global applications. The opportunity to commercialize IP in the AI space has, therefore, never been higher.

The business world is rushing to patent AI developments. The American research firm, Gartner,[10] released a new report on AI-derived business value forecasts from 2017 to 2025. The firm predicts that the AI industry will be worth USD 1.2 trillion in 2018, and USD 3.9 trillion by 2022. Since a full 26 of the top 30 patent applicants in the AI field are companies, according to the WIPO report, (with the other four being universities or public research organizations), this is a playing field in which top companies are competing fiercely and thus accelerating the pace of AI innovation. To date, IBM, Microsoft, Samsung and Google have patented most of the fundamental AI technologies.[11]

However, there is more to IP than just commercialization and money-making. In the race for AI supremacy, many academics, entrepreneurs and private companies are teaming up to stake their claims on new AI developments. There are financial incentives, of course, but there is also a desire to be the first to reach new technological and research milestones to garner international reputation and to obtain investment. 17

CBS NEWS (21 Jul. 2016, 7:05 AM), (describing Stanford University freshman Joshua Browder and how the robot already saved drivers an estimated $4–5 million).

7. WIPO (2019). *WIPO Technology Trends 2019: Artificial Intelligence*. Geneva: WIPO.
8. Google's artificial intelligence chief, John Giannandrea, stated that '[w]e're in an AI spring' as opposed to the AI winter of the 70s discussed by Cristina Warren in May 2016: https://mashable.com/2016/05/20/google-ai-spring/?europe=true#KxSalpvSAGqD.
9. UN News, *'Boom in Artificial Intelligence patents, points to 'quantum leap' in tech'*, UN report https://news.un.org/en/story/2019/01/1031702.
10. Gartner Newsroom, 'Gartner Says Global Artificial Intelligence Business Value to Reach $1.2 Trillion in 2018', https://www.gartner.com/en/newsroom/press-releases/2018-04-25-gartner-says-global-artificial-intelligence-business-value-to-reach-1-point-2-trillion-in-2018.
11. *See supra* note 7 WIPO (2019). *WIPO Technology Trends 2019*, reference to IBM having the largest portfolio of patent applications in the AI field, with 8290 inventions at the end of 2016, followed by Microsoft with 5930 inventions, Toshiba with 5223, Samsung with 5102 and NEC with 4406.

out of every 20 universities that apply for patents are Chinese.[12] The big economies[13] are investing significant amounts in AI since most of them have realized that the nation's leading AI might be the future leaders or rulers.[14]

The boom in AI's technological advancement is due to increased computer power, made less expensive as a result of cloud-based computing, the advent of big data analytics and the fact that algorithms are increasingly more powerful.

The creation of new technologies always implies its protection through IP. The protection and enhancement of the results of these investments in research and development are essential: the sustainability of their economic model and the improvement of their innovations depend on it.

The economic stakes surrounding AI are extreme,[15] but are the current IP tools adequate and efficient enough to protect those investments? If we consider the existing mechanism for protecting AI components, patents seem to be the most obvious form of protection, as the same considerations that apply to traditional technologies are relevant.

As AI-based technologies gain capacity, they are likely to play an increasingly important role in the creation of new IP rules and in the challenging of existing IP rules. There are several key aspects of AI technologies involved in developing patent, copyright and trade secret protection.

There is currently no country with an IP, legal or regulatory framework dedicated to AI. The European Parliament in its 16 February 2017 resolution regarding civil law rules on robotics, did make a recommendation that as long as there is no specific regulation, the currently applicable IP rights should be applied to AI.[16] Nonetheless, existing regulations seems to be adapted only to certain forms of AI, namely those without autonomy.

§7.02 PROTECTING AI: IS THE EXISTING SYSTEM ADEQUATE AND EFFECTIVE?

It is evident that IP protection is critical. Currently, companies are using several legal tools to protect their innovations, considering that AI is usually made up of three main components: Software, Algorithms and Data. This section covers the framework for the acquisition of IP rights, with a principal focus on Europe.

12. *See supra* note 7 *WIPO report*.
13. Rapport Villani, '*Donner un sens à l'intelligence Artificielle – Pour une stratégie nationale et européenne,*' March 2018.
https://www.aiforhumanity.fr/pdfs/9782111457089_Rapport_Villani_accessible.pdf.
14. Putin commented that the nation that leads in AI '*will be the ruler of the world,*' *The Verge* 24 Sep. 2017.
15. McKinsey Global Institute, 'Notes from the AI Frontier: Modelling the Impact of AI on the World Economy,' September 2018, which states that by 2030, 70% of companies may have adopted AI technology and that AI may deliver a global economic activity of USD 13 trillion by the same year.
16. European Parliament Legislative Initiative (INL) 2015/2013, 'Resolution of 16 February 2017 with recommendations to the Commission on Civil Law Rules on Robotics,' http://www.europarl.europa.eu/doceo/document/TA-8-2017-0051_EN.html.

[A] Patents or Copyright & Software

As the skeleton of AI, the software is of fundamental importance: by transforming algorithmic modalities into instructions that can be understood by a machine, it becomes possible to configure the functioning of AI and provide it with capabilities. Most of the legal systems provide little protection for its innovations because of the alleged incompatibility of software and patents. However, AI pushes the boundaries of patentability on several fronts. Patents seem the most logical way of protecting AI[17] and recovering investment.

Although the existing legal framework might seem unprotective of AI, big companies are using patents to protect their inventions.[18] This does not seem impossible since Apple has protected the unlocking of an automatic gate by fingerprint recognition on an iPhone[19] and Facebook protected access to an online community by the scanning of a QR code printed on a poster.[20]

Protection of software is treated in different ways by patent offices around the world. At the moment, AI innovations, and mainly software, are probably more difficult to protect in Europe (and in some EU countries more than others) than in the United States.

Although Article 52 of the European Patent Convention (EPC)[21] excludes computer programs 'as such' from patentability, the jurisprudence of the European Patent Office (EPO) chambers over the last twenty years has defined relatively stable and predictable rules of law regarding the patentability of computer-implemented inventions. Like any invention, a computer creation must comply with the basic conditions of patentability, namely novelty, inventive step and industrial application. In addition, it must be established that such an invention has a technical character which makes distinguishable from computer programs as such. However, this exclusion does not imply that software exclusion is systematic, but rather that a more rigorous examination of the technical nature of these inventions is required.

In a recent report, the EPO[22] conceded that the AI introduces a significant change and says it is 'prepared to deal with the patentability of 4th Industrial Revolution inventions (resulting from the AI) within the framework of applicable European patent

17. Artificial Intelligence by EPO – 14 Jun. 2019.
18. *See supra* note 7 WIPO (2019). *WIPO Technology Trends 2019*, reference to AI patent portfolios of IBM and Microsoft: 'IBM and Microsoft are leaders in AI patenting across different AI-related areas IBM has the largest portfolio of AI patent applications with 8,290 inventions (2,700 related to AI), followed by Microsoft with 5,930. Both companies' portfolios span a range of AI techniques, applications and fields, indicating that these companies are not limiting their activity to a specific industry or field.'
19. Apple US9342674, Abdallah David S. and Johnson Barry W., 'Man-Machine Interface for controlling Access to Electronic Devices,' 2015. https://patents.google.com/patent/US9342674.
20. Facebook US9740372, George, John-Alistair C. and Connelly, Adam, 'Enabling Participation in an Online Community Using Visual Machine-readable Symbols,' 2016, https://patents.google.com/patent/US9740372.
21. The European Patent Convention, Article 52.
22. The EPO (report) 'Patents and the Fourth Industrial Revolution – The inventions behind digital transformation', December 2017.

legislation and to create the necessary legal certainty for innovative companies in the sector'. This means that the gap between the United States and Europe may narrow for AI.

The protection of software suffers from certain shortcomings. Indeed, in most European countries software is protected by a dedicated copyright regime,[23] based on a criterion of originality adapted to its specificities: it will be a question of demonstrating the existence of choices made by the creator testifying to a 'personalized intellectual effort.' But this protection will only benefit the *structure* of the software, i.e., the program architecture, source code, object code and preparatory design material.[24]

On the other hand, the interfaces and functionalities, which are the ideas behind the software, will escape any protection by copyright.[25] Even though they are the key to innovation, the functionalities (e.g., the robot arm that rises) could thus be reproduced employing new coding without infringing copyright. Only patent law would then be able to rescue the software, provided that it is included in an invention that is itself patentable.

[B] Copyright and Algorithms (or Trade Secret Protection)

Like the main industrial revolutions, which were mostly spurred by the exploration of a new type of energy, algorithms are the new gold of AI innovations. The algorithm is at the heart of daily life, and a new sort of 'Algorithm governance' is emerging. From Google's search engine to Netflix's recommendation system, to video surveillance based on facial recognition: most of the latest technologies work with advanced algorithms. Algorithms are not much different from a cooking recipe: both are methods, describing the steps and instructions that must be carried out in order to achieve a result. The algorithm is to AI what the neural network is to humans. The development of powerful algorithms that are capable of efficiently exploiting 'Big Data' or being able to reproduce motor skills has become the main challenge for robot designers. The economic value of algorithms makes it logical that their creator - who is not necessarily the creator of the machine (the robot, etc.) in which the algorithms will be integrated – is concerned with their legal protection.

At first sight, neither copyright nor patent law extends its protection to algorithms. The former considers them to be non-protectable ideas, principles and methods because of their capacity to freely evolve. The latter expressly excludes scientific theories, mathematical methods and computer programs from its scope. In the EU, the exclusion of algorithms from copyright protection is contemplated in the Directive 2009/24/EC[26] in Recital 11, which states that 'in accordance with this principle of

23. French IP Code, Article L.112-2 13.
24. French IP Code, Article L.112-2 13 states that any multimedia elements embedded in the software (e.g., the robot's voice, images, etc.) are protected by other provisions of the IP Code.
25. *Official Journal of the European Union*, Directive 2009/24/EC of the European Parliament and of the Council of 23 April 2009 on the legal protection of computer programs.
26. *See supra* note 25.

copyright, to the extent that logic, algorithms and programming languages comprise ideas and principles, those ideas and principles are not protected under this Directive'.

Indirect, but imperfect, copyright protection would, however, be possible but through software protection. When the algorithm is integrated into the 'original' software in the sense of copyright, the software, and therefore the algorithm (its intelligent core) will be protectable. But since the protection only concerns the software and not the algorithm itself, a third party who could legally extract the algorithm from the software would be free to reuse it.[27] However, in France, the National Centre for Space Studies (CNES) was able to get a patent on a method for detecting the atypical behaviour of telemetry parameters for satellites that were based on Machine Learning (ML) algorithms.[28]

Patent law would also protect an algorithm integrated into a machine and whose implementation 'produces an additional technical effect.' However, the advantages of such protection are offset by two major disadvantages inherent in the filing: (i) the claims of the said patent must contain a detailed description of the algorithm which will, therefore, be revealed to the public and competitors; (ii) the filing will only protect the version of the algorithm described in the claims, each new version being the subject of a new patent for improvement, which is impossible in practice. Algorithms, due to their nature, will always evolve and therefore, change!

A possible alternative and viable solution for protection might be trade secrets that can also be used for other elements of AI. Most jurisdictions around the world protect trade secrets, although to varying degrees.[29] In 2016, the EU approved a Directive aiming to harmonize national regimes on the protection of confidential information.

In their paper on the robotic industry, Andrew Keisner, Julio Raffo, and Sacha Wunsch-Vincent write that '[t]here are multiple reasons why a ... company may prefer to keep certain technologies ... as trade secrets rather than seeking patent protection',[30] including the complexity and cost of the patent filing and prosecution. The protection relies on the innovating companies who must establish and maintain secrecy since they are not required to file any application. This protection will last as long as the inventor keeps the secret (since it does not require any disclosure) by taking the necessary steps (e.g., firewalls, encryption, restricting employee access to a company's confidential and trade secret information, etc.). Protection via trade secret is by no means perfect either and has its limitations.

---

27. EU Court of Justice ruling C-406/10, 'SAS Institute Inc. v. World Programming Ltd.,' 2 May, 2012.
28. CNES FR3045170 is an AI solution used by France's National Centre for Space Studies (CNES) to learn satellite behaviour, monitor it and generate alerts when predefined borders are exceeded since the number of measurements has become too large to be tracked.
29. *Official Journal of the European Union*, Directive 2016/943 of the European Parliament and of the Council of 8 Jun. 2016 on the protection of undisclosed know-how and business information (trade secrets) against their unlawful acquisition, use and disclosure.
30. Keisner, C. Andrew, Raffo, Julio and Wunsch-Vincent, Sacha, 'Breakthrough technologies – Robotics, innovation and intellectual property,' *Economic Research Working Paper No. 30* (WIPO publication).

[C] Copyright and Databases

As analysed previously, certain elements of AI could be protected by copyright because the EU has harmonized such protections for software since 1991.[31] But what about databases? They have been protected at the European level both in terms of the right to prohibit the use of the database as a whole and the right of the database holder.[32] One of the goals of this directive was to promote database creation at a European level. The real issue is not the ownership of the database but the ability to access the collected data.

According to this European Directive, if a database is an original intellectual creation, then it can be protected via copyright, guaranteeing the exclusive rights (the IP right holders can exclude any other person from the use of this right.) to reproduce, adapt and distribute the database or any variant thereof. Copyright protects the structure of a database, not its content.

The European legislators saw that copyright might not provide an ideal solution to the protection of creators of databases and introduced a new right called sui generis, which is unknown in some legal systems, such as that of the United States.[33] According to this right, if the structure of a database is not an original creation, its content can be protected under sui generis, a right that recognizes the effort invested in building a database, even if it does not cover the creative aspect protected by copyright. To benefit from this protection, the creator of the database must be an EU national or reside in the EU. It must also be proven that obtaining, verifying or presenting the content of the database required a substantial investment (financial, material and/or human).

The economic agents and the doctrine both agree that regarding AI that moves in Big Data environments, this directive has not reached its objective. Currently, the European database market is far from being among the leading markets, such as the US, Japan, Canada and South Korea.[34]

---

31. *Official Journal of the European Union*, Directive 91/250/EEC of the European Parliament and of the Council of 14 May 1991 on the legal protection of computer programs (repealed by Directive 2009/24/EC).
32. Copyright Directorate, The Patent Office, Directive 96/9/EC of the European Parliament and the Council of 11 Mar. 1996 on the legal protection of databases, giving specific and separate legal rights (and limitations) to certain computer records. The law calls these database rights. Rights afforded to manual records under EU database rights laws are similar in format, but not identical, to those afforded artistic works. Database rights last for 15 years. Each time a database is substantially modified, however, a new set of rights are created for that database. An owner has the right to object to the copying of substantial parts of their database, even if data is extracted and reconstructed piecemeal. Database rights under the EU are created automatically, vested in the employers of creators (when the action of creation was part of employment), and do not have to be registered to have effect.
33. Yu, Peter K., 'Data Producer's Right in the Platform Economy,' *Texas A&M University School of Law Legal Studies Research Paper No. 18-12*, 16 Jul. 2018.
34. Hargreaves, Ian, Guibault, Lucy, et.al., *European Commission Expert Report: Standardization in the area of innovation and technological development notably in the field of text and data mining*, 2014.

[D] Trademarks and Industrial Design

Robots are fast becoming part of our everyday life[35] – from the retail to the hospitability industry – and it is only logical that their aesthetic, or 'look & feel', should be protected. This can be achieved through the protection of industrial designs for any AI-based technology product, such as robots, as long as the requirements of new and specific characters are met.

Siri, Alexa and iRobot have all been registered as brands. The name given to an AI can be protected under the trademark's regime: this means subject to availability and distinctiveness of the name.

[E] Conclusion

There are still several varied existing legal mechanisms that protect AI innovation, depending upon the part of the AI component that needs protection. It goes without saying that the existing IP legal corpus everywhere must evolve, or it risks becoming inadequate and ineffective. There must be a harmonization of certain elements, such as the duration of the protection rights for all the components of AI. Currently, copyright protection lasts seventy years after the death of the creator, whereas the patent gives an exclusive right to exploit the patented innovation for twenty years.

There is considerable engagement around the need to modify or create a new IP framework for AI, but caution is required. At the European level, as previously mentioned, there are suggestions coming from the European Parliament, some of which are found in its resolution of 16 February 2017,[36] containing recommendations to the Commission on civil law rules on robotics, and the Communication from the Commission to the European Parliament on AI for Europe of 25 April 2018.[37]

§7.03 AI CREATIONS AND INVENTIONS: CHALLENGING COPYRIGHT AND PATENT

[A] Introduction

This section covers the unpredictable creations and innovations that can be protected by IP. By definition, AI simulates human cognitive processes (and even surpasses them in many areas); creativity is undoubtedly one of these processes. New forms of creation of works and of interaction between the public and the creations have become possible

35. Bensoussan, Alain and Bensoussan, Jérémy, IA, robots et droit, Bruylant, 2019.
36. European Parliament Legislative Initiative (INL) 2015/2013, 'Resolution of 16 February 2017 with recommendations to the Commission on Civil Law Rules on Robotics,' http://www.europarl.europa.eu/doceo/document/TA-8-2017-0051_EN.html.
37. Communication from the Commission to the European Parliament, the European Council, the Council, the European Economic and Social Committee and the Committee of the Regions on Artificial Intelligence for Europe of 25 Apr. 2018.

with AI. AI is now involved in creating paintings, writing poems, novels and news,[38] composing music,[39] producing full-length movies, writing articles in newspapers or movie scripts,[40] creating perfumes,[41] or games and other artworks and doing so it challenges the 'scepticism that an algorithm can be creative, or innovate'.[42]

Works created by AIs that can be described as artistic or considered as new, are flourishing. They, therefore, raise several questions regarding the recognition of intellectual property rights (IPR) and the ownership of these rights (e.g., when technology, a machine or robot goes from being a 'mere tool', like a pen and a paper, to an 'inventor' or 'author', nor even a collaborator of the human being). AI has evolved so fast that we can entertain the possibility that AI has reached a stage in which 'machines,' themselves, may create original or patentable material.

AI-generation used simply as a tool in the creative or inventive process of a human does not yield uncertainty with regards to IP protection; the work results from a collaboration between man and machine. The author, therefore, is human.[43] But what happens when the work is a pure AI creation or innovation? It then becomes about the system itself 'creating' without any human intervention, which may result in comparable or even superior originality. This is a technical possibility nowadays. Although AI has not yet reached that stage, it may be conceivable in the near future (perhaps within twenty years). At the same time, there is the insistence upon first establishing protocols concerning the ethical development of AI technologies (which is covered in Chapter 3). The only moment humans may be involved is at the upstream of the AI application, when creating the software, or the algorithm or robot.

How will current IP regimes recognize the fruits of some of the creative and inventive processes coming from AI technologies? Are they adequate to deal with the ownership of works generated by AI systems? Should they give the same protection to the AI creations as those created by human authors?

Even if legal protection under the IP regime were granted to AI-generated works under the terms of IP, it is not clear how the issue of the ownership of existing IPR

38. James Vincent, 'Google is helping fund AI news writers in the UK and Ireland: 30,000 local stories a month will be created with the help of AI for the Press Association,' *The Verge*, July 2017.
39. *Deep Mind, a Google-owned artificial intelligence company, has created software that can generate music by listening to recordings*. Devin Coldewey, 'Google's WaveNet uses neural nets to generate eerily convincing speech and music,' *TechCrunch.*
40. An AI called 'Benjamin' wrote an entire script for a short movie, coherent enough to be interpreted by actors. *See* the court film 'Sunspring a surreal delight, upchucked eyeball included' produced for the UK festival 'Sci-Fi London'. Annalee Newitz, 'Movie written by algorithm turns out to be hilarious and intense,' *Ars Technica*, 6 Sep. 2016.
41. Bernard Marr, 'Artificial Intelligence Can Now Create Perfumes, Even Without A Sense of Smell', *Forbes*, 29 Jul. 2019. A company was looking for a fragrance for the millennials. They used Philyra, an AI, created by IBM and a perfumer David Apel. This collaboration officially launched AI into the fragrance industry.
42. Bouchared, Anthony and Cann, George H., 'Raiders of the Lost Art,' September 2019 https://arxiv.org/pdf/1909.05677.pdf .
43. McCormack, Jon, et. al., 'Ten Questions Concerning Generative Computer Art,' Leonardo E-book, 2014 – Leonardo. 'Generative procedures have a long history in art that predates the computer by thousands of years. Additionally, much contemporary generative art does not involve digital computers at all.'

would be far from resolved, given that computers do not currently have the legal capacity to own property.

[B] AI-Created Works and Copyright

There are unlimited examples cropping up daily in the news that demonstrate AI's engagement in creative activities (music, film, painting, writing, etc.) without any human intervention. Each one is more surprising than the last: some AIs are capable of bringing deceased artists to life, others generate things of incredible economic value, and some produce works that fool humans into thinking they are a human creation.[44]

In 2019, a neural network retrieved and finished a lost Picasso painting using the colours the Spanish artist used in that creative period.[45] In April 2016, The Next Rembrandt project unveiled a 3-Dimensional (3D) painting created by an AI algorithm that imitates the subject and style of the famous Dutch dead artist in an almost indistinguishable way[46] through a collaboration between Microsoft, Internationale Nederlanden Groep ("ING"), Delft University of Technology, the Mauritshuis, and the Rembrandt House Museum. In 2017, the American YouTuber, Taryn Southern, released her album 'I am AI'[47] for which she used an AI platform called AMPER[48] to compose her music. Thanks to a wide range of available online software, it is now possible to generate a piece of instrumental music in a few clicks, sometimes for free. Taryn Southern used the AMPER platform, but there are many others, including

44. 'A wounded deer leaps highest', is a ten-verses poem written by a 'robot-poet' created by the researcher R. Kurzwell – 'Additional Poems Written by Ray Kurzweil's Cybernetic Poet', http://www.kurzweilcyberart.com/poetry/rkcp_poetry_samples.php. Michelle Starr, 'Bot or not? Try to tell a human poet from a computer,' (61% of people who were surveyed about Raymond Kurzweil's AI-generated 10-verse poem 'A Wounded Deer Leaps Highest' said they believed it was written by a human), 10 Mar. 2014.
45. *See supra* note 42 Bouchared & Cann. 'La femme perdue' was found beneath a Picasso's Masterpieces from the blue period in 1998, through the conventional x-ray system by the conservators at the Art Institute of Chicago. However, what A. Bourached and G. Cann have achieved by using a machine vision technique called neural style transfer is to retrieve the lost Picasso painting in colour.
46. https://www.nextrembrandt.com/_The Next Rembrandt is a 3D painting created by computer using a facial recognition algorithm. Eighteen months of work were required to produce this painting after 346 works known to the Dutch painter had been scanned. The portrait was made out of 168,263 fragments taken from the artist's works and stored in a database designed for this purpose. The project was sponsored by the Dutch banking group ING, in collaboration with Microsoft, the marketing consultancy firm J. Walter Thompson and consultants from Delft University of Technology, Mauritshuis and the Rembrandt House Museum.
47. Dom Galeon, 'The World's First Album Composed and Produced by an AI Has Been Unveiled', 21 Aug. 2017, https://futurism.com/the-worlds-first-album-composed-and-produced-by-an-ai-has-been-unveiled/.
48. Dani Deahl, 'How AI-Generated Music Is Changing the Way Hits Are Made,' *The Verge*, 31 Aug. 2018.

Jukedeck[49] or AIVA, to name a few.[50] The Portrait of Edmond de Belamy was the first AI-created work sold at an auction house in 2018.[51] It was sold for over USD 400,000.

Science fiction is fast becoming a reality. The tension between creative work and AI technologies is no longer a future concern, but a present one. If copyright law is included in the equation, then the current AI copyright protections adhered to by the main copyright regimes (the EU and the US) should apply to conditions in which AI creations are generated. Should the traditional copyright standards – such as originality – apply to AI? Could AI be considered an author according to traditional copyright standards? Although this protection might be granted, who would be considered the author, and who would be the right holders, and what prerogatives would come with this protection? AI-created works force a rethinking of the fundamental concepts upon which copyright has been built.

B.1 Could AI Technology Be an Author? How Should the Originality Standard be Applied?

Copyright as a legal instrument serves two main functions: it provides adequate protection to authors and right holders, and it provides the public access to content.[52] To be protected by copyright, creation must be in a fixed, tangible form (as opposed to in the author's mind) and based on a free flow of ideas, which makes it 'original.'[53] The originality could be either subjective or objective. In the case of the music created by the AI Orb Composer,[54] an AI composition tool, there is a subjective conception of originality since the platform clearly states that each composition created with the program is marked by the artistic imprint of the human composer, who is an actor in its creation and only receives support from the AI. Categorizing the originality of these AI creations is difficult, and more so when the majority of the doctrine has generally agreed that AI is not endowed with a spirit or a personality in the legal sense of the term.[55]

---

49. https://www.jukedeck.com/.
50. https://www.aiva.ai/.
51. Obvious (http://obvious-art.com). The portrait was made with machine learning algorithms called Generative Adversarial Networks (GANs) by the Paris-based art collective Obvious Art who inserted 15,000 portraits dating from the 14th to the 20th century into the software, enabling it to make portraits itself. The artwork was signed min G max D Ex[log(D(x))] + Ez[log(1-D(G(z))]. The AI tool used is Ian Goodfollow (Google Brain).
52. Stamatoudi, Irini, and Torremans, Paul, *EU Copyright Law: A Commentary*, Edward Elgar Publishing, 2014.
53. World Intellectual Property Organization (WIPO), Summary of the Berne Convention for the Protection of Literary and Artistic Works (1886).
54. https://www.orb-composer.com/ (According to the site's information leaflet, the Orb Composer AI is not completely autonomous but an assistant to the composer – the program is based on a combination of the composer's creative ability and the capacities of AI – but it is the composer who controls the AI.
55. Caron, Christophe, *Droit d'auteur et droits voisins*, LexisNexis, 2017 (which states that '[t]he duo formed by the notion of creation and a physical person is inseparable...[a]s a result, the creator is necessarily a physical person.'

Computer-aided creations are one thing, but works generated solely by AI are another.[56] For works created by totally autonomous AI, over which humans have no control, and over which one cannot anticipate the result produced, the application of a subjective conception of originality is less obvious because it is not possible to perceive the imprint of the author's personality. If the subjective imprint would prevail, then those works would be deemed free of copyright, and that would put anyone investing in those AI systems in a risky position. In the EU, the notion of originality has evolved through case law, and it requires the work to be the author's own intellectual creation.[57] Today, the objective dimension of originality applies to all works eligible for copyright.[58] Nonetheless, the evolution of the notion of originality makes it possible to overcome this difficulty through case law. Whereas in a subjective approach to originality, it is the approach that prevails, it is the result that counts in an objective approach. The objectification of originality, therefore, makes it possible to extend copyright protection to AI-generated works without referring to the author's personality or the process of creation. Under these conditions, it is possible to accept that creativity is not the exclusive domain of the human brain.

However, the originality requirement is intertwined with the concept of authorship. Most copyright legal frameworks, particularly in Europe, were conceived in a humanistic way, placing the human being at the heart of creation. Spanish[59] and German law[60] provide that authors are only the natural person creating the work; French law[61] states that only a human can be an author and the US copyright office only registers a work '... provided that [it] was created by a human being'[62] and this was clearly established in the widely publicized 'Monkey Selfie' case, in which an American court determined that an animal cannot be the author of a photograph, only a human can.[63]

56. Abbott, Ryan, *Artificial Intelligence, Big Data and Intellectual Property: Protecting Computer-Generated Works in the United Kingdom* Edward Elgar Publishing, 2017.
57. *European Court Reports,* Case C-5/08, 'Infopaq International A/S v. Danske Dagblades Forening,' 19 Jul. 2009.
58. *European Court Reports,* Case C-145/10, 'Eva-Maria Painer v. Standard Verlags GmbH and Others,' 1 Dec. 2011 (the court case held that portrait photographs enjoy the same copyright protection as any other work and extended the originality standard from computer programs, databases, or photographs to all literary, musical, artistic, and dramatic work.
59. *Official Bulletin of the Government of Spain,* IP Law of Spain, Article 5.1 22 of April 1996, (which provides that an author must be a natural person).
60. *Bundesministerium der Justiz und für Verbraucherschutz,* §2(2) of the German Copyright Act (Urheberrechtsgesetz).
61. French IP Code, Article L. 111-1, which refers to the 'work of the mind.'
62. *The Compendium of U.S. Copyright Office* Practices, Section 313.2, 'Works That Lack Human Authorship. As discussed in Section 306, the Copyright Act protects 'original works of authorship.' 17 U.S.C. § 102(a) (emphasis added). To qualify as a work of 'authorship' a work must be created by a compendium: Copyrightable Authorship: What Can Be Registered Chapter 300 | 17 revised 09/29/2017 human being. *See* Burrow-Giles Lithographic Co., 111 U.S. at 58. Works that do not satisfy this requirement are not copyrightable.
63. United States Court of Appeals, Ninth Circuit, Naruto *v.* Slater (a case in which a Crested Macaque named Naruto picked up a photographer's camera and took photos of himself. The photographer, David Slater published the 'Monkey Selfies' in a book and claimed copyright ownership in the photographs. People for the Ethical Treatment of Animals (PETA) sued on

In the creation of the AI-generated Portrait of Edmond Belamy, or Le Comte de Belamy, it was art collective Obvious that created the AI behind the painting. In this case, if the artist is the one who created the image, then the machine is considered the author, whereas if the author is the one who holds the vision, then the author is Obvious.[64] Under the EU copyright law, as well as the US law, deciding whether a work qualifies for copyright protection requires assessing the level of human as opposed to any technological input.

B.2 Ownership & Infringements

While it is possible to consider granting the status of intellectual works to 'computer-generated' works, the question of copyright ownership remains. In the same way, we should raise the question of who bears the responsibility for protecting rights from infringements by others and, on the other hand, who will be accountable for the infringements? While there is currently much active discussion, no unanimous conclusions have been reached.[65]

Just as in the monkey selfie case, in which an American court refused to recognize the animal or the owner of the camera as the author, a creative AI does not have a legal personality, which makes it unclear who holds the rights – if there are any – or if rights fall into the public domain.

There are a variety of possible copyright holders for AI-generated works: Should copyright belong to the designer and / or programmer(s) of the AI (who are the creators of the AI)? Should the owner of the AI (who is the operator) get the copyright? Or is it the users? Should the copyright be shared between parties, or should it be attributed to the AI itself, thus granting the machine a legal personality?[66] The following is an exploration of all possible angles.

(i) Let's start with the option of granting the rights to the user. The contribution of the user is limited to 'pushing the button'. This could be a strong possibility when the user is a necessary agent to trigger the creative process. In the gaming industry, for instance, this may be an apt solution since the players/users have an increasing role.[67] But what if the user intervention is very limited, as in the case of the script of the short film 'Sunspring?' The film was written by an AI named Benjamin, and the resulting creation is a product that is almost entirely software-generated, and the user only determined inconsequential elements related to minor

behalf of Naruto, claiming he was the author of the photographs. The US Court decided that 'to qualify as a work of authorship, a work must be created by a human being,' 23 Apr. 2018.

64. *See supra* note 51 *Obvious* (http://obvious-art.com).
65. Yanisky-Ravid, Shlomit, *Generating Rembrandt: Artificial Intelligence, Copyright, And Accountability in the 3a Era – The Human-Like Authors Are Already Here – A New Model*, Michigan State Law Review, Number 659, 2017.
66. *See supra* note 35 Bensoussan A.
67. Ramalho, Ana, 'Will Robots Rule the (Artistic) World? A Proposed Model for the Legal Status of Creations by Artificial Intelligence Systems' *Journal of Internet Law*, July 2017.

constraints[68]? Granting the copyright to the user would severely distort its purpose.

(ii) Granting the authorship and the corresponding economic rights to the AI creator. There are already a few countries - all of them belonging to the common law legal tradition - which have agreed to this solution, including the UK,[69] New Zealand,[70] Ireland[71] and Hong Kong. This approach was best captured already over 30 years ago in the UK copyright law, in section 9(3) of the Copyright, Designs and Patents Act (CDPA). The British law refers to 'computer-generated works' which are those that are 'generated by computer in circumstances such that there is no human author of the work' and the author is then 'the person by whom the arrangements necessary for the creation of the work are undertaken'. The idea behind such a provision is to create an exception to all human authorship requirements by recognizing the work that goes into creating a program capable of generating works, even if the creative spark is undertaken by a machine.

(iii) Granting the rights to the owner(s) of the AI whoever they are (e.g., the investors or the licensees). There is a major trend advocating in favour of the doctrine of 'work made for hire'[72] (WMFH) under copyright law, mostly in the USA. This labour approach secures investor rights, making sure they recoup their investments. This principle is set out in section 201 of the *Copyright Law of the United States* (U.S.C),[73] which provides that, '[i]n the case of a work made for hire, the employer or other person for whom the work was prepared is considered the author for purposes of this title, and, unless the parties have expressly agreed otherwise in a written instrument signed by them, owns all of the rights comprised in the copyright.' Robotic creations, subject to meeting the legal conditions, could eventually be qualified as 'work made for hire,' and thus the copyright that is potentially attached to them could be vested in the 'employer,' which means the investor. However, not all works that have been created as part of the ordered work can be included in the definition of work made for hire. The list of works eligible for this qualification is provided for in section 101.[74]

---

68. *See supra* note 40 about the movie Sunspring.
69. UK Copyright, Designs and Patents Act, Section 178, 1988.
70. New Zealand Copyright Act, Section 2, 1994.
71. Irish Copyright Act and Related Rights Act (2000), Part 1, Section 2 and Chapter 2, paragraph 21.
72. *See Supra* note 65 Yanisky-Ravid, Shlomit, *Generating Rembrandt.*
73. United States Congress, *Copyright Law of the United States*, USC, 17, A. 201(a) Ownership of copyright, 30 Jul. 1947: '*Copyright in a work protected under this title vests initially in the author or authors of the work.*': 'In the case of a work made for hire, the employer or other person for whom the work was prepared is considered the author for purposes of this title, and, unless the parties have expressly agreed otherwise in a written instrument signed by them, owns all of the rights comprised in the copyright.'
74. Section 101 of the Copyright Act defines a 'work made for hire' in two parts:

   (i) a work prepared by an employee within the scope of his or her employment; or

This doctrine, in the field of AI and robotics, would give a clear advantage to anyone investing in this field, but at the same time, these investors would be held accountable for any infringement.

(iv) Granting the rights to the AI themselves. The legal personhood of robots has become a popular topic of today's debate on the normative challenges brought about by AI. More and more voices are advocating for a new legal personality for robots.[75] This position is defended in particular by Mady Delvaux-Stehres, a Luxembourgish MP, and states that robots 'must be able to have a unique legal personality in order to be considered as electronic persons with rights and duties, including the right to repair damage caused to others.'[76] Delvaux-Stehres made a proposal to the European Commission to adopt a common definition of the different categories of autonomous and intelligent robots.

A robot called Sofia[77] became the first AI application to receive citizenship-granted rights in Saudi Arabia, and in fact, has more of certain rights than Saudi women do. But would a robot actually be able to enjoy economic and moral rights, such as the economic exploitation of its work or the exercise of its right to respect the integrity of its work? Could robots have obligations like any human being with legal personality granted?

The European Parliament adopted a proposal in February 2017, which invites the European Commission 'to explore, analyse and consider the implications of all possible legal solutions, (including) ... creating a specific legal status for robots in the long run, so that at least the most sophisticated autonomous robots could be established as having the status of electronic persons responsible for making good any damage they may cause, and possibly applying electronic personality to cases where robots make autonomous decisions or otherwise interact with third parties independently'.[78]

Pending acceptable legislative responses and in view of the economic stakes that AI represents, the protection by the secrecy of works created appears to be a possible solution in order to prevent them from immediately falling into the public domain.

Another key IP issue is the use of potentially protected data by robots in their learning processes, such as images or text. This would raise the question of whether the use of this information by AIs would require designers to obtain the consent of their authors, in that it would constitute an act of reproduction or communication to the

---

(ii) a work specially ordered or commissioned for use as a contribution to a collective work, as a part of a motion picture or other audio visual work, as a translation, as a supplementary work, as a compilation, as an instructional text, as a test, as answer material for a test, or as an atlas, if the parties expressly agree in a written instrument signed by them that the work shall be considered a work made for hire.

75. *See supra* note 35 A. Bensoussan.
76. *European Parliament News*, 'Rise of the robots: Mady Delvaux on why their use should be regulated,' December 2017.
77. Agnieszka Kraińska, 'Legal personality and artificial intelligence,' (article references makers of the robot Sophia: https://www.hansonrobotics.com/sophia/) 2 Jul. 2018.
78. *European Parliament Legislative Initiative (INL) 2015/2013 (recommendations to the Commission on Civil Law Rules on Robotics).*

public. On the contrary, it could fall under one of the exceptions provided for, in the sense that the use of such data would only be a private or temporary copy used for learning purposes.

This is the path that seems to be taken to solve the problems of robot civil liability, but which divides public opinion. On the one hand, the European Parliament, supported in particular by car manufacturers, proposes the creation of a specific legal personality for robots capable of taking autonomous decisions or interacting independently with third parties. The attribution of this personality, called 'electronic', would hold the robots responsible for any damage caused to a third party. On the other hand, AI experts, academics and business leaders find this approach inappropriate and point to ethical issues.

[C] The Protection of AI Works: The Patent

The same debate that has already emerged in the area of copyright extends to patents. AI challenges the patent standard; can an AI application be an inventor and who will be deemed the owner? But more importantly, will these inventions be protected by patent laws?

Do machines actually invent? Machines are usually seen as providing technical solutions to technical problems.

Again here, the focus is on robots that generate inventions without any human intervention. Recently, it has been widely reported in the press that several patent applications have been filed designating a ML algorithm as an inventor.[79] The AI called 'DABUS AI' created by Dr Stephen Thaler was not trained to solve particular problems, unlike some machine learning systems.

AI seeks to devise and develop new ideas which are 'traditionally considered the mental part of the inventive act', according to the Dabus creator.[80] Two professors from the University of Surrey teamed up with Dr Thaler, and along with a legal team set out to file patents in the United Kingdom, Europe and the United States on behalf of the AI system and force the issue. However, for the current legal regime, a machine or algorithm cannot be favoured with the recognition of a patent since the latter is reserved exclusively for human beings. Dr Thaler had tried once before to file a US patent for a so-called Creativity Machine, but, in the end, the designated inventor was not considered to be the AI application, but Dr Thaler himself.[81] DABUS is certainly not the first robot that has come up with inventions.[82] However, in December 2019, the

79. Martin Coulter, 'Patent agencies challenged to accept AI inventor' *Financial Times*, 1 Aug. 2019.
80. For more information about DABUS on Dr Thaler's site, *see* http://www.imagination-engines.com/.
81. Thaler, Stephen L., *The Creativity Machine Paradigm: Withstanding the Argument from Consciousness*, January 2013. This machine is credited with an invention which is covered by US patent 5,852,815 issued in 1998, the first known patent on an AI-generated invention. The '815 patent lists Dr Thaler as the sole inventor, though his Creativity Machine is credited with generating the invention.
82. Hattenbach, Ben and Glucoft, Joshua, 'Patents in an Era of Infinite Monkeys and Artificial Intelligence,' *Stanford Technology Law Review 32*, October 2015.

EPO issued a negative response and did not grant the status of inventor to DABUS.[83] The EPO concluded 'After hearing the arguments of the applicant in non-public oral proceedings on 25 November the EPO refused EP 18 275 163 and EP 18 275 174 on the grounds that they do not meet the requirement of the EPC that an inventor designated in the application has to be a human being, not a machine.'

Despite the patent eligibility issues, many patent applications for inventions attributed to AI are being filed in the US Patent Office.[84] However, the patents are only being issued on AI inventions by humans. Many industries, such as the pharmaceutical sector,[85] are increasingly investing in AI dramatically speed up the process of discovering new drugs.

Even if the EPC[86] has harmonized patent laws at a procedural and pre-grant stage, other matters have been left to national jurisdictions and therefore operate on multiple levels. Regarding the definition of the term 'inventor', the EPC states in Article 60(1) that '[t]he right to a European patent (...) belong[s] to the inventor or his successor in title.' Neither the EPC nor its case law or the national laws provide a clear definition of the nature of an inventor – and whether it has to be human or not – except perhaps the UK law.[87] Nevertheless, under European patent law, there is a presumption that inventions are made by natural persons only. Indications that the EPC intended to refer to inventors as human beings can also be found in patentability requirements such as novelty, inventiveness and disclosure. An invention is new if it is not included in the state-of-the-art,[88] i.e., if it was not accessible to the public before the filing date by written or oral description, use or any other means. The question remains: can an AI machine or a robot satisfy this requirement?

On the other hand, the US Patent Law defines an 'inventor' as 'an individual or a set of individuals who invented or discovered the subject matter of the invention.'[89] Neither the US Congress nor its courts have addressed the patentability of AI-generated inventions. From a legal standpoint, China seems to be ahead of the USA since China's New Generation AI Development Plan refers to AI IPR.[90]

---

83. European Patent Register - (1) EP3564144 Food Container (2) EP3563896 - DEVICES AND METHODS FOR ATTRACTING ENHANCED ATTENTION; EPO, '*EPO refuses DABUS patent applications designating a machine inventor*', December 2019.
84. United States Patent and Trademark Office, 'Class 706, Data Processing – Artificial Intelligence,' 10 May 2018), https://www.uspto.gov/web/patents/classification/uspc706/defs706.htm.
85. DiMasi, J.A., Grabowski, H.G., and Hansen, R.W., 'Innovation in the pharmaceutical industry: new estimates of R&D costs' *Journal of Health Economics*, 2016.
86. Convention on the Grant of European Patents (European Patent Convention) of 5 Oct. 1973.
87. UK Patent 1997 Section 7 (3).
88. Convention on the Grant of European Patents (European Patent Convention) of 5 Oct. 1973, Article 56.
89. Consolidated Patent Laws, Section 100 (f), U.S.C 35, https:// www.uspto.gov/web/offices/pac /mpep/consolidated_laws.pdf.
90. State Council's Plan for the Development of New Generation Artificial Intelligence, 20 Jul. 2017.

§7.04 CONCLUSIONS

The current situation of IP laws is complicated and not yet prepared for AI's new steps or phases of development. What awaits this fascinating technology depends on how IP regimes handle AI and whether its implications, both societal and legal, are understood. As AI theorist Eliezer Yudkowsky wrote, '[b]y far, the greatest danger of artificial intelligence is that people conclude too early that they understand it'.[91]

More and more voices are emerging to recommend that the IP laws should be rethought or even replaced in order to address how Robots, AI-computers, are creating and innovating.[92] Most of the standard copyright and patent notions will have to evolve as AI becomes increasingly advanced.

Francis Gurry of the WIPO stated that 'from a strictly economic point of view if we set aside the other objectives of the IP system, such as "fair compensation" and moral rights, there is no reason why we should not use IPto reward inventions or creations generated by artificial intelligence.' Let us see how IP systems evolve. The best solution is still unclear.

91. Yudkowsky, Eliezer, 'Artificial Intelligence as a Positive and Negative Factor in Global Risk,' from *Global Catastrophic Risks*, edited by Nick Bostrom and Milan M. Ćirković, 308–345, New York: Oxford University Press.
92. *See supra* note 65, Yanisky-Ravid, Shlomit, *Generating Rembrandt.*

CHAPTER 8

Legal Responsibility of Intelligent Systems

Grzegorz J. Nalepa & Michał Araszkiewicz

§8.01 INTRODUCTION

Artificial Intelligence (AI) has been around for over sixty years (as mentioned in Chapter 1, the term was originally coined in 1956). It came through several phases of optimism and hype as well as disillusionment about its capabilities, scope, and the speed of progress. Currently, we are witnessing one of the greatest AI hypes so far. This is due to the recent advancement in several AI-related fields, predominantly machine learning (ML), but also other important and often controversial new applications of AI. These current applications, as well as the soon expected ones, raise a number of concerns regarding the legal responsibility of intelligent systems (IS).

The structure of the chapter is the following. We start introducing some key concepts and distinctions in the field of AI relevant to the possible legal conceptualization. We will continue with the analysis of certain features that incorporate systems with intelligent features, which make them different from regular computer systems. We will then review some recent applications of AI technologies that are particularly important for our case, and we will continue with the discussion of factors that are crucial for the design of liability norms and regulations. Furthermore, we identify the features that differentiate artificial agents from human beings. We will also discuss the different types of legal liability as applied to AI technology operations. Finally, we will centre our analysis in the concept of explainable AI, as central for the discussion, since we believe that it will be crucial for future legal considerations and regulations.

§8.02 DISTINCTIVE FEATURES OF AI-BASED COMPUTER SYSTEMS

Let us begin with the concept of AI itself. Among AI researchers there seems to be a consensus, that due to the lack of specific and precise definition of intelligence, AI research is oriented to the development of complex computer systems that can be considered 'intelligent' in some sense.[1] Such systems can possess a number of features that can make them expose the intelligent operation of behaviour, e.g., the capability of drawing inferences from the available knowledge, ability to process the natural language, adaptation of the system's operation to the changing environment, or ability to generalize the available information to obtain new information. It is important to realize that IS have been mostly developed to solve specific problems or address specific tasks. As such, they always have only a certain subset of these features. Therefore, it is important to distinguish between the existing technology of task-oriented IS and the so-called general AI.[2] We will not consider the latter here, as it is a hypothetical concept, whereas we wish to focus on existing or close-to-market technologies.

In general, one can assume that an IS solves a given task (or a class of tasks), or achieves a given goal based on a certain model of knowledge about the task/goal and/or domain, using its appropriate methods, or taking adequate decisions over time. This perspective was one of the first ones (but not the only one) in the early decades of AI. The dominating group of such models are the logical ones, including decision rules, trees or tables. Consequently, the logical inference is applied as the means of using the knowledge to solve the task. This approach is commonly referred to as knowledge representation and reasoning, and the overall approach as knowledge engineering.[3] An IS built in this manner is called a knowledge-based system (KBS).[4] An important feature of knowledge models in KBS is that thanks to being symbolic ones, they are understandable and transparent. Moreover, the inference process is observable and traceable. Finally, these methods are closer to high-level human reasoning. This is why they are the preferred means of representing explicit human knowledge, often expert domain knowledge.[5]

Another important group of models are sub-symbolic ones, where knowledge is not explicitly represented, but instead implicitly coded by a low-level numerical (not symbolic) representation.[6] This approach to building IS using sub-symbolic models is called *computational intelligence* (CI).[7] Examples of numerical models include probabilistic methods, including Bayesian networks, evolutionary computation, and artificial neural networks (ANN). Furthermore, there are some important sub-symbolic approaches which offer a higher level of abstraction and reasoning, such as fuzzy logic and rough sets. Compared to KBS, CI methods offer flexibility, as well as the capability of partially solving computationally hard problems (from the perspective of search

1. I. S. Torsun, Foundations of Intelligent Knowledge-Based Systems, (Academic Press 1995).
2. Nick Bostrom, *Superintelligence: Paths, Dangers, Strategies* (Oxford University Press, 2014).
3. Ronald Brachman & Hector Levesque, *Knowledge Representation and Reasoning* (Morgan Kaufmann, 2004).
4. Jeffrey D. Ullman, *Principles of Database and Knowledge-Base Systems* (Computer Science Press, 1988).
5. Grzegorz J. Nalepa, *Modeling with Rules Using Semantic Knowledge Engineering*, Intelligent Systems (Springer International Publishing, 2018).
6. These two approaches to building models are also sometimes called data-driven and knowledge-driven (for symbolic ones), as in Chapter 1.
7. Adrian A. Hopgood, *Intelligent Systems for Engineers and Scientists* (CRC Press, 2001).

complexity). Due to the reasoning they provide, they are sometimes called *soft computing*[8] methods. Their flexibility has an impact on their transparency and understandability, which is generally lower than in the case of KBS. However, it is important to emphasize that many of them are well formalized and provide predictable reasoning within certain boundaries.

The concept of learning has been present in the field of AI from the very beginning. The capability of learning is one of the most relevant features of an IS. It is crucial to understand that, in general, it has very little to do with the specific model to be used. This means that models from both aforementioned groups can be used with learning capabilities. Under certain conditions, ML algorithms allow building models of knowledge in a semi- or fully automated manner. ML methods can select and tune the parameters of the models and improve their operation based on experience, i.e., the data they use. Therefore, they offer a convenient alternative to manual construction of knowledge models by experts if relevant and good quality data is available. In general, all of the models used in KBS can be learned, although it is not always easy. Furthermore, some of the models in CI basically require learning. The most notable case is the one of ANN, as their manual configuration would not be feasible. In general, the use of ML can have an impact on the transparency and understandability of the resulting is. However, what matters most are the models that are used. The important features for the legal analysis of the operation of an IS are their transparency and understandability to humans building and using them, as well as those monitoring or auditing them. Another important feature is the predictability of operation of IS. Computers were commonly considered as predictable machines, but the fact is that the algorithms computer systems execute can make the results of their operation unpredictable. Predictability, in a broad sense, can also be related to the determinism of the system, i.e., Its feature to generate the same results under the same given conditions. Traditionally, most algorithms produce deterministic results. One can argue that one of the distinctive features of many AI algorithms is their indeterministic operation. But it does not have to result in unpredictable behaviour of an IS based on them. While predictability can be related to rationality of IS and human beings, it is often the indeterminism which is related to human intelligence, including heuristic reasoning, intuition, or creativity. In a way, this is a natural design, considering that we want the system to operate in a robust manner in a complex, changing, and generally indeterministic environment. Furthermore, recent advances of AI, especially in the field of ML, are changing the game.

The use of ML bears an important consequence for IS, i.e., the capability of changing the future behaviour of IS. In fact, in many settings, training using ML leads to behaviour which is not fully predictable. Consider one of the most typical tasks addressed by models built using ML, i.e., the classification task. It is expected that the model will be able to generalize over the data that was used for training, in order to perform as well as possible on the new data, unseen before. However, it is also clear

8. Soft computing is a loosely defined area of methods and paradigms that can provide solutions for computationally complex problems, exploiting certain level of uncertainty or imprecision. Examples include fuzzy logic, evolutionary computation, rough sets and artificial neural nets.

that the model will not perform perfectly, i.e., there will always be some errors. As such, the intended outcome of the ML process is by design a not fully predictable behaviour of the is being trained. However, an important challenge is a tacit bias that can always be present in the training data. This bias can, in fact, lead to an unintended change of the behaviour of the system.[9]

In a certain way, we are not only programming IS to be indeterministic, but also not to be fully predictable. This is not only due to the algorithms being employed, but mostly to the data they use (e.g., in the learning process). Furthermore, this can also be somehow related to the task the IS supposed to solve. Finally, the degree of unpredictability, and its possible negative character and consequences, i.e., unintended behaviour and possible harm resulting from it, are critical in the case of autonomous intelligent systems (AIS). By developing and using such systems, we delegate certain tasks and goals to them, expecting them to develop proper solutions or to take appropriate decisions on their own.

To conclude, as IS are different from traditional computer systems, assessing liability issues in relation to it is especially challenging. In many cases IS are by design not fully predictable, since this opens up the possibility to operate in an 'intelligent' manner. While being unpredictable, they should still demonstrate generally expected and useful behaviour. However, training them with data containing implicit bias can lead to unintended and harmful behaviour. This can have profound consequences, especially if IS operates autonomously to a certain degree. In such a case, its harmful operation can lead to substantial damage. This is why we put emphasis on the features of transparency and understandability of IS. Thanks to them, it should be possible not only to explain the unintended operation of the system but also to correct it, and, finally, to assess the possible damage. Ultimately, it should be possible to predict and evade their mis-operation and its legal consequences.

These issues are especially important in some recent applications of IS that we discuss next.

§8.03 LEGALLY CHALLENGING APPLICATIONS OF INTELLIGENT SYSTEMS

The legal responsibility of IS becomes an especially important issue when one considers its growing use in certain areas. Central to our discussion are not so much the technical challenges related to these applications, but rather their high societal impact, and thus, their possible legal consequences.

One highly controversial and widely discussed area of application of AIS is transport, where there is a growing degree of automation. In general, automation can be understood as follows: 'whenever the legal moves of a formal system are fully determined by algorithms, then that system can be automated'.[10] In the case of

9. Consider the famous 'accidents' of some chatbots making racist comments, *see*: Aylin Caliskan, Joanna J. Bryson & Arvind Narayanan *Semantics derived automatically from language corpora contain human-like biases*, 356 Science 183, Issue 6334, 2017.
10. John Haugeland, *Artificial Intelligence The Very Idea* (MIT Press, 1985).

autonomous vehicles, the international society of automotive engineers (SAE) has defined six levels of vehicle automation (0–5). Current technologies are at level 3 (conditional automation) where the human driver is still required, but the vehicle can execute several manoeuvres on its own. In fact, level 4 technologies are currently field-tested, and it is estimated that they are not more than 10 years to the market. A level 4 vehicle does not need the human driver, although s/he could still intervene. In the postulated level 5 (the highest one), humans would only be passengers. It is important to note, that while economic factors could slow down the adoption of this technology in the customer market, it is already being deployed by large transport companies for tracks and some public transport systems (e.g., subways, buses). It is clear that, in the case of an accident, such vehicles can cause substantial damage. Thus, the issues of liability are already today very relevant.

Another important area of application of AI is the military, especially for autonomous weapons. This is one of the most controversial areas of application of AIS that poses not only legal but also grave ethical concerns. In fact, it requires a completely different regulatory approach from international law.

However, our concerns rely even more on the IS categories that are not embodied, such as the ones that are already being applied by financial organizations in the financial markets. The prime examples are the automated trading systems in the stock markets, which can be considered, at least partially, as autonomous. Some of the unpredicted consequences of their use contributed to the stock market flash crash in 2010. And besides, these large-scale applications are also commonly used as support tools in the decision-making process of a growing number of banks and other financial agents.

The medical domain is also using a new generation of AI-based decision support systems. Some of the most important tasks to be solved by it are disease diagnosis, drug development, and personalized medicine which can include risk analysis, disease prediction, and personalized treatment. AI is also widely applied in genetics. While so far AI mostly supports but not replaces doctors,[11] it can be expected that in the future such replacement would not only be technically possible but also sometimes societally beneficial and acceptable.[12] However, a proper legal framework is an obvious prerequisite for this to become true.

Finally, there is a growing use of IS in the fields of law enforcement and security. Indeed, there are several countries, including the United States of America, that are deploying IS for tasks ranging from data analysis (mostly image analysis) to classification, decision support, and, more controversially, prediction of future behaviour of individuals. This is especially challenging in the wake of the widespread use of AI-based on hardly transparent models, which are often referred to as *black-boxes*. These issues are discussed in more detail in the next section.

---

11. Varun H. Buch, Irfan Ahmed, Mahiben Maruthappu, *Artificial intelligence in medicine: current trends and future possibilities*, 68 (668) Br J Gen Pract 143 (2018).
12. In interesting discussion of the overestimated impact of the IBM Watson in medical applications can be found in Eliza Strickland, *How IBM Watson Overpromised and Underdelivered on AI Health Care*, IEEE Spectrum (2019).

§8.04 DESIGN OF INTELLIGENT SYSTEMS AND ITS ROLE IN THE LEGAL ANALYSIS

When considering the impact of legal analysis of liability, it can be observed that while understanding and certifying hardware, including computer hardware, is a somehow feasible and mature activity, software assessment is not so obvious but necessary for a complete system assessment. Software companies have established themselves in an almost unique position in the market, as they explicitly use a waiver of liability for the software they create. This applies to virtually all software, even the most basic and predictable. This said if we consider that intelligent software is, as we already stated, programmed to be unpredictable to some degree, the situation is particularly challenging. Furthermore, as we emphasized, some models of knowledge in IS are hardly understandable even for their creators, not mentioning the users. Thus, if we consider the societally important and intrusive applications of IS, this conceptual and legal loophole can have a very high impact.

Furthermore, for considering the legal liability of IS, it is instrumental in understanding the general features of the design and development of IS that make it different from more traditional software systems. In order to do this, we consider and analyse several aspects such as embodiment, non-physicality, connectivity, and distribution.

Let us consider two cases of *embodiment* in IS. The first one is the kind of IS since it is very different if the IS constitutes a complete stand-alone system (e.g., a robot), or just a component of a larger (non-intelligent) system, e.g., a navigation system in an electric car. The second one is the case when the IS located in some physical container, e.g., a robot or IS consists of is a larger system of connected and communicating components. This, in fact, brings forward two next issues.

Considering the *physical aspect* of construction, it can be observed that the nature of IS differs when it is composed of both hardware and software components than when it is an only software-based IS.

On the other, the *connectivity* of IS and data required for its functioning must be considered. As we know, nowadays, there is a tendency to interconnect when possible hardware and software systems in order to create a large grid, i.e., the Internet of Things paradigm. It is often the case that the data circulating in such large networks of devices and software systems do not have a predefined structure that allows the IS to operate.

The final issue that should be brought to attention is the *distribution*. Today, computing architectures, including cloud, but also dedicated systems for supporting the training of ANNs, are massively parallel and distributed. Therefore, it is mostly challenging to localize the software to be purely and only operating in some specific and well-localized hardware system.

The AI community realizes these challenges regarding the design of IS. One of the most important efforts to tackle them is being deployed by the IEEE[13] global initiative

13. Institute of Electrical and Electronics Engineers, http://ieee.org.

on ethics of AIS. They have produced *the ethically aligned design (EAD)* report, which is a result of wide consultation in several sensitive areas related to the development of AI[14] (IEEE 2017). Within this document, a special emphasis is put on the autonomous IS. As the authors have stated, the objective of the EAD report is to 'provide insights and recommendations that provide a key reference for the work of technologists in the related fields of science and technology in the coming years.' This key document addresses several topics, including the role of classical ethics in the analysis, embedding values into IS, treatment and use of data in IS, economic and humanitarian dimensions, as well as the legal ones. Furthermore, several disruptive technologies are identified, including autonomous weapons, mixed reality[15] and affective computing[16]. The analysis is based on the general principles of well-being, accountability, transparency, and awareness of misuse. While it is only a collection of proposals and recommendations, it is an important voice in the engineering community.

Today, data used in the development of IS plays a paramount role in the quality of the design. Data, in a broad sense, becomes basically the main source of knowledge to be used in the building of the IS. It applies both to the use of knowledge engineering in the building of KBS, but more importantly, to the use of ML methods for training. Considering the latter practice, one of the challenges is the volume, but even more importantly, the quality of data used for training.[17] However, as we mentioned earlier, the real challenge is not so much the question of the technical quality of the data, but in fact, the bias in the data.[18] This bias can impact many dimensions of the system on the ethical and societal level.[19] While one of the assumptions of the IS designers is the design for values, i.e., embedding certain ethical values into the system, it is the use of biased data and non-transparent training methods that make it challenging.

We are of the opinion that the allocation of liability following from the operations of IS depends on fundamental choices concerning purposes to be achieved through regulation and predictions concerning the real consequences of the regulation. As in the case of any complex societal phenomena, it is necessary to find the path to properly balance the interests of involved stakeholders, which means, in particular, taking into account promoting innovation, on the one hand, and protecting the safety and privacy of the consumers, on the other hand. Finding such a path requires the analysis of a multi-level structure of factual and normative factors that may influence the liability attribution, choice of proper liability regime, and finally, the allocation of liability. The role of IS design in this context is crucial, and the key question is whether general standards should be adopted for IS design and what should be the role and the content

14. *Ethically Aligned Design: A Vision for Prioritizing Human Well-being with Autonomous and Intelligent Systems, Version 2* (IEEE, 2017).
15. The mixed reality technology combines virtual reality and augmented reality to create immersive environments combining physical objects with virtual ones.
16. Affective computing is an interdisciplinary paradigm devoted to the computer-based methods for modelling, recognition and synthesis of emotions.
17. Doug Patterson & Kord Davis, *Ethics of Big Data* (O'Reilly Media 2012).
18. Aylin Caliskan, Joanna J. Bryson & Arvind Narayanan *Semantics derived automatically from language corpora contain human-like biases*, 356 Science 183, Issue 6334, 2017.
19. Frank Pasquale, *The Black Box Society, The Secret Algorithms That Control Money and Information* (Harvard University Press 2015).

of such standards. There are several important questions: What should be the consequences of a producer failing to comply with the standards in the process of IS design? If the design process complies with the standards, who should bear liability if the IS produces any harm? To what extent should the user take precautions in order to minimize the risk of harm? It should also be emphasized that in the case of autonomous systems, they also may make their own assessment of situations they are involved in and decide on the action to be taken. This holds irrespective of attributing them any type of legal personhood. The question is how the autonomous systems' decision-making process can be constrained on the level of IS design in order to maximize the likeliness of them following the proper rules and minimizing adverse consequences of their conduct.

There are three basic mechanisms that may be used to implement the norms in IS: enforcement, sanctions and coordination mechanisms.[20] The first technique, *enforcement mechanisms*, simply excludes the system from performing certain actions; however, the scope of its application may be reduced in case of systems interacting with the real world. The *sanctions mechanisms* may prove effective where the system is adequately 'motivated' to avoid them, which is a complex issue in the case of agents whose constitution is different from humans. Potentially, the most fruitful technique is the latter one, the *coordination mechanisms*, where the system autonomously adjusts its behaviour considering the relevant circumstances. However, the implementation of such a technique in the design of a system, and its proper reflection in legal regulation, is quite a complex task.

In our opinion, the proper path to discuss the standards of IS design and the content of appropriate regulation of liability should begin with careful investigation of the types of IS and mechanisms of their behaviour in given environments, including the possibility to implement reasoning with norms into the systems. Only such analysis may provide solid grounds for the anticipated consequences of different legal liability regimes. In the next section, we discuss the features of IS to be considered when defining its legal framework.

§8.05 LEGAL-PHILOSOPHICAL OUTLOOK ON THE PROBLEM OF LIABILITY REGULATION DESIGN OF INTELLIGENT SYSTEMS

The notion of legal responsibility is ambiguous in the legal-philosophical language, and the different senses of this term have been discussed thoroughly.[21] In the following, we focus on the understanding of legal responsibility as liability: attaching legal consequences to certain acts, performed by certain entities. We also follow Hage[22] to assume the position of liability *attributivism*: legal liability is a feature attributed to a subject,

20. Trevor Bench-Capon, *Analysing Norms with Transition Systems*, (in: Rinke Hoekstra ed., Legal Knowledge and Information Systems - JURIX 2014: The Twenty-Seventh Annual Conference, 271, Frontiers in Artificial Intelligence and Applications, Amsterdam: IOS Press, 29–38 2014).
21. Herbert L.A. Hart, Punishment and Responsibility. Essays in the Philosophy of Law (Oxford: Oxford University Press, 2nd edition, 2008): 210ff.
22. Jaap Hage, Theoretical foundations for the responsibility of autonomous agents, 25 Artificial Intelligence and Law, 255–271 (2017).

rather than 'discovered'. Evidence following from history reveals that legal liability has been attributed, in accordance with the general world view of policymakers, also to non-existent entities (supernatural forces) or, for instance, to animals, who were criminally punished for their 'acts'. Even though deciding on liability is essentially about attribution, this does not mean that this process is simple or unconstrained (arbitrary). The contrary is the case. Attribution of liability is a complex and constrained decision.

Liability attribution is complicated, mainly because it presupposes the existence and coordination of several institutions, such as the lawmakers, the system of judiciary and the law enforcement system. Moreover, the structure of each of these institutions is extremely complex, subject to evolution, and it changes in the different jurisdictions. Additionally, relations between this system and external institutions (political, economic, societal) that may influence the process of liability attribution are even more complicated. In case of policy design related to attribution of liability in the context of a new type of phenomena having a huge influence on the economy, the sources of this complexity are, in particular, as follows: (1) the problem of assuming political responsibility for the introduction of the new rules, (2) the potential impact of the rules on the markets and lack of possibility of actual trial and error, (3) the dynamics of the environment in which the rules will operate.

Liability attribution is constrained by different factual and normative factors, to mention a few: the current state of scientific knowledge, the general common-sense worldview shared by the members of each community, the content of the valid law and the political considerations concerning the goals that the law should have and how they should be achieved. It is also constrained differently on several levels: recognizing the legal personhood of a new type of legal entity or establishing a new type of liability requires different justification than attribution of liability to an already acknowledged legal entity.

Attribution of legal liability to non-human agents (which presupposes acknowledging non-human agents) has a long and continuous history. Juridical persons such as foundations and corporations were already established in ancient Rome. Therefore, it should be emphasized that it is in principle perfectly possible to attribute legal personhood and in consequence of legal liability to IS – they could, for instance, become a new type of legal entities. However, irrespective of the fact whether they should be recognized as a new type of legal entity, or whether liability should rely on IS producers or other relevant actors, the specific features of IS have to be taken into account in the process of relevant liability rules design.

Legal systems, in general, and regimes of legal liability, in particular, were developed and have evolved in principle in connection with the liability of human beings. This consideration is also relevant to the existence and activities of legal persons. Even though the decisions of the latter count legally as their own decisions, on the fundamental level, they are made by humans who act in the role of representatives of these legal persons. Therefore, the existing liability regulations were developed ultimately taking into account the specific features of humans as liability subjects. Any legal system, in order to operate properly and efficiently, has to take into account the specific features related to human beings and the general context in which they operate. Let us enumerate the list of these features, following Hart:[23]

(1) human vulnerability. It is relatively simple for one human agent to injure or cause death to other human beings. In addition to this remark of hart's we may add that bringing a human being to adulthood is, in contrast, a time-consuming, costly and emotionally engaging process;
(2) approximate equality. Despite the big differences amongst human individuals, the divergences from the average values of certain parameters characterizing people are not significant enough to interfere with the functioning of a legal system consisting of general rules. In connection with the above, let us also note that human beings are approximately equal in their vulnerability. Hart rightly notes that the situation is different in international public law where there are significant differences between particular states and let us add that also in the case of legal persons, especially corporations, the relevant differences with regard to income and assets may be drastic. This remark is critical because traditional legal regulation has proven at least not entirely effective regarding operations of international, extremely wealthy corporations, and the entities of this type are primarily involved in the development of IS;
(3) limited altruism. Taking into account the general aim of survival, typically people are neither overly altruistic nor excessively intrusive towards other people. However, coercive regulation seems to be necessary to curb the tendency of aggressive behaviour and to foster better cooperation;
(4) limited resources. The resources human beings need are not available in unlimited amounts. In larger groups of people, the need to supply the participants with adequate resources implies division of labour. Hart rightly notes that the division of labour naturally leads to the emergence of legal institutions that secure the exchange of goods, including the law of obligations and coercive regulations. Let us add that in this context, the role of time, understood as a specific, irrecoverable resource, cannot be overestimated;
(5) the limited ability of understanding and strength of will. Obviously, human cognitive and volitional powers are limited. The last decades brought unprecedented progress in connection with identification and analysis of different limitations concerning the rationality of human decision-making, memory, attention etc. The lack of ability to recognize the nature of a situation where a human agent is involved, or to control its behaviour, is acknowledged in numerous jurisdictions as an excuse from liability under the label of the insanity defence.

The features discussed above should be taken into account in the process of design of any well-functioning regime of human agents' legal liability. Although these

23. Herbert L.A. Hart, The Concept of Law (Oxford: Oxford University Press, 2nd edition, 1994): 193ff.

features are contingent, their 'natural' character motivated hart to refer to them as 'minimal content of natural law' (we will abbreviate it as MCNL).

Any discussion concerning legal regulation of activities involving IS should take into account similar constraints. The consideration of these factors is more important for the design of appropriate regulation than the discussion of whether legal personhood should be ascribed to IS because the latter is largely a technical decision. Irrespective of whether legal personhood is attributed to IS, we have to consider what are the *conditions* of effective enforcement of liability related to the operation of such systems, and what *purposes* do we expect to achieve through such regulation. As in the case of any regulation concerning relatively novel technology, it is a complex and difficult task to attempt to predict the effects of such regulations, including externalities.

In addition to the above five points referred to as the MCNL, we should also note the following general characteristics of human beings: self-awareness, the ability to identify themselves and other human beings as possessing certain features characteristic for humans, including the MCNL features, and the ability to process natural language. These features were not discussed by Hart in connection with the MCNL because there he was interested in such features that influence the content of law rather than its very existence, while the general characteristics mentioned in the preceding sentence are conditions of emergence and functioning of any known legal system. Let us refer to them as 'basic conditions'.

Both basic conditions and the MCNL should serve as the point of departure for a discussion concerning the design of legal regulation related to AI. As we have noted above, AI is a rather broad concept encompassing different types of objects. In the following, we will focus on the regulation design concerning the activities of autonomous agents, capable of adaptive, not entirely predictable behaviour.

As far as the basic conditions are concerned, IS are not self-aware, and it is very disputable whether self-awareness or human-like intentionality may emerge in an artificial environment.[24] In connection with this, no IS are driven by the basic aim of survival, and unless they are appropriately programmed, they do not recognize the protection of themselves as a goal. Even though it may relate to the external world, they do not have intentional states similar to those experienced by human beings.

These findings have far-reaching consequences for the discussion of MCNL features:

> Vulnerability: If IS interacts with human beings in the physical world, it has to be taught about human vulnerability, and appropriate constraints have to be applied in order to prevent the occurrence of bodily harm in connection with the agent's activities. Similarly, IS are not motivated by the awareness of their own vulnerability. This finding has specific significance in connection with the design of the sanctions system related to IS causing personal injury.

24. John R. Searle, Minds, Brains and Programs, 3 The Behavioral and Brain Sciences, 417–457 (1980); *see also* Roger Penrose, The Emperor's New Mind: Concerning Computers, Minds and the Laws of Physics (Oxford: Oxford University Press 2002).

Approximate equality: As emphasized above, the concept of AI refers to numerous, very diverse entities. IS are, therefore, not approximately equal among themselves, and they are also very different from human beings. This remark leads to a tentative conclusion that it may be futile to discuss the general principles of regulation concerning the AI-related liability in the first place. A potentially more fruitful path consists of careful analysis of the features of a certain subtype of IS and considering what liability rules would be appropriate in connection with their operation. The possibility of developing a set of general principles of AI-related liability is not excluded, but it should be reasonably considered after more specific regulations are designed and tested.

Limited altruism: As far as the limited altruism problem is concerned, and the IS does not have the goals consciously intended as their own goals, but it obviously may be programmed to attempt to realize certain aims and behave as if these goals were its own. This remark is particularly important in connection with adaptive, learning systems which may choose an unpredicted, surprising path to achieve a certain goal. Therefore, it is necessary to consider constraints that could restrict the types of actions taken by an agent in order to realize the goal, not only on the level of IS design but also on the level of appropriate legal regulation design (which may, in turn, influence the design of the IS itself). Further, the legal regulation should take into account not only the risks related to the realization of goals but also define the space of appropriate goals and values. In this connection, an important discussion is one of IS 'own' goals, that is, the goals that the system itself may be able to come up with, irrespective of, and in some cases, in conflict with, the goals assumed by the developers or the users of the system. At any rate, socially responsible regulation of IS operations should take into account the values and aims of all relevant stakeholders.

Limited resources: An IS functions in a world of limited resources, but it is not aware of this fact. Therefore, the legal regulation pertaining to these systems should take this fact into account by prompting them to respect legal institutions that follow from it (for instance, property, rights and duties following from obligations, etc.) Legal regulation may provide in this context the feedback for the engineering aspect of systems' design.

Intellectual and volitional powers: Perhaps the most evident differences between human agents and artificial agents concern the fifth MCNL feature discussed by Hart: the limited ability of understanding and strength of will. The reasoning of both knowledge-based systems and data-driven (ML) systems differ considerably from the reasoning performed by human beings. On the one hand, IS are able to process a significantly greater amount of information in definitely a shorter time than human beings. On the other hand, in spite of continuous development of this field, KBS is relatively weak in processing common sense reasoning, while most ML methods (e.g., ANNs) are not able to explain their behaviour in a manner understandable by humans. The problem of (free) will, one of the most troubling issues in legal and moral philosophy,[25] seems not to apply directly to the IS decision-making process. However, the notion of control should be taken into account in the context of the risk of a cyberattack on a system. These remarks are relevant in connection with the discussion of potential defences and excuses in connection with AI-related liability, including the debate of the potential counterpart of the insanity defence in this field.

We are convinced that the 'minimal content of AI natural law' is a subject worth extensive and deepened investigations. The careful recognition of features of a given type of IS becomes an essential condition for any informed discussion of legal liability related to the operation of IS.

§8.06 AI AND THE TYPES OF LEGAL LIABILITY

The general discussion concerning the grounds of legal liability following from the operation of IS has been hampered by the fact that different jurisdictions employ diverging regulations of liability. In particular, there are far-reaching differences between the models used in Anglo-American legal culture, on the one hand, and in continental European legal systems, on the other hand. A more detailed investigation requires an extensive study: criminal liability of AI was discussed, for instance, by Hallevy;[26] and Pagallo[27] presents a broad analysis of criminal, contract and tort liability of AI. The grounds for AI legal liability have also attracted considerable attention in the industry[28] and are a subject of interest in the European Union (EU), as a part of a broader AI strategy framework.[29] In the following, we restrict our investigations to the four abstract models of liability: civil liability based on negligence, strict civil liability, criminal liability and administrative liability, focusing on certain specific issues related to the conditions of liability. We discuss civil liability on a general level, abstracting from the important details between contractual, tort and product liability. Finally, we focus on the consequentialist approach towards the choice of liability type,[30] compatible with the legal-economic analysis of legal liability,[31] although we stress that

25. Kevin Timpe, Meghan Griffith & Neil Levy (eds.), The Routledge Companion to Free Will (Routledge 2016).
26. Gabriel Hallevy, When Robots Kill. Artificial Intelligence under Criminal Law (Boston: Northeastern University Press 2013); Gabriel Hallevy, Liability for Crimes Involving Artificial Intelligence Systems (Cham: Springer 2015).
27. Ugo Pagallo, The Laws of Robots. Crimes, Contracts and Torts (Dordrecht: Springer 2013).
28. For instance, Allianz Global Corporate and Specialty, The Rise of Artificial Intelligence: Future Outlook and Emerging Risks, https://www.agcs.allianz.com/news-and-insights/news/artificial-intelligence-report.html (2018) (accessed 21 May 2019).
29. European Commission, Communication from the Commission to the European Parliament, the European Council, the Council, the European Economic and Social Committee and The Committee of the Regions. Artificial Intelligence in Europe, https://ec.europa.eu/digital-single-market/en/news/communication-artificial-intelligence-europe (2018) (accessed 1 May 2019).
30. The discussion of different purposes of liability may be found in Jaap Hage 2017, *ibid.*
31. For a thorough overview, *see* Michael Faure (ed.), Tort Law and Economics, Volume 1, Encyclopedia of Law and Economics (2nd edition) (Cheltenham: Edward Elgar 2009), Nuno Garoupa (ed.), Criminal Law and Economics, Volume 3, Encyclopedia of Law and Economics

economic efficiency should not be the sole criterion for AI-related regulation assessment.

The basic conditions of civil liability are the occurrence of damage, a certain event and a causal link between this event and the occurrence of damage. In case of negligence-based liability, there is an additional necessary condition of liability, which may be referred to as a breach of duty of care, lack of adequate diligence, or fault on the side of the perpetrator of the damage. In case of strict liability, the entity is responsible for the occurrence of damage irrespective of its acts of diligence; hence, this entity bears the risk of its activities. Typically, a legal regulation provides a list of circumstances which enable the perpetrator to release itself from liability, such as the exclusive fault of the victim.

One of the most important challenges is *the problem of causality* in connection with the operation of IS. As any of the terms related to legal liability, causality is also an attributed rather than a discovered feature. However, in most jurisdictions, a certain type of empirical connection between the event and the damage is considered as one of the causality conditions.[32] The crucial question is what in the operation of the IS caused the damage: an error in algorithm design, a flaw in the data the algorithm was trained on, or another factor, and what tests should be used in order to determine whether there was a causal link. In particular, it is doubtful whether the foreseeability test is of any use in connection with damages related to the operation of IS, taking into account the expected added value following from these systems that relies precisely on the possibility of unpredictable actions.

As for the *negligence* standard, the perpetrator of the damage is released from liability once it is not possible to determine that it is at fault (for the sake of conciseness, we omit the issues related to the burden of proof distribution).[33] Therefore, the potential perpetrator will be *ceteris paribus* motivated to exercise the standard of diligence required by the law. This leads to a challenging question: what acts of diligence should be performed and by whom. In particular, the IS should not only be adequately protected from cyberattacks but also should be possible to show that it was 'properly' trained and tested before it was placed on the market and used. It is vital to note that if the standard of adequate diligence is too severe, it may hamper the development of IS, but if it is too low, it will lead to harm to the overall welfare of the society because the damages will not be adequately compensated. Taking these doubts into account, it is worth considering strict liability as the standard of civil liability, but

(2nd edition) (Cheltenham: Edward Elgar 2009) and Gerrit De Geest (ed.), Contract Law and Economics, Volume 6, Encyclopedia of Law and Economics (2nd edition) (Cheltenham: Edward Elgar 2011).

32. For the jurisprudential discussion, *see* Herbert L.A. Hart & Anthony M. Honoré, Causation in the Law (London: Oxford University Press 1959); recent knowledge-based analysis of the concept of causal link may be found in Michał Araszkiewicz, Incorporation of complex doctrinal theories in a model of statutory interpretation: an example of adequate causal link, in: Ted Sichelman, Katie Atkinson (eds.) Proceedings of the 15th International Conference on Artificial Intelligence and Law, ICAIL 2015, ACM, New York, 161–165 (2015).

33. For instance, Henry Prakken & Giovanni Sartor, A logical analysis of burdens of proof. In: Hendrik Kaptein, Henry Prakken & Bart Verheij (eds.) Legal Evidence and Proof: Statistics, Stories, Logic. Farnham: Ashgate Publishing, Applied Legal Philosophy Series, 223–253 (2009).

its disadvantage is, in turn, that it may discourage the agent from undertaking the activity because it will be potentially too costly.

A particularly challenging issue is how to implement the elements concerning the exercise of an adequate level of care into the reasoning of the AI algorithm itself. Irrespective of whether such algorithm is attributed or not to legal personhood, the implementation of such mechanisms may be an important factor in finding an involved stakeholder liable (if a negligence standard is adopted) and, under both regimes, delimiting the scope and amount of harm done by the algorithm. However, as standards of diligence are essentially context-sensitive, implementation of such standards into the IS constitutes a challenging task.

The emergence of IS does not invalidate the traditional distinction of inherently dangerous activities and other types of activities. Therefore, it is justified to argue that the application of strict liability is appropriate wherever the operations of IS classify as dangerous ones. This contention opens a question concerning adequate insurance policies and the definition of exemptions from insurance protection. We are of the opinion that the development of such insurance policies should be preceded by careful investigation concerning, in particular, how the reasoning with levels of diligence is implemented in the IS. Such discussion has already been started in the academic circles.[34]

Criminal liability is by default the most onerous type of legal responsibility because criminal punishment is designed to interfere with the most important goods such as individual freedom, or, in case of capital punishment, the life of an individual. Moreover, the status of the criminal convict is typically connected with the prohibition of involvement in certain types of activity; moreover, on the level of social relations, this status carries a heavy burden of stigma. The conditions of criminal liability are defined differently in the Anglo-American world (the notions of *actus reus* and *mens rea*) and in continental Europe. However, it is a basic requirement that the activity being the subject of criminal sanction should be well-defined in the statutory provision and that a person may be punished only if found guilty. Importantly, while these conditions were designed to assess the criminal liability of human beings, criminal (or quasi-criminal) responsibility of juridical persons has also been recognized in different jurisdictions. This opens the possibility to discuss the criminal liability of juridical persons responsible for the design, use or placing the IS on the market, and eventually the criminal liability of IS if they are assigned with a type of legal personhood. In this connection, challenging questions pertain to the subjective (intellectual and volitional) conditions of criminal liability. In particular, it is vital to investigate under what conditions could the notion of intent be attributed to IS and to what extent such criminal liability defences as insanity or error could be applied in this context.

The last type of legal liability we intend to discuss is *administrative liability*. There is a visible tendency in contemporary legal systems to sanction more and more types of legally non-compliant behaviour with administrative means, including fines; the sanctions following from Article 83 of the general data protection regulation

34. For instance, Henry Prakken, On the problem of making autonomous vehicles conform to traffic law, 25 Artificial Intelligence and Law, 341–363 (2017).

(GDPR) are the most notorious recent example of this direction, although administrative penalties are ubiquitous in numerous domains of law (transportation, pharmaceuticals, trade, environment protection, medical services, etc.) The application of administrative fines is *ceteris paribus* less complicated for the authorities than the imposition of criminal punishment, and it does not carry a similar moral stigma for the liable entity, although economically, it may be very onerous. The use of this type of regulation presupposes the existence of certain standards with which the agent in question should be compliant with. While such standards may increase certainty in a given sphere of social interaction, the sanctions are the risk associated with them that may hamper the innovation.

In summing up the above considerations, any type of existing model of liability regime is problematic in case of considering liability following from the operation of IS or direct liability of IS if it is acknowledged as a type of legal entity. In any particular case where liability depends on determining a causal link between event and damage, determining what subject is liable and to what extent, may be extremely complicated. A similar conclusion holds for the notion of civil and criminal fault. A more detailed inquiry into the mechanisms of IS operation is necessary in order to provide for factors relevant in connection with the interpretation of these classical legal concepts in connection of AI liability. Such an inquiry may also lead to the development of certain IS design standards. In this context, a particular role should be assigned to the idea of explainability.

§8.07 THE IMPACT OF EXPLAINABILITY

In 2016, American Defense Advanced Research Projects Agency (DARPA) announced the program DARPA-BAA-16-53 on explainable artificial intelligence (XAI).[35] This was a response to a growing concern regarding the use and development of certain IS. Furthermore, the possible legal consequences of their applications were grave. The agency acknowledges the problems with models built with modern ML techniques. The main challenge is the tension between model performance and explainability. DARPA asserts that there is a clear trade-off between both. On the other hand, in practical applications, there is a growing need for explainability; consequently, there should be a kind of a balance between these two.

Although DARPA XAI program sparked many discussions in the AI community, the problem of XAI is not new. Not only were the early symbolic IS explainable but also the research on XAI-related topics has been around for almost fifteen years. Paradigms like explanation-aware computing were proposed over a decade ago.[36] In fact, now, the ML community faces the challenge that the KBS community solved a long time ago. It

35. DARPA, *Broad Agency Announcement – Explainable Artificial Intelligence (XAI)* (DARPA-BAA-16-53, 10 Aug. 2016).

36. Thomas Roth-Berghofer, Stefan Schulz Eds., *Explanation-Aware Computing, Papers from the 2005 AAAI Fall Symposium, November 4–6, 2005, Arlington, Virginia, USA* (AAAI Technical Report, FS-05-04, AAAI Press, 2005).

is the time now, for these two approaches to work together on delivering hybrid solutions.

The topic of XAI in IS should be regarded as clearly relevant to the discussion of their legal liability. Today, it is often the case that if an IS makes an error that possibly causes damage, not only the user does not understand why, but even the creators cannot explain it. Furthermore, removing the flaw or improving the system is not always possible. Such systems appear to be as black-boxes to both the users and to a large extent to the engineers who built them. The use of black-boxes has already been identified as a threat in some domains like medicine[37]and discussed in the IEEE EAD document.

Let us now consider that these black-boxes are mostly common purely software entities (i.e., non-physical, as we defined it before). Moreover, as we stated previously, the software companies include the waiver of liability in the software licences. This makes it particularly difficult to claim that IS or its creators are legally liable. It also demonstrates the urgent need to provide legal means to do so. Furthermore, there is an even more concerning use of black-boxes than medicine. It is the law itself. During the last two decades, significant progress has been made in AI and law in connection with the development of legal data analysis, information retrieval and extraction, and argument mining.[38] Commercial computer programs are aiming at supporting lawyers in problem-solving or even replacing them in performing certain, at this moment, simple tasks, with learning mechanisms based on statistics. Such systems may give accurate answers in terms of classification and prediction but lack the ability to provide adequate (legal) justification for the solution.

It seems that the delivery of appropriate legal means for solving the problem of liability of IS currently dominated by black-boxes needs actions on several fronts. The very concept of explainability (and cognate terms as transparency or intelligibility) need further elaboration. The models of explanation need to be considered on engineering, ethical and legal levels. As far as the latter is concerned, the notion of 'right to explanation' calls for broad jurisprudential analysis. As far as the approaches are concerned, a technology that has been around in both the area of AI and law are argumentation models, including the paradigm of argumentation frameworks initiated by Dung.[39] Nowadays, argumentation frameworks are one of the most investigated approaches to computational modelling of argumentation.[40] Even though the degree of explainability of results generated by these and similar systems is subject to debate, their advantage in this context is that they operate with symbolic information. They

37. Varun H. Buch, Irfan Ahmed, Mahiben Maruthappu, *Artificial intelligence in medicine: current trends and future possibilities*, 68 (668) Br J Gen Pract 143 (2018).
38. Kevin D. Ashley, *Artificial Intelligence and Legal Analytics. New Tools for Law Practice in the Digital Age* (Cambridge: Cambridge University Press 2017).
39. Phan Minh Dung, *On the acceptability of arguments and its fundamental role in nonmonotonic reasoning, logic programming and n-person games*, 2 Artificial Intelligence, 321–357, issue 77 (1995).
40. For a broad outlook, *see* Iyad Rahwan & Guillermo R. Simari (eds.), Argumentation in Artificial Intelligence (Dordrecht: Springer 2009) and Pietro Baroni, Dov Gabbay, Massimiliano Giacomin & Leendert van der Torre (eds.), Handbook of Formal Argumentation (London: College Publications 2018).

begin to be applied in the context of an explanation of IS[41] and offer a promising direction also because of the existing tradition of their application to the field of legal reasoning.[42]

Looking at some preliminary solutions to the DARPA challenge, another problem arises. It is the domain of biases. Most of the current prominent applications of black-box IS lie in the area of pattern recognition in general, and in particular for image classification and recognition. As such, some of the 'solutions' seem also limited or at least targeted at this domain. On the other hand, in a general sense, an explanation should most commonly be understood at the linguistic level. Furthermore, if we consider the legal perspective, giving an explanation requires a more profound approach than just generating a simple answer to the question of why, it requires a proper normative argument, and in many cases, a presentation of balancing of different pro and contra reasons will be required. And this is something that many of IS used today cannot provide as they lack appropriate explanation modules.

We argue that certain methods of assessment of explainability of IS should be proposed and defined in a legal manner. Furthermore, we assert that these methods could serve as a foundation for both dedicated liability insurances, as well as guidelines in the legal reasoning about the liability of IS. Finally, we are convinced that the explanatory aspect of AI that is being introduced into the society should be investigated and evaluated by interdisciplinary communities combining lawyers, engineers and ethicists.

§8.08 CONCLUSIONS

We began our analysis by demonstrating that AI is a complex and ambiguous concept. We proposed instead the use of the concept of IS, which is common in the engineering community and, more importantly, is better defined. Recent applications of IS, some of them mentioned in this chapter have societal impacts that have to be addressed on the legal level. To consider and conceptualize legal liability of IS, one must consider specific aspects of its design, such as unpredictability, autonomy, embodiment, physicality, connectivity, distribution, and finally the role of training data. It can be asserted that on the one hand the features of the design of IS have to be considered in future legal regulations, but on the other hand, legal regulations should shape the design and development of IS. Finally, we emphasized the role of the above-mentioned aspects, as well as the transparent models of knowledge used during the design that impact the final explainability of IS. We are strongly convinced that in fact, explainability is crucial for considering legal liability.

---

41. Kristijonas Čyras, David Birch, Yike Guo, Francesca Toni, Rajvinder Dulay, Sally Turvey, Daniel Greenberg & Tharindi Hapuarachchi, Explanations by arbitrated argumentative dispute, 117 Expert Systems with Applications, 141–156 (2019) and Qiaoting Zhong, Xiuyi Fan, Xudong Luo & Francesca Toni, An explainable multi-attribute decision model based on argumentation, 117 Expert Systems with Applications 42–61 (2019).
42. Henry Prakken & Giovanni Sartor, Law and logic: A review from an argumentation perspective, 223 Artificial Intelligence, 214–245 (2015); Douglas Walton, Argumentation Methods for Artificial Intelligence in Law (Berlin: Springer 2005).

CHAPTER 9
AI and Cybersecurity

Ignacio Arnaldo

§9.01 INTRODUCTION

In the past years, the number of reported cyberattacks has unfortunately increased.[1] On the one hand, according to the Breach Level Index, data breaches have led to the theft or loss of more than 14 billion data records since 2013.[2] [3] On the other, major malware outbreaks have disrupted operations of government and corporate organizations across the spectrum of business sectors, causing not only financial and reputational damage but also the disruption of critical services.[4] Perhaps, the best example is the WannaCry malware outbreak (May 2017), which impacted more than 250K machines in over 115 different countries. The disruption of the normal operations of the United Kingdom's National Health Service (NHS) was particularly alarming: the attack caused the cancellation of 19,000 appointments and an estimated financial cost of GBP 100 million.[5]

While some of the reported attacks correspond to simple mistakes that should have been avoided, the soaring number of attacks is arguably an indicator of a systemic issue, caused by a confluence of several factors:

1. Victor Reklaitis. How the number of data breaches is soaring – in one chart. MarketWatch, https://www.marketwatch.com/story/how-the-number-of-data-breaches-is-soaring-in-one-chart-2018-02-26, 2018.
2. Lily Hay Newman. The Wired guide to data breaches. Wired, https://www.wired.com/story/wired-guide-to-data-breaches/, 2018.
3. Breach Level Index. Online, https://breachlevelindex.com/, 2019.
4. Josh Fruhlinger. The 5 biggest ransomware attacks of the last 5 years. CSO Online, https://www.csoonline.com/article/3212260/the-5-biggest-ransomware-attacks-of-the-last-5-years.html, 2017.
5. Danny Palmer. This is how much the WannaCry ransomware attack cost the NHS. ZDNet, https://www.zdnet.com/article/this-is-how-much-the-wannacry-ransomware-attack-cost-the-nhs/, 2018.

(1) The growing number of devices (mobile phones, tablets, etc.) and the shift towards cloud services are increasing the threat surface and generating greater volumes of data that need to be protected.
(2) Adversaries have gained sophistication, and a profit-oriented underground economy has emerged in which threat actors have a monetary incentive to perform the attacks.[6]
(3) There is a shortage of cybersecurity professionals, making it difficult for organizations to hire the talent needed to implement appropriate defensive strategies.[7]

Despite the current situation, it is not all negative news; the cybersecurity community keeps striving to provide ever more efficient prevention, detection, and remediation solutions to mitigate cyber risks, and to enable the continuity of business operations. In this difficult and uneven situation for defenders, Artificial Intelligence (AI) can play a significant role: to restore the balance by increasing the efficiency of security devices and processes. However, AI has not yet permeated many state-of-the-art defensive strategies, resulting not only in opportunities for improvement but also in scepticism about AI matching these elevated expectations.

In this chapter, we provide a high-level introduction to the cybersecurity landscape, introducing the different categories of threat actors and attacks (§9.02), common defensive strategies (§9.03), and existing and foreseen applications of AI in the cybersecurity domain (§9.04).

§9.02 CYBERSECURITY PRIMER

In this section, we describe the different threat actors behind cyberattacks (note that we adopt the classification introduced by Anthony Giandomenico[8]), and we provide a brief introduction to offensive techniques. Given that it is not possible to deep dive into the wide range of documented cyberattacks in a short chapter, we focus on common threats that any internet user faces on a daily basis and point to resources where the interested reader will find more detailed information.

[A] Threat Actors

(1) Opportunistic actors: Derogatorily referred to as *script kiddies*, these individuals are generally motivated by a desire for notoriety but are not necessarily

6. Pierluigi Paganini. Cybercrime and the underground market. Infosec Institute, https://resources.infosecinstitute.com/cybercrime-and-the-underground-market/, 2018.
7. Steve Morgan. One Million Cybersecurity Job Openings In 2016. Forbes, https://www.forbes.com/sites/stevemorgan/2016/01/02/one-million-cybersecurity-job-openings-in-2016/#c59eb3727ea2, 2016.
8. Anthony Giandomenico. Know Your Enemy: Understanding Threat Actors. CSO Online, https://www.csoonline.com/article/3203804/know-your-enemy-understanding-threat-actors.html, 2017.

technically skilled. In fact, they rely on the reuse of existing programs or *scripts* to exploit common security flaws.

(2) Internet activists: Also known as *hacktivists*, these groups perform attacks with a political agenda. Their targets are either states or large organizations, and the goal is often to either raise awareness for social causes such as freedom of speech or human rights or to simply cause damage to the targeted organizations. Examples of attacks carried out by these groups are denial of service campaigns, in which many synchronized requests are sent to the same server to overload it and interrupt its normal functioning. Successful campaigns have managed to take down websites of major organizations, causing a disruption in business operations that translates into both a reputation cost and direct financial losses.[9]

(3) Organized crime: With monetary profit as the end goal, these cybercriminals engage in a variety of criminal activities.[10] For instance, the year 2016 saw *ad fraud* become the most lucrative cybercrime.[11] Other activities comprise the illegal trade of personally identifying information such as social security or credit card numbers, or the compromise and ransom of digital resources.

The elevated number of resources managed by these organizations gives an idea of their sophistication. For example, in November 2016, a joint international operation dismantled *Avalanche*, an international criminal infrastructure that managed more than 800 thousand domains.[12] Moreover, to maximize profits, these actors monetize their resources via the offering of a variety of products and services that run on top of their managed infrastructure. Examples of so-called *services* sold in this criminal marketplace are spam and flooding, denial of service, file encryption, malware and malware distribution, dedicated servers, exploits, and even professional services. In summary, these organizations adopt a business-oriented approach to cybercrime.

Insider threats:

Attackers in this category operate from the inside of an organization and generally correspond to employees or ex-employees. They can act alone or in cooperation with external actors and can be motivated by a sense of revenge or by a promise of monetary gains.

9. Sandra Laville. Anonymous cyberattacks cost PayPal GBP 3.5m, court told. The Guardian, https://www.theguardian.com/technology/2012/nov/22/anonymous-cyber-attacks-paypal-court, 2012.
10. Aditya Sood and Richard Enbody. *Targeted Cyber Attacks: Multi-staged Attacks Driven by Exploits and Malware.* Syngress Publishing, 1st edition, 2014.
11. Hewlett Packard Enterprise. *The Business of Hacking: Business innovation meets the business of hacking*, 2016.
12. The United States Department of Justice. Avalanche Network Dismantled in International Cyber Operation. Online, https://www.justice.gov/opa/pr/avalanche-network-dismantled-international-cyber-operation, 2016.

Industrial and state espionage:

These sophisticated adversaries often work in state-sponsored groups and pursue political, economic, or military advantages. These groups have been reported to use highly stealthy attacks[13] and to exploit unreported vulnerabilities (aka *zero-day attacks*) to gain access to the targeted systems.[14]

[B] Common Threats

[1] Social Engineering Attacks

Social engineering[15] is the act of manipulating people into performing actions devised by the attacker, or into providing confidential information. Note that while social engineering is not exclusive to cybersecurity, it is a prevalent technique in this domain given that online services, namely emails and social networks, enable adversaries to maximize the reach of their attacks. Moreover, threat actors often rely on social engineering techniques because it is usually easier to exploit the natural human inclination to trust than it is to discover ways to bypass existing security defences. In the following, we drill down into frequent social engineering techniques.

Phishing:

Phishing websites are fake replicas of legitimate websites maintained by malicious actors. This way, users are tricked into either entering their login credentials or their credit card information, which are collected and used by the attackers at a later time.

Spear-Phishing:

The key difference with respect to the regular phishing attacks is the use of messages customized to the targeted victims. These messages often include the three following ingredients: an unusual ask from an unusual sender, a sense of urgency, and a statement of negative consequences if the user does not perform the requested actions. Note that, to prevent these frequent attacks, organizations implement training programs to teach their employees or users to recognize fraudulent emails. The requests included in these messages range from visiting a link (leading to a malicious website) to downloading and opening a malicious file, or *malware*, attached to the message.

13. FireEye Threat Intelligence. HAMMERTOSS: Stealthy Tactics Define a Russian Cyber Threat Group. Online, https://www2.fireeye.com/rs/848-DID-242/images/rpt-apt29-hammertoss.pdf, 2015.
14. Matt Burgess. Everything you need to know about EternalBlue - the NSA exploit linked to Petya. Wired, https://www.wired.co.uk/article/what-is-eternal-blue-exploit-vulnerability-patch, 2017.
15. Christopher Hadnagy. Social Engineering: The Art of Human Hacking. Wiley, 1st edition, 2010.

[2] Malware (malicious software) and Malware Distribution Networks

The term malware encompasses any software designed to control or cause damage to computing resources (laptops, desktops, mobile phones, servers, etc.). As described in the introduction of this chapter, there have been recent outbreaks of *ransomware*, a type of malware that encrypts the hard disk of the compromised machines and asks for a ransom to be paid in exchange of the restoration of the file system.

The presence of malware is arguably the most common manifestation of malicious activity in a compromised system. In fact, similar to content delivery networks, attackers maintain so-called *malware distribution networks* to deliver malware at Internet scale.[16]

[3] Vulnerability Exploits

Software applications can present weaknesses that can be leveraged by attackers to perform unauthorized actions (often code execution) on a targeted machine. The so-called *zero-day exploits* (exploits that take advantage of either unreported or unpatched software vulnerabilities) are arguably the most challenging threats to prevent because attackers do not rely on bad user practices (other than not keeping systems updated) to compromise and control systems. Since its launch in 1999, the Common Vulnerabilities and Exposures (CVE) initiative[17] has documented more than 148 thousand vulnerabilities in mainstream software applications.

[C] Targeted Attacks

Targeted attacks are tailored to a particular organization and correspond to threats that readers can face at their workplace. In the following, we provide a simplified breakout of the steps involved in these attacks (although attackers do not always need to perform each of these steps to meet their goals). Note how the cybersecurity community has adopted military terminology to describe and classify the different stages of sophisticated attacks.

Reconnaissance

This step involves gathering information or *intelligence* about the target organization. This intelligence ranges from employee role and contact information to the infrastructure and software versions used by the organization. With the retrieved information, attackers can decide how to best craft a tailored attack.

16. Li Qing and Gregory Clark. Security Intelligence: A practitioner's Guide To Solving Enterprise Security Challenges. Wiley, 2015.
17. The MITRE Corporation. Common Vulnerabilities and Exposures (CVE). Online, https://cve.mitre.org/about/index.html, 2019.

Initial Access

There are multiple techniques adversaries can leverage to gain an initial foothold within a network. The most common initial access techniques, or *vectors*, are spear-phishing, malware delivery, and zero-day exploits (*see* descriptions above).

Privilege Escalation

Once attackers establish a foothold in the organization, they might need to obtain higher privileges to access the targeted information or to perform the next steps of the attack. For instance, attackers often need elevated permissions to execute the malicious software devised to perform the attack.

Persistence

Advanced attackers often use persistence mechanisms to maintain remote control of the machines in cases where the initial connection is interrupted, or the compromised machine is restarted.

Defence Evasion

Adversaries may use techniques to evade existing detection and prevention mechanisms. For instance, attackers can disrupt monitoring and logging services to hide their activity traces.

Lateral Movement

As part of the quest to the targeted resource or information, adversaries may move laterally, that is, pivot from the compromised machine to other machines inside the organization.

Command and Control

Attackers maintain one or more communication channels to control the compromised machines remotely and provide instructions for next steps. These communications usually rely on open channels such as web traffic,[18] the Domain Name Server (DNS),[19] or social networks

Actions on Objective

Once the attacker gains access to the objective, the last step corresponds to executing the attack. As mentioned above, the ultimate goal of adversaries is often the exfiltration of sensitive data (user credentials, credit card information, intellectual property (IP),

18. Daniel Plohmann, Khaled Yakdan, Michael Klatt, Johannes Bader, and Elmar Gerhards-Padilla. A comprehensive measurement study of domain generating malware. In 25th USENIX Security Symposium (USENIX Security 16), pages 263–278, Austin, TX, 2016. USENIX Association.
19. Wil Allsopp. Advanced Penetration Testing: Hacking the World's Most Secure Networks. John Wiley and Sons, Inc., 2017.

etc.). In other cases, the action consists of disrupting the normal operation of the resource.

For a more in-depth description of offensive techniques, the interested reader is invited to deep dive into MITRE's ATT&CK initiative,[20] which as of March 2019 describes more than 250 attack techniques, classified into 10 attack stages or *tactics*.

§9.03 DEFENSIVE STRATEGIES

Given the breadth of the potential attacks, defending organizations represents a challenging task. In this section, we introduce some of the most common solutions and processes adopted to protect enterprises. It is important to note that organizations consider the risks associated with potential attacks and the cost of implementing defences to define a security strategy that enables the organization to meet a series of business objectives.

[A] Common Security Solutions

Antivirus

Antivirus are software programs installed in endpoints (desktops, laptops, or mobile devices) that aim at identifying malware. To this end, these programs analyse new files and perform periodic scans of all the files present in the endpoint's file system.

Firewalls

These systems are generally deployed at the organization's network perimeter to control all inbound and outbound connections. Organizations generally block inbound traffic (attempts to connect to the organizations' systems originated from the outside) and limit outbound connections to the minimum necessary to enable business operations.

Network Intrusion Detection Systems

These systems inspect the organization's internal network traffic to identify malicious activities.

Threat Intelligence

Threat intelligence encompasses information about the capabilities, motivations, infrastructure, and methods of active threat actors. Many security applications and monitoring devices rely on curated lists of Indicators of Compromise (IoCs) (known malware, URLs, IP addresses, etc.) to alert on the presence of adversaries in the monitored environments.

20. MITRE. Adversarial tactics, techniques & common knowledge. https://attack.mitre.org, 2019.

Authentication and Authorization frameworks

These frameworks verify the credentials of the organization's users (typically employees) and grant or deny, based on predefined policies, access to the organization's services and resources.

The listed security solutions generate alerts when anomalous activity is detected. These alerts are then triaged, investigated and if needed, remediated at a Security Operations Centre.

[B] Security Operation Centres

Security operations centres (SOCs) are facilities where information security teams continuously monitor and analyse the alerts generated by the organizations' threat detection mechanisms. The SOC team goal is to systematically detect and respond to attacks. To this end, the team relies both on technology solutions as well as on curated human-centric processes.

SOCs split their analysts in three tiers, where the first tier is composed of the junior-most analysts and the most skilled analysts are in tier three. This way, first-tier analysts perform a first screening and filtering of the alerts to discard false positives and remediate common threats. For example, a common tier-1 workflow is to match alerts against blacklists of known malicious entities and to add rules to block further connections to the matched entities. In cases where the first-tier analysts cannot conclude whether an event is malicious or whether it requires additional action, they escalate the event for further investigation by a higher-level analyst. This way, tier-2 analysts perform investigations and remediation of escalated alerts and can in turn pass on events to tier-3 analysts. Generally, only critical alerts requiring advanced investigation skills such as reverse-engineering malware are escalated to the last layer.

Apart from the layered investigation workflows, SOCs adopt continuous improvement strategies to maintain appropriate detection rates as the threat landscape evolves. This way, there is a management of the mechanisms (detection strategies, threat intelligence sources, etc.) that generate alerts, in such a way that mechanisms with inadequate detection rates are either updated or switched off. Update procedures include subscription-based feeds as well as in-house continuous improvement processes developed by the operations team. Similarly, new detection mechanisms are constantly added as information on new attacks is available.

§9.04 APPLICATIONS OF AI IN CYBERSECURITY

As reported in the recent US Government of Accountability Office (US GAO) technology assessment '*Artificial Intelligence: Emerging Opportunities, Challenges, and Implications*',[21] AI systems can help cybersecurity professionals in multiple tasks such as

21. US GAO. Artificial Intelligence: Emerging Opportunities, Challenges, and Implications. Online Technology Assessment, https://www.gao.gov/products/GAO-18-142SP, 2018.

identifying vulnerabilities and defending against active attacks. This chapter summarizes the state-of-the-art of the most common applications of AI in cybersecurity, namely threat detection techniques based on data analytics, and human-machine interaction frameworks leading to a reduced human workload. We also introduce the potential uses of AI for offensive purposes.

[A] Threat Detection

The last years have yielded a large corpus of research focused on tackling a wide range of cybersecurity use cases with machine learning (ML).[22] In particular, there are two cybersecurity problems for which the availability of labelled datasets has resulted in a proliferation of ML applications: file analysis for malware detection and the malicious domain or URL detection problem. In addition, the cybersecurity industry has developed monitoring solutions coined as *behavioural analytics* that leverage Big Data techniques to analyse the activities of all the entities (i.e., users, machines etc.) observed at a given organization.

[1] Malware: File Analysis

The identification of malware has historically relied on antivirus that performs signature-based detection, that is, that compare the files observed in the defended system against a curated list of known malicious files. However, adversaries can bypass these detection strategies by introducing modifications to a malicious file in such a way that its functionality remains unchanged, but the performed alterations result in a different file signature. This defence evasion strategy has been commoditized through the release of a wide range of antivirus evasion tools,[23] leading the cybersecurity community and industry to develop more robust detection mechanisms based on AI.

The application of AI for malware detection enables quick and automated analysis of file contents and even runtime behaviours to determine whether a file is malicious or not. This AI application is arguably at a mature stage; not only because there are commercial applications, but also because this particular problem has been addressed and validated by a large research community. For instance, in 2015, Microsoft led a malware detection research initiative coupled with the release of a large malware classification dataset.[24] The dataset is composed of more than 20K malware

---

22. Heju Jiang, Jasvir Nagra, and Parvez Ahammad. Sok: Applying machine learning in security – a survey. arXiv preprint arXiv:1611.03186, 2016.
23. Srinivas. Antivirus evasion tools. Infosec Institute, https://resources.infosecinstitute.com/antivirus-evasion-tools/, 2019.
24. Royi Ronen, Marian Radu, Corina Feuerstein, Elad Yom-Tov, and Mansour Ahmadi. Microsoft malware classification challenge. CoRR, abs/1802.10135, 2018.

samples and has helped advance the research on modelling and detection of malicious files. In fact, researchers were able to classify malware into different categories with almost perfect accuracy.[25]

[2] The Malicious Domain or URL Detection Problem

Current networking defensive mechanisms rely predominantly on simply blocking a list of known malicious domains (aka *blacklist*) to prevent malicious connections. As a reaction to this defensive mechanism, attackers continuously register new domains that bypass the defences. This way, there is a dwell time in which malicious domains can operate until they are identified (note that in the worst case, malicious domains remain undetected throughout their life-cycle). Given the scale at which some malicious actors operate (sometimes managing hundreds of thousands of domains, it is safe to assume that the generation and registration of a large number of malicious domains are performed in an automated manner. As a consequence, the generated domains exhibit distinctive patterns that can be leveraged for automated identification. Thus, in addition to the list, a ML model trained with examples of malicious and benign domains can be used to dynamically detect new malicious domains.

Several works[26] use lexical analysis to detect and categorize spam, malware hosting, and phishing URLs. A recent work by Woodbridge et al. proposes to use deep learning models to detect domains generated by DGA-malware[27] (note that DGA stands for domain generation algorithm). Other works rely on character-level convolutional networks for URL classification.[28] It is worth mentioning that open data initiatives such as the Centralized Zone Data Service by the Internet Corporation for Assigned Names and Numbers (ICANN)[29] or the Certificate Transparency,[30] as well as access to labelled

25. Mansour Ahmadi, Giorgio Giacinto, Dmitry Ulyanov, Stanislav Semenov, and Mikhail Trofimov. Novel feature extraction, selection and fusion for effective malware family classification. CoRR, abs/1511.04317, 2015.
26. M. Darling, G. Heileman, G. Gressel, A. Ashok, and P. Poornachandran. A lexical approach for classifying malicious URLs. In 2015 International Conference on High Performance Computing Simulation (HPCS), pages 195–202, July 2015. *See also*, Mohammad Saiful Islam Mamun, Mohammad Ahmad Rathore, Arash Habibi Lashkari, Natalia Stakhanova, and Ali A. Ghorbani. Detecting malicious URLs using lexical analysis. In Network and System Security – 10th International Conference, NSS 2016, Taipei, Taiwan, September 28–30, 2016, Proceedings, pages 467–482, 2016.
27. Jonathan Woodbridge, Hyrum S. Anderson, Anjum Ahuja, and Daniel Grant. Predicting domain generation algorithms with long short-term memory networks. ArXiv e-prints, abs/1611.00791, 2016.
28. Joshua Saxe and Konstantin Berlin. eXpose: A Character-Level Convolutional Neural Network with Embeddings For Detecting Malicious URLs, File Paths and Registry Keys.CoRR, abs/1702.08568, 2017.
29. ICANN. The centralized zone data service. Online, https://czds.icann.org, 2019.
30. Certificate Transparency. Online, https://www.certificate-transparency.org/, 2019.

data[31,32] have enabled researchers to create models that reduce the dwell time of malicious domains, sometimes performing the detection even before the domains are used by attackers.[33,34,35]

[3] Behavioural Analytics

This generic category of detection approaches relies on the observation that many attacks exhibit a distinctive activity or *behavioural footprint*. This footprint, which comprises the series of steps involved in committing an attack, leaves a trace in activity logs and can be leveraged for detection with data analytics. The implementation of these detection mechanisms represents a challenge because, on the one hand, the information required for attack identification is often buried deep in the raw data and, on the other, this approach requires a Big Data computing infrastructure to process and analyse activity logs. Note that large organizations currently generate several terabytes of data relevant to security analysis on a daily basis.

Given the variety and changing nature of the cyberattacks targeted with behavioural analytics, it is often difficult to collect large datasets of attack examples to build sophisticated AI detection models. Instead, many applications resort to anomaly detection for threat detection.[36] This way, an AI system learns a *baseline*, i.e., a series of frequent activities assumed to be *normal* and reports new activities that differ from the learned patterns. While most of the research on this area focuses on improving anomaly detection models,[37] recent works explore interactive AI frameworks that not only detect attacks but also boost the efficiency of human analysts.

[B] Improving the Efficiency of Cybersecurity Professionals

As stated in the US GAO report cited above[21] AI systems can help cybersecurity professionals in multiple ways. For example, AI systems can learn from

31. VirusTotal. Online, https://virustotal.com/, 2019.
32. Google SafeBrowsing. Online, https://safebrowsing.google.com/, 2019.
33. x0rz. Catching phishing before they catch you. Online, https://blog.0day.rocks/catching-phishing-using-certstream-97177f0d499a, 2017.
34. Wes Connel. StreamingPhish. Online, https://github.com/wesleyraptor/streamingphish, 2018.
35. I. Arnaldo, A. Arun, S. Kyathanahalli, and K. Veeramachaneni. Acquire, adapt, and anticipate: continuous learning to block malicious domains. In 2018 IEEE International Conference on Big Data (Big Data), pp. 1891–1898, Dec 2018.
36. Aaron Tuor, Samuel Kaplan, Brian Hutchinson, Nicole Nichols, and Sean Robinson. Deep learning for unsupervised insider threat detection in structured cybersecurity data streams. CoRR, abs/1710.00811, 2017.
37. Benjamin J. Radford, Leonardo M. Apolonio, Antonio J. Trias, and Jim A. Simpson. Network traffic anomaly detection using recurrent neural networks. CoRR, abs/1803.10769, 2018.

human-machine interactions to facilitate or even automate human tasks.[38,39,40] Figure 9.1 shows a schematic representation of the *AI* system was proved to improve alert fidelity over time, which translates into more efficient use of the analyst bandwidth.

38. K. Veeramachaneni, I. Arnaldo, V. Korrapati, C. Bassias, and K. Li. AI^2: Training a Big Data Machine to Defend. In 2016 IEEE 2nd International Conference on Big Data Security on Cloud (Big Data Security), pages 49–54, April 2016.
39. S. Das, W. Wong, T. Dietterich, A. Fern, and A. Emmott. Incorporating expert feedback into active anomaly discovery. In 2016 IEEE 16th International Conference on Data Mining (ICDM), pages 853–858, Dec 2016.
40. Anaël Beaugnon, Pierre Chifflier, and Francis Bach. ILAB: An Interactive Labelling Strategy for Intrusion Detection. In *RAID 2017: Research in Attacks, Intrusions and Defenses, Atlanta, United States,* September 2017.

Figure 9.1 AI: A ML System with Human Feedback for Cybersecurity[41]

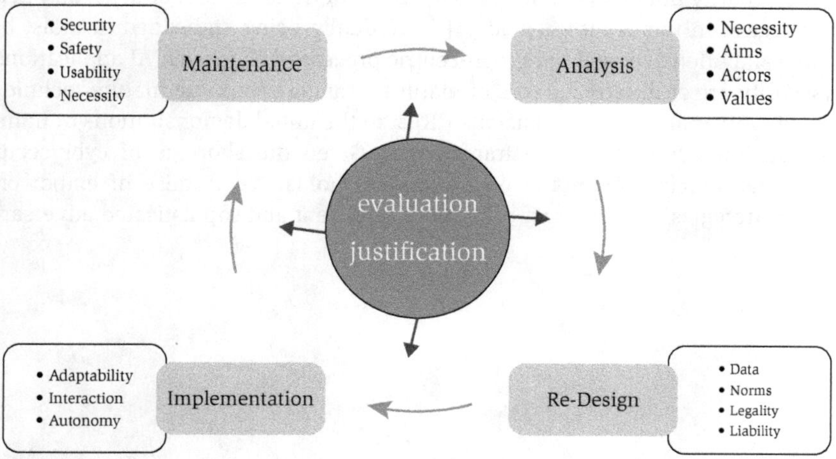

[C] Offensive AI

While the era of AI-powered attacks has been forecasted in the past years,[42] the use of AI for offensive purposes presumably remains limited. This being said, researchers have demonstrated the feasibility of AI approaches to improve password guessing attacks[43] or to generate phishing sites that bypass security defences.[44] The community has also identified several other low-hanging opportunities for attackers.[45] In particular, there seems to be a consensus on the capability of AI methods to improve reconnaissance (in particular, to identify vulnerabilities in a targeted system), to automatically customize social engineering attacks, and even to generate fake user activities and data to confuse data-driven detection systems.

41. As illustrated in the US GAO report Artificial Intelligence: Emerging Opportunities, Challenges, and Implications. Online Technology Assessment, https://www.gao.gov/products/GAO-18-142SP, 2018.
42. Keren Elazari. Hackers are on the brink of launching a wave of AI attacks. Wired, https://www.wired.co.uk/article/hackers-ai-cyberattack-offensive, 2017.
43. Briland Hitaj, Paolo Gasti, Giuseppe Ateniese, and Fernando Pérez-Cruz. PassGAN: A Deep Learning Approach for Password Guessing. CoRR, abs/1709.00440, 2017.
44. Alejandro Correa Bahnsen, Ivan Torroledo, Luis David Camacho, and Sergio Villegas. DeepPhish: Simulating Malicious AI. Online, https://albahnsen.files.wordpress.com/2018/05/deepphish-simulating-malicious-ai_submitted.pdf, 2018.
45. Doug Drinkwater. 6 ways hackers will use machine learning to launch attacks. CSO Online, https://www.csoonline.com/article/3250144/6-ways-hackers-will-use-machine-learning-to-launch-attacks.html, 2018.

§9.05 CONCLUSIONS

The cybersecurity domain encompasses a variety of threat actors, attacks, and defensive strategies. In this complex field, AI is gradually being embedded in tools, both defensive and offensive, and in human-centric processes. This way, AI applications in cybersecurity are at different stages of maturity, ranging from the mature techniques used to identify malware and malicious URLs, to the initial demonstrations of human-in-the-loop interactive defensive frameworks. Given the shortage of cybersecurity professionals anticipated for the next years, AI holds the promise of empowering defensive strategies to counteract even more proficient and sophisticated adversaries.

CHAPTER 10
AI and Data Protection

Paloma Aparicio

Algorithms, by preferring behaviours over aspirations, impose this effective realism on us. They imprison us in our conformism. (...) If they are predictive it is because at all times they abide by the hypothesis that our future will be a reproduction of our past.

Dominique Cardon[1]

§10.01 INTRODUCTION

The purpose of this chapter is to outline some of the personal data protection issues that should be examined by those who are applying technologies incorporating Intelligent or Artificial Intelligence (AI) systems or those who wish to develop and implement them in the future, irrespective of the specific regulatory framework[2] to be addressed in each case. These considerations may also be useful for all of us that as clients, users, consumers or citizens are already affected by AI solutions in many facets of our life since AI is behind a growing number of activities of both online and offline businesses.

Many AI systems are already in place, and many others are still in a phase of the investigation, trial and error. AI systems are evolving incredibly fast. Algorithms are able to perform, at an enormous speed, a set of calculations on Big Data in order to obtain predictive results or make expert decisions. Algorithms are able to 'learn' (not yet to 'understand') automatically from the processing of this mass of data. Algorithms are also becoming autonomous in decision-making. More recently, newly developed algorithms are becoming capable of making contextual sophistication, abstraction, and

1. Dominique Cardon, *À quoi rêvent les algorithms. Nos vies à l'heure des big data.*, Le Seuil, Paris, 2015).
2. *See* as a general guide, the Organisation for Economic Cooperation and Development (OECD) *Privacy Framework* (2013), with reference to other international initiatives in this line.

explanation.[3] In this context, we may dare to expect that algorithms will be able to explain the reason behind their decisions.

AI is built on other technologies, and it is those companies that are dedicated to the massive processing of large-scale data or Big Data which have already integrated advanced data analytics techniques and reached a critical level of digital skills and use of technologies (e.g., cloud computing, mobile, and the web), who are the ones that are more likely to adopt AI and thus, differentiate themselves and become more competitive.

In all these cases and regardless of their level of development in the implementation of AI systems (leaders and laggards), the common raw material for automatic learning, supervised or not, more or less deep, in all AI technologies is data.

Moreover, a huge amount of this data usually relates to people's being or doing, both in the physical and digital worlds and may, or may not, ultimately serve to identify, directly or indirectly, a particular individual.

Likewise, such data may have very diverse origins, which can be classified fundamentally under two headings: data consciously and expressly provided by the individual to the developer of the AI technology for the specific purpose for which they will be processed (i.e., as an ideal proposition) and, the rest of collected and processed data, which may have been obtained without their consent and, in many cases, even without their conscious knowledge (i.e., which is not an unusual situation).

Additionally, the incorporation of sensors to all things, imaginable or unimaginable, that can be connected to the Internet, the so-called Internet of Things (IoT),[4] will undoubtedly increase the amount and heterogeneity of data sources, the calculation capacity of the intelligent systems based on them and also, the risk of cyberattacks.

In this context, here are some considerations to take into account from the perspective of data protection for those who believe in the development of intelligent systems for a sustainable digital economy.[5]

§10.02 DATA-DRIVEN AI

AI systems and applications have been introduced into our lives silently and have taken root in such a way that we, as users, could hardly want to renounce their benefits, apart

3. Timothy M. Persons, United States Government Accountability Office (GAO), on *Artificial Intelligence: Emerging Opportunities, Challenges, and Implications for Policy and Research*, available at https://www.gao.gov/assets/700/692793.pdf following former opinion of John Launchbury, GAO-18-644T (June, 2018), accessed 15 Sep. 2019.
4. European Commission, *Definition of a Research and Innovation Policy Leveraging Cloud Computing and IoT Combination* study available at https://ec.europa.eu/digital-single-market/en/news/definition-research-and-innovation-policy-leveraging-cloud-computing-and-iot-combination (May 2015), accessed 15 Sep. 2019.
5. For instance, the OECD, under the project Going Digital, is promoting studies such as *Artificial Intelligence in Society* accessible online in http://www.oecd.org/sti/ieconomy/artificial-intelligence-in-society-eedfee77-en.htm (June, 2019) and declaring the *OCED Principles on Artificial Intelligence* (May, 2019), available at http://www.oecd.org/going-digital/ai/principles/ which were adopted by G20 (June, 2019).

from those who want to return total control to individuals and advocate digital disconnection.

Nor do countries and companies want to stop the progress of innovation and new technologies because of the strategic impact they have on the global economy, society and politics. Numerous initiatives and declarations are emerging in favour of the promotion of a legal and responsible AI and among the various challenges posed by the AI, the fact that it must respect privacy or the protection of personal data.

[A] Data Related to Individuals

The raw material for intelligent systems is Big Data, i.e., large-scale data processing. And, within it, data relating to individuals is also included.

Regarding data, the first consideration is that it is necessary to distinguish between non-personal data and personal data because of the different legal protections that each category deserves. When data is personal data, a stronger level of protection is legally required.

Many privacy and data protection scholars are worried because the scope of personal data is expanding and becoming equivalent to *any information related to an identified or identifiable natural person (data subject)*. The importance is given to the element of data identifiability with a specific natural person to consider it a personal data, together with technological development (i.e., re-identification and de-anonymization algorithms), advances in data analysis (i.e., tracking and profiling or custom audiences tools) and the existence of increasingly interconnected (i.e., IoT) or smart environments (e.g., smart cities), leads us to the possibility that all information could be related to a natural person in the near future.

Specifically, in the European Union (EU), the Regulation 2016/679 of the European Parliament and of the Council of 27 April 2016 on the protection of natural persons with regard to the processing of personal data and on the free movement of such data and repealing Directive 95/46/EC (the so-called GDPR) has used a broad and extensive concept of personal data,[6] in line with what was being interpreted by Article 29 Working Party (Article 29WP)[7] and with the jurisprudence of the Court of Justice of the EU, with guaranteed protection of the individual, which is probably praiseworthy and justified in 2016 but which, in a few years, may generate the danger of turning the GDPR into the 'law of everything'[8] and, consequently, into a regulation impossible to comply with, in practice.

We do not believe that the EU's intention was to make the GDPR the 'law of everything' or to hinder the free movement of personal data, quite the opposite.

6. GDPR, Article 4 (1).
7. Article 29WP, WP136 *Opinion 4/2007 on the concept of personal data, available at* https://ec.europa.eu/justice/article-29/documentation/opinion-recommendation/files/2007/wp136_en.pdf, accessed 15 Sep. 2019.
8. Nadezhda Purtova, *The law of everything. Broad concept of personal data and future of EU data protection law*, Law, innovation & Technology Journal, Volume 10, 2018, available at https://www.tandfonline.com/doi/full/10.1080/17579961.2018.1452176, accessed 15 Sep. 2019.

In fact, the EU subsequently adopted another regulation for the free movement of non-personal data[9] that was much less demanding and restrictive and, therefore, much less protectionist. On the other hand, the GDPR trusts[10] as an effective security measure for reducing the scope of personal data subject to the GDPR restrictions, the application of techniques[11] of effective pseudonymization of the personal data, as well as, the application of the protocols of privacy by design and by default. One step further, the GDPR also recognizes the definitive effectiveness, if irreversible, of the techniques of anonymization of personal data so that the anonymous or anonymized data would remain outside the scope of application of the GDPR.

Pseudonymized data are personal data for the controller, processor or any other person who has the additional information that allows such data to be attributed to a particular natural person or, *any means reasonably likely to be used to identify a natural person, account should be taken of all objective factors, such as the costs and the amount of time required for identification, taking into consideration the available technology at the time of the processing and technological developments.*[12] Conversely, the same data would be considered non-personal data for any third party who does not have such additional information or reasonable means to use them to identify the data subject. The possibility of pseudonymized data being treated by third parties as non-personal data in the form of totally dissociated or aggregated data would enable a much freer use of such data as if they were anonymous, anonymized or non-personal data *ab initio*. Pseudonymization techniques would create AI-based applications' developers and operators a set of business opportunities.

The problem may arise when technological progress may develop so far that, emerging techniques of re-identification or de-anonymization render reversible, and thus useless, the present existing techniques of pseudonymization or anonymization. As a consequence, GDPR's existing measures would become obsolete, and those non-personal data AI systems will happen to enter into the scope of the GDPR and its stringent regime.

Thus, it is worth to bear in mind that data can change in nature (from personal to non-personal and vice versa), not only during its life-cycle due to the techniques to which it is submitted but also within the function of who is carrying out the data processing.

The advances in data analysis techniques, especially by those companies with big capacity to attract and process data (e.g., Google, Apple, Facebook, Amazon and Microsoft, jointly called GAFAM, or others, such as Alibaba, Tencent or Baidu) make it possible to trace data from different origins and attribute them to the same natural person and, at the same time, compare them with the data of millions of other people in order to create profiles according to different parameters and purposes.

9. Regulation (EU) 2018/1807 of the European Parliament and of the Council of 14 Nov. 2018 on a framework for the free flow of non-personal data in the EU.
10. GDPR Article 4 (5) and Article 32.
11. Article 29WP, WP216 *Opinion 05/2014 on Anonymisation Techniques, available at* https://ec.europa.eu/justice/article-29/documentation/opinion-recommendation/files/2014/wp216_en.pdf, accessed 15 Sep. 2019.
12. GDPR Recital 26.

It is also interesting to analyse the different origins of data (e.g., taxonomy data 'Provided, Observed, Derived and Inferred')[13] and the data life-cycle. Entering into such detail helps to understand the evolution that has taken place in the sense that many data that were formerly considered as non-personal data (e.g., statistics, energy, traffic, agriculture, sales, weather, etc.) have now become data that identify or can identify a natural person and so, individuals can currently be categorized into many more profiles of people and form part of many more processes that involve automated decision-making that impact their lives. This exercise also shows that in many occasions the data subject is not aware, nor will be able to be aware, nor would probably want to be aware, that his/her personal data is being subject to one or more specific treatments (e.g., credit scores, facial images from CCTV, Wi-Fi readers in buildings from geolocation tools, classification based on common attributes of buyers, risk of developing a disease-based multifactor analysis, etc.).

Finally, it will be interesting to *see* the effect that the 'sensorization' of all things and cities (i.e., IoT or smart cities) is going to have on the expansion of personal data, in volume, in the birth of new possible data origins, as well as, in the emergence of new types of personal data. The state of people in this hyperconnected reality in which we enter has been defined by Luciano Floridi[14] under the interesting term 'onlife' as follows:

> The new experience of a hyperconnected reality within which it makes no longer sense to ask whether one may be online or offline.

Consequently, given the broad and expansive scope of the term personal data, many of the AI's usage applications should be conducting privacy impact assessments or establishing privacy by design and by default protocols to examine other issues specific to the area of data protection (some of which will be mentioned below).

[B] Right for Protection

The question of what is, or is not, a personal data worthy of special protection against the risk that any information could become personal in a hyperconnected reality subject to AI technologies, forces us to take a step back and reflect on what is the legal asset or value to be protected, its limits and exceptions.

It seems that in the EU, within the European territory and even beyond its borders, personal data deserves protection per se, regardless of its relevance (whether or not it is sensitive data), whether or not it provides information in the sphere of private and family life, on the identity, honour or privacy of someone and regardless the interest of the data subject to preserve his or her intimacy.

The right to the protection of personal data in the European GDPR is considered a fundamental right that derives from the consideration that is set out in the EU Chapter

13. Martin Abrams, *The Origins of Personal Data and its Implications for Governance*, The Information Accountability Foundation, available at http://informationaccountability.org/wp-content/uploads/Data-Origins-Abrams.pdf, accessed 15 Sep. 2019.
14. Luciano Floridi, *The Onlife Manifesto. Being Human in a Hyperconnected Era*, Springer (2015).

of Fundamental Rights and in the EU Treaty, but this is not a unanimous consideration at an international level.

However, it is worth noting that the same EU Chapter of Fundamental Rights also establishes that *everyone has the right to respect for his or her private and family life, home and communications* in line with Article 8 of the European Convention of Human Rights (ECHR).[15]

The sphere of private life[16] is not limited to an 'inner circle' in which the individual may live his own personal life as he chooses and excludes the outside world but, as the right to personal development, whether in terms of personality or of personal autonomy. Thus, private life embraces (i) a person's physical, psychological or moral integrity, (ii) his privacy and (iii) his identity and autonomy.

The reason for giving special protection to personal data is to protect the person both in their private and public life spheres.

Just as we previously adopted the term 'onlife' to describe the state of people in which it is difficult and probably already irrelevant to distinguish between the offline and online world for the purposes of whether or not they deserve different protection, we should coin a term to refer to that state of people in which it is difficult and probably also irrelevant to distinguish between private and public life: 'wholelife'. The almost total digitization of life and of the relationships of people and things has produced an effect of overlapping and confusion of private life with public life that forces the debate on whether it makes sense for one and the other to receive different protection, to what extent and how to arbitrate it in a balanced way.

The right to data protection or privacy (following the Anglo-Saxon terminology prevailing before the GDPR) of a person is not an absolute right but coexists with the fundamental rights and freedoms of other persons and society as a whole (e.g., vital, legitimate or public interests, legal obligations, the right to one's own defence, reasons of health or public safety, etc.) being all of them what make up its limits and exceptions.

Depending on who carries out the data processing, whether a public or private entity, it may be presumed whether allegedly they have or not legitimacy to carry out certain data processing. However, the appropriate way to do it would be to enter into a prior examination that analyses the prevalence between rights, freedoms and interests, on a case-by-case basis whenever a conflict is detected. Also, there should be clear criteria to guide in this examination at both public authorities and private companies to reduce uncertainty.

There is a perception that under the banner of public interest almost anything can be done while private companies, under their legitimate interest, can do almost nothing. If this were actually the case, AI initiatives developed under public aid programs or projects sponsoring innovation and development of new technologies would have a clear competitive advantage by avoiding part of the legal burden that

15. ECHR, Article 8, (1) and (2).
16. Guide on Article 8 of ECHR available at https://www.echr.coe.int/Documents/Guide_Art_8_ENG.pdf, accessed 15 Sep. 2019.

means obtaining a legal basis and the fierce scrutiny of the supervisory authorities over private companies.

This reflection leads to another parallel debate on the desirability of encouraging open data initiatives so that states and public authorities share citizens' data with private companies for the benefit of technological progress itself and, in particular, for the benefit of small- and medium-sized enterprises and society as a whole. There are even those who call for the large private corporations to share the data obtained in their activity in order to avoid the risk of situations of abuse for their capacity to enjoy a dominant position in the market, based on the processing (and possession) of data and, in particular, of data relating to individuals.

Before closing this section, it is worth to note two remarkable concepts inserted in the wider private life sphere of a person: his identity and his autonomy, which were already mentioned and that will be subject to further analysis.

To sum up and conclude, many of the AI applications, which operate in an Internet without frontiers, should ultimately be designed with full awareness on the data processing they carry out and what is the legal asset or value to be protected in their case so that, regardless of the specific regulations that apply to them, people are always respected to the fullest extent in both their private and public lives.

[C] Data Legitimation

The question of which is the legal asset to be protected in each case also leads us to the question of fair treatment or the legitimacy for data processing and to what is the real and effective power of control that the different stakeholders have in the management of the data.

The data subject is the individual to whom the data relates to and whom the data identifies or can identify. The concept of personal data defined in this way is therefore linked to the concept of identity,[17] i.e., to what extent it is useful for others to identify an individual in their relations with third parties in his/her sphere of public life.

In a way, it is desirable that the individual has or recover control over his/her personal data management even before data is captured by third parties. In fact, primacy has always been given some to consent and, lately, also reinforced[18] (by requiring that consent is explicit) as a legitimate basis for the use of data.

At the same time, the exercise of rights by the data subject has always been guaranteed (i.e., revocation of consent, access, rectification, cancellation and opposition) and recently the scope of the rights of the data subject in terms of data protection (i.e., suspension, limitation, portability, the right to be forgotten and the right of explanation) has been extended.

However, at the same level as express consent or at a superior level in certain circumstances, other legitimate bases coexist for the processing of data of individuals

17. Borja Adsuara Varela, *El ciudadano ante el RGPD y la nueva LOPDGDD, Capítulo 31;* Jose López Calvo (ed.), *La adaptación al nuevo marco de protección de datos tras el RGPD y la LOPDGDD, Wolters Kluwer 845 (2nd edition, 2019).*
18. GDPR, Article 4 (11).

(e.g., performance of a contract, legal obligations, vital interests, public interests and legitimate interests). This fact distorts, in theory, and in practice, the prevalence of consent and allows a myriad of possible legal justifications. This requires prior examination for the analysis of preference among rights, freedoms and interests and the desirability of having clear criteria for the guidance of public authorities and private companies.

The complexity and sophistication of data processing involved in the use of Big Data and the application of intelligent systems in an interconnected reality, the different possible legitimate bases, the different actors involved (i.e., owner, controllers or processors), their different status (e.g., public authorities or private entities) and the real and effective power of control that each of them has as interested parties in data management lead us to ask ourselves, at each moment of the data's life-cycle, who are the real 'owners' of the data.

The concept of data owner should not be used because there is no property right or patrimonial right over personal data, but perhaps this denies the evidence before us. Reality shows that data use has a relevant economic value, that its exploitation is carried out with a clear profit motive, and that its use can generate a benefit or advantage for those who exploit them. There are entities that monetize the data through sale to third parties and this 'secondary use' is the clearest proof that data is susceptible to economic traffic.

In relation to this concept of data ownership, there are voices who ask for the right to total digital disconnection so that the natural person becomes the sole owner of their data (an aspiration that we consider unrealistic given the level of digitalization nowadays) and those who claim that, as a minimum, each natural person should be the main owner of his data in the digital world. In this respect, it is worth mentioning self-sovereign digital identity initiatives based on blockchain technology, among others.

Regarding data legitimation, there are various initiatives like the ones within the Fintech sector, for test-safe environments or regulated 'sandboxes', with special focus on data protection matters, that may legitimate AI projects to test their prototypes of products or services in a controlled and safe way so that, at least, in the preliminary phase of research, less restricted data protection protocols could be adopted while maintaining risks under control within the limited environment.

Thereof, many of the AI's use cases, which are based on or will be based on the Big Data of personal data from many different origins, should review the bases that legitimize their use in each case and, if necessary, arbitration procedures for the exercise of rights by the data holders to the extent that they do not impede innovation.

[D] Profiling and Automated Decisions

Probably the most characteristic and controversial issue in the use of AI over Big Data is the ability of intelligent systems to analyse huge amounts of data, track them and combine them with other data to produce profiles for very diverse purposes, among others, in order to make better decisions, preferably, in an automated way.

Here lies the competitive advantage of AI, the use of algorithms with techniques of advance analytics and Big Data, which can also be adapted through automatic learning, supervised or not, and more or less deep, and thus be able to accurately predict behaviours and make decisions that will influence people and their future behaviour.

Here we reflect on what is the protected legal asset or value, the concept of protection of a person's private life that encompasses the right to personal development, whether in terms of personality or personal autonomy.

From the point of view of data protection and without going into depth in the underlying ethical issues, there is a general concern about profiling and decision-making processes that are purely automatic and about how to avoid errors, biases, discrimination or manipulation of data. The risk that these automated processes could be used to manipulate behaviour is also a common concern.

As an example, to combat the risks derived from the automation of processes, the European GDPR provides[19] the right to object to being subject to profiling, the right not to be subject of a solely automated decision that can be decisive on someone's life (i.e., which can cause significant legal effects or other similar equivalent impacts) and the right to obtain human intervention. This right to oppose solely automated decisions is not absolute. It has explicit exceptions in the GDPR and so, it can be dismantled if it is justified that there are other prevailing rights, freedoms or interests.[20] Needless to say, human intervention is not necessarily a guarantee for better and fairer decision-making.

In this respect, there are two additional issues that deserve some extra consideration.

First, what some studies have called the 'privacy paradox',[21] that is, the fact that people may express concerns about the impact on their privacy of 'creepy' uses of their data, which in practice they have provided anyway via the use of the online services. In other words, they provide the data because it is the price of using certain services. People may be resigned to allowing any use of their data because they feel that there is no alternative – mainly because they do not want to renounce the benefits that they may get. Therefore, they are consciously engaging in trading their personal data. The first person interested in protecting their data should be the data owner. Legislators should better analyse the scope of the protection that certain data deserve or that individuals require in order to be not too restrictive if it is not necessary. Or, maybe legislators are committed to protecting individuals even from their own actions.

Second, I would also like to highlight the impact of automated processes and AI on the autonomy of will, i.e., on the information and advertisements that people

19. GDPR, Article 21 and 22.
20. Matthias Avocats, *Artificial Intelligence and the GDPR: how do they interact?*, Available at https://www.avocats-mathias.com/technologies-avancees/artificial-intelligence-gdpr, accessed 15 Sep. 2019.
21. Information Commissioner's Office (ICO), *Big Data, artificial intelligence, machine learning and data protection*, available at https://ico.org.uk/media/for-organisations/documents/2013559/big-data-ai-ml-and-data-protection.pdf, 24, accessed 15 Sep. 2019.

receive, and, therefore, on shaping their criteria for making decisions or on the lack of choices for making some decisions that algorithms make, replacing human will.

The example used by Dominique Cardon[22] in this regard is illustrative of the impact of AI in human free will:

> Driving with GPS has been so strongly inscribed in the practices of drivers that they have sometimes lost all idea of map, of the ways of reading it, of the diversity of their roads and of the joys of getting lost.
>
> Like GPS in vehicles, (...) the algorithms come from a desire for autonomy and freedom. But they also contribute to subjecting the Internet user to this calculated, efficient, automatic route, which adapts to our destination by secretly adapting to the traffic of others. With the route we have lost the map. The path we follow is the "best" for us.

AI systems initiatives, as carrying out high data risk activities, when doing automated profiling with personal data on a large scale and when taking decisions automatically that can significantly affect people's lives, will have to implement the strictest possible actions and measures that their regulations require of them, such as carrying out privacy impact assessments, the appointment of data privacy officers, issuing protocols for responding to the exercise of rights and procedures for managing information security incidents, among others. AI systems will need to meet the accountability principle, to guarantee privacy compliance and to provide proper evidence as appropriate.

[E] Other Data Challenges

Finally, and very briefly, below are mentioned some other considerations to be taken into account from the perspective of data protection and which show the complexity of the implementation of AI in real life.

In opposition to the concept of Big Data is the data minimization principle, which means to only process those data that are essential in order to legitimately achieve a predefined purpose. AI is built on Big Data (the biggest data, the better AI), and as it is based on automated learning, it makes no sense at all to reduce and use scarce data at front. The use of any potential data available in AI technologies is what ensures the richest results. Despite regulations in force, AI essence is based on using as much data as possible. There might be proper exceptions and risk minimization measures that enable a legal way to reconcile data minimization with AI and Big Data analytics, otherwise, these advanced technologies will not be able to progress much further.

Big Data would better assist AI systems development if it can improve data labelling.[23] For AI proper development purposes, it is essential to improve and ensure the collection of high-quality labelled data, without any buzz, with the goal of reducing

22. *See supra* note 2, 134.
23. United States Government Accountability Office, *Artificial Intelligence: Emerging Opportunities, Challenges, and Implications for Policy and Research*, available at https://www.gao.gov/assets/700/690910.pdf, GAO-18-142SP (March, 2018).

bias and becoming more comprehensive and organized and, in a manner that facilitates machine learning (ML) and produces more accurate outcomes.

Another frequently debated topic is to what extent AI systems should be able to explain the 'how' and the 'why' algorithmic works in automated individual decision-making processes, i.e., if there is a right to explanation[24] that should cover 'information' around the algorithmic 'method' 'used rather than an explanation about the rationale' of an automated decision (only *meaningful information about the logic involved*[25]). As of today, it is commonly understood that there is no need to explain the source code, or 'how' and 'why' a specific decision was made.

This problem is also known as the 'opacity' of algorithms and has become inevitable with the more recent deep learning systems, which need vast quantities of data through non-linear neural networks that classify the data based on the outputs from each successive layer, and that produces a 'black box' effect. The term 'black box' illustrates opacity, that is, the difficulty to understand the reasons for decisions made as a result of deep learning. Notwithstanding, at this state-of-the-art, the challenge and the expectation are that new 'imaginative' algorithms resulting from automated complex processes may finally be able to unlock the 'mysteries' behind.[26]

Building on former challenges, AI systems struggle to achieve the transparency principle and to provide information upfront to individuals on what data will be subject to processing and for what purposes. It is common that AI applications use or re-use the same data for different purposes than the one for which it was originally collected. This is because the analytics are able to mine data for new insights and find correlations between apparently disparate datasets and also to learn from databases in an unexpected manner. The re-use of data will require a refresh of information to be provided to individuals and/or a refresh of the legal basis applicable depending on whether the new purposes are compatible or not with the initial ones. Moreover, it may deserve a renewal of an individual's consent, something that may result in a serious difficulty considering the volume of data used in these intelligent systems.

Improving the safety and security of AI system applications from cyberattacks is another challenge. Probably, the costs of cybersecurity measures to prevent breaches are much lower than dealing with security incidents. Big Data and AI may improve security by detecting patterns and anomalies and rapidly identifying security threats. On the other hand, Big Data and AI themselves have created new security risks and threats,[27] as well as those derived from the IoT incremental use.[28]

These brief examples do not pretend to be exhaustive but illustrative of the many issues that AI can face from a data protection perspective.

---

24. GDPR 'Meaningful information about the logic involved'.
25. GDPR, Article 13 (2) (f).
26. Ed Finn, *La búsqueda del Algoritmo. Imaginación en la Era de la Informática (original: What Algorithms Want. Imagination in the Age of Computing)*, Alpha Decay 321–328 (2018).
27. Damiani, Ernesto, *Big Data Threat Landscape and Good Practice Guide*. ENISA, January 2016, available at https://www.enisa.europa.eu/publications/bigdata-threat-landscape, accessed 15 Sep. 2019.
28. José Villarino Marzo, *El Internet de las Cosas y el Reglamento y la Ley, Capítulo 39;* Jose López Calvo (ed.), *La adaptación al nuevo marco de protección de datos tras el RGPD y la LOPDGDD, Wolters Kluwer 997–1009 (2nd edition, 2019.*

§10.03 ROADMAP AND CONCLUSIONS

From the above, we can easily conclude that data protection matters must be taken into consideration from the very beginning of an AI initiative or from the first step of an AI project and, with a long term and holistic view.

Having said that, AI initiatives will probably not succeed unless they are well data-driven.[29] In a sustainable digital economy, any company might acquire core digital capabilities and master Big Data and advance analytics before testing or implementing AI solutions. Data culture needs to be promoted, and data protection experts might be part of the interdisciplinary teams for AI development.[30]

Privacy by design and by default attitudes are critical in the AI strategy of a company and will help to anticipate problems, make correct risk analysis, implement adequate security measures, minimize or prevent further risks, design and prepare a responsive scenario for emerging incidents or for dealing with claims from individuals or official investigations or sanctioning proceedings from control authorities.

It is probable that 100% compliance with all data protection specific legal requirements in all applicable jurisdictions is almost impossible. AI needs to join forces.[31] This is the reason why corporations and countries are developing proper codes of conduct for AI solutions or are joining collective partnerships[32] on AI best practices for the future.[33]

Finally, due to the particularities of AI, authorities from different regions, institutions or countries will need to work together to clarify the framework for AI development at the global basis and to find the right balance to have protective regulations which will not slow or stop ambitions.[34] There are plenty of good intentions and diverse initiatives,[35] but, I suggest, there could certainly be more concrete proposals and more strategic agreements among all stakeholders influencing AI.

---

29. Jacques Bughin and Nicolas van Zeebroeck, *Artificial Intelligence: Why a Digital Base is Critical*, Data Culture, McKindsey Quarterly no. 3, 13 (2018).
30. For instance, the European Commission, among others, is promoting a Smart Specialization Platform to get diverse collaboration at many different levels, information available at https://s3platform.jrc.ec.europa.eu/, accessed 15 Sep. 2019.
31. European Commission, Communication on Artificial Intelligence, COM(2018) 237 final, (April 2018) available at https://ec.europa.eu/digital-single-market/en/news/communication-artificial-intelligence-europe?utm_source = POLITICO.EU&utm_campaign = fb25ba8e0f-EMAIL_CAMPAIGN_2018_04_25&utm_medium = email&utm_term = 0_10959edeb5-fb25ba8e0f-189679453, accessed 15 Sep. 2019.
32. *See* Partnership on AI in https://www.partnershiponai.org/about/, accessed 15 Sep. 2019.
33. Among others, it is worth to mention AI4EU on demand platform, https://www.ai4eu.eu/#about; ALLAI for responsible AI, http://allai.nl/; Responsible Robotics, https://responsiblerobotics.org/, accessed 15 Sep. 2019.
34. European Commission, *Towards an innovation Principle Endorsed by Better Regulation*, (June 2016) available at https://ec.europa.eu/epsc/publications/strategic-notes/towards-innovation-principle-endorsed-better-regulation_en, accessed 15 Sep. 2019.
35. For example, the European Commission, Enhance European Innovation Council (EIC) pilot in https://ec.europa.eu/research/eic/index.cfm?pg = home, accessed September 2019.

CHAPTER 11
Artificial Intelligence in the Judicial

María Jesús González-Espejo

§11.01 THE APPLICATION OF AI IN THE JUDICIAL FIELD

The coordinators of this handbook could not fail to dedicate a few pages to one of the fields that could be described as being the closest to justice and where we are certain that AI will have a very large impact: the judicial.

First, we need to specify what we mean when we talk about AI in relation to this particular field. As it is well known, the granting of justice requires the participation of several actors: judges, prosecutors, lawyers, experts, court personnel and lawmakers. Moreover, a judicial conflict requires the handling of documentation and other materials, such as videos, which are submitted by the lawyers, shared with and analysed in depth by the judge. In turn, this requires document and knowledge management. A trial can be recorded and, in some cases, retransmitted. Testimonies can be key in a trial. In short, around any legal procedure, there are processes of communication, search and filing of documentation, drafting based on precedents, rules or doctrine, and building of innovative arguments. And as we have already seen in the previous pages, for the accomplishment of all these activities AI offers innovative solutions, which can make the work of the different agents of justice more efficient and of better quality, whether through its functionalities of search of information and detection of patterns; the detection of information or false declarations; the analysis of information or the application of this to the prediction of future behaviours.

Additionally, AI applications can not only help judicial proceedings actors do their job better but also potentially replace them in one or all its functions, especially for repetitive and well-specified tasks. We will analyse the state-of-the-art in the so-called robot judges.

In a discipline that is still being defined, classification is essential to its development. As we shall see, AI is being applied to the development of different types of solutions for judicial purposes, which we have classified in 3 groups[1] considering the segment of users they serve to:

(1) Technology to support the function of judges and courts in the performance of their functions. Within this category, we find different kinds of applications that can be classified as follows:
 - Search and research tools. Among others, this category includes AI that supports the search for information like advanced case law search engines. This is a mature family of tools.
 - Tools that assist judges in their drafting tasks.
 - Tools that assist judges in their decision-making. These tools support judges in making more informed decisions. An example within this category of tools is the Correctional Offender Management Profiling for Alternative Sanctions or COMPAS developed by the private company North Point and used in several states in the US. COMPAS is a risk assessment software that aims to contribute to rendering data-centric decisions through an evaluation, based on 137 questions answered by the offender during an interview and his/her criminal history. We will further discuss COMPAS and the conflict that arises from the fact that it is a privately owned tool rendering a public service, later on, the so-called black-box effect.Another category of tool that could serve judges to take better decisions is the system that covert automated deception detection in real-life courtroom trial videos. These systems use vision, audio and text to do tasks such as classify video features which predict human micro-expressions that can be used as features for deception prediction.[2]
 - Tools to detect implicit or explicit bias. This category is composed of AI that helps to detect implicit or explicit racial or gender bias in order to dictate better resolutions. As analysed by Daniel L. Chen[3] 'much empirical work observes inconsistencies in judicial behaviour.' In this regard, AI has the capacity to analyse facts and influence judgments dispassionately, without human bias, irrationality, or mistakes creeping into the process. It is undiscussable that we humans can be swayed and convinced by emotion.

1. For further information on available tools: María HERNÁNDEZ GIMÉNEZ, INTELIGENCIA ARTIFICIAL Y DERECHO PENAL* INTELLIGENCE AND CRIMINAL LAW, Actualidad Jurídica Iberoamericana N° 10 bis, ISSN: 2386–4567, pp. 792–843, http://www.revista-aji.com/wp-content/uploads/2019/06/792-843.pdf (June 2019), last accessed 17 Dec. 2019.
2. More information about this project can be found at https://doubaibai.github.io/DARE/ and here: Zhe Wu, Bharat Singh, Larry S. Davis, V. S. Subrahmanian, Deception Detection in Videos in AAAI (2018).
3. Daniel L. Chen Machine Learning and the Rule of Law, Computational Analysis of Law, Santa Fe Institute Press, ed. M. Livermore and D. Rockmore, Forthcoming (2019).
 See also, David Abrams, Marianne Bertrand, Sendhil Mullainathan, Do Judges Vary in Their Treatment of Race?, Journal of Legal Studies, volume 41, issue 2, p. 347–383.

- Tools to detect a conflict of interests. As L. Kugler indicates,[4] conflict of interests is 'a big problem...according to an investigation by U.K.-based newspaper The Guardian, local, state, and federal courts in the U.S. are rife with judges who' routinely hide their connections to litigants and their lawyers. The investigation learned that oversight bodies found wrongdoing and issued disciplinary action in nearly half (47%) of complaints about judge conflict of *interest they investigated. However, oversight bodies rarely look into complaints at all—90% of over 37,000 complaints investigated were dismissed by state court authorities 'without conducting any substantive inquiry,' according to that same investigation.*
- Tools to handle massive cases. AI can help to handle those cases that demand the management and processing of tons of documents. The processing of most of these cases requires the realization of repetitive tasks that can better be performed by Machine Learning (ML).
- Tools that help in the categorization of legal documents according to different criteria.

(2) Technology to support other legal professionals, such as lawyers, in carrying out tasks related to judicial proceedings.

- Prediction tools (or as some suggest probability) of judicial results: Among other things, it is worth mentioning here those technologies which support lawyers, by predicting results on the basis of historic judicial data, allows for the detection of patterns, as well as the performance of other lawyers in similar cases. This is also a rather mature category of technology, where several tools are available:

Case Quant	UK	https://www.casequant.com/
Case Law Analytics	FR	http://caselawanalytics.com
Case Crunch	UK	http://www.case-crunch.com/
Emerita Legal	SP	https://www.emerita.legal/
Eunomia	SP	https://vlex.es/p/eunomia/
Jurimetria	SP	https://jurimetria.wolterskluwer.es/content/Inicio.aspx
Icebert platform	SP	https://vlex.es/p/iceberg/
Lex Machina (	USA	https://lexmachina.com/
Predictice	FR	http://predictice.com
Premonition	USA	https://premonition.ai
Ravel Law	USA	http://ravellaw.com/
Tyrant Analytics	SP	https://analytics.tirant.com/analytics/

4. Logan Kugler, AI Judges and Juries, Communications of the ACM, Vol. 61 No. 12, pp 19–21 (December 2018).

Vincent	SP	https://vlex.es/p/vincent/
Vlex Analytics	SP	https://vlex.es/p/spain-court-analytics/

- Legal documents builders: Likewise, we would include in this category tools that serve to find arguments with more probability of success. Within this category, a group of Lawyers and big data experts of the University of Zaragoza[5] in Spain are working side by side on a pioneering project that uses Natural Language Processing (NLP) for the automated extraction of knowledge from legal texts. The pilot is being done with sentences referring to the custody (shared or individual) of minor children. If results are positive, researchers would be given a powerful tool for 'argument mining' applied to legal argumentation, as well as for analysing – both from an academic and sociological perspective – the judicial decisions of the Aragonese and Spanish courts.
- Detection of false allegations: As we know, AI serves to analyse big amounts of data and to detect patterns. AI can also serve to detect patterns of fake information or false allegations. An interesting example of this kind of technology is the one developed by the Spanish National Police VeriPol,[6] a model for the detection of false robbery reports based solely on text. The tool combines NLP and ML methods in a decision support system that provides police officers with the probability that a given report is false.[7]
- Virtual environments (VEs), immersive virtual environments (IVEs), and collaborative virtual environments (CVEs) are different categories of technologies that can be applied in different ways in the courtroom. These technologies can be used to aid in trial preparation, to present evidence and support argument during trials, to impeach witnesses and provide an additional form of record-keeping during trials. The recreation of crime and accident scenes, when a site visit is not possible for whatever reason; the Remote Witness/Remote Expert testimony or the recognition by witnesses of suspects in line-ups are some of the uses of

---

5. https://www.heraldo.es/noticias/sociedad/2019/11/11/inteligencia-artificial-para-analizar-sentencias-1343452.html, last accessed 17 Dec. 2019.
6. LaraQuijano-Sánchez, Federico Liberatore, José Camacho-Collados, Miguel Camacho-Collados, Applying automatic text-based detection of deceptive language to police reports: Extracting behavioral patterns from a multi-step classification model to understand how we lie to the police, Knowledge-Based Systems, Volume 149, 1 Jun. 2018, Pages 155–168, https://www.sciencedirect.com/science/article/abs/pii/S095070511830128X?via%3Dihub last accessed 17 Dec. 2019.
7. VeriPol has been tested on more than 1,000 reports from 2015 provided by the Spanish National Police. Empirical results show that it is extremely effective in discriminating between false and true reports with a success rate of more than 91%, improving by more than 15% the accuracy of expert police officers on the same dataset. The underlying classification model can be analysed to extract patterns and insights showing how people lie to the police (as well as how to get away with false reporting). In general, the more details provided in the report, the more likely it is to be honest. Finally, a pilot study carried out in June 2017 has demonstrated the usefulness of VeriPol on the field.

this kind of AI. An example of which is the use of AI in a Chinese court to simulate the scene of a crime.[8]

(3) Technology aimed to service the final users of Justice, citizens and corporations. Within this category, we have found:
   - Online dispute resolution platforms. There are several examples of this kind of platforms which in some cases have demonstrated to be extremely successful in solving conflicts.[9]
   - 'Chatbots' to inform litigants or support them in their legal proceedings. An interesting example of this is PJ-Bot the chatbot of the *Poder Judicial* of Costa Rica launched in August 2018, which aims to help citizens solving their doubts about the institution.[10] Another example is Gavel,[11] the bilingual, English-Spanish, chatbot developed by the Arizona Courts with the same purposes of guaranteeing 24/7 information and transparency to its users.
   - Lawyer platforms with information on their experience and win rate in court: examples of this kind of tools are, for instance, these two: Premonition AI[12] or Emerita Legal.[13]

§11.02 THE MAIN ISSUES REGARDING AI USE IN JUDICIAL SYSTEMS

What do judges think about the use of AI? This is an interesting question, given that the speed and fluidity of AI tools' implementation in the judiciary are dependent on the answer to this question. If we were to summarize in one word how they seem to feel we would probably choose bewildered.

Two main issues are being central for the discussion by the judiciary: on one side whether judges could and/or should be replaced by robots. On the other, whether the use of AI to assist their decision-making is good as well as how should these tools be beneficial for Justice Administration. These two questions are the object of the report published by *The Mission de Recherche Droit and Justice* in July 2019, entitled *Comment le numérique transforme le droit et la justice vers de nouveaux usages et un bouleversement de la prise de decision.*[14] This report analyses whether robot judges could or

8. Witness visualization systems is the name given to the AI technology developed by the First Branch of the Beijing People's Procuratorate in order to present evidence in a more clear and visual way. *See*: https://www.sixthtone.com/news/1001846/vr-technology-called-to-the-stand-in-beijing-court.
9. Online dispute resolution: An artificial intelligence perspective, Artificial Intelligence Review 41(2) . (February 2014).
10. https://pj.poder-judicial.go.cr/index.php/component/sppagebuilder/?view = page&id = 4, last accessed 17 Dec. 2019.
11. https://www.azcourts.gov/, last accessed 17 Dec. 2019.
12. https://premonition.ai/, last accessed 17 Dec. 2019.
13. https://www.emerita.legal/, last accessed 17 Dec. 2019.
14. The research included a survey conducted among the presidents of the regional courts and courts of appeal of metropolitan France and overseas France, as well as the Court of Cassation, to find out their perception of these tools, their expectations and their suggestions as to their use

should replace judges and concludes that judges are both expert and impartial human beings, that can empathize with the feelings of both parties when making a decision, while robots fail to do so until now. According to the report, 'Society is not ready to delegate this kind of power to a computer, and that is good. Indeed, we are ready to accept the sentence of a judge, because he/she is both an expert and an impartial human being: he/she can apprehend the facts and organize them according to the appropriate rules of law, but he/she is also able to empathize with the feelings of both parties when making his/her decision, seeking beyond the rule of law a fair solution, which a machine cannot do to date.'

Not without standing the veracity of this statement, we could ask ourselves if their assessments are really always true: Are judges always impartial? Are they always experts about the fields for which they make decisions? Do they always remain empathetic in regard to both parties? What is more, we could ask ourselves if maybe robots can be empathetic with human beings too.

Measuring bias and its impact in judges is not simple, but in the cases where research has been done to prove its existence, the results show that judges are humans and therefore, not always impartial. As pointed out by Dyevre and Wijtvliet,[15] 'assessing how personal attributes such as ideology influence judicial behaviour is often made difficult by the unavailability of votes and other common proxies for judicial preferences'. This is why they designed a project that proposes an alternative measurement approach to leverage the knowledge of legal experts. In fact, they asked European Union (EU) competition law experts to rate General Court judges on a number of dimensions and then use these ratings to construct judicial scores for Europhilia, competition law expertise and business-friendliness. They showed that, unlike Europhilia and competition law expertise, the pro-business score of the panel median is a significant predictor of General Court decisions in competition and state aid cases. Their analysis suggests that expert ratings constitute a viable and promising alternative in settings where other measurement methods are unavailable.

Another interesting project that analysed influencing factors in judges' decision-making is the one deployed by which results were published on 24th October 2016 in Predicting judicial decisions of the European Court of Human Rights: a Natural Language Processing perspective.[16] This has been the first systematic study of case law texts of the European Court of Human Rights (ECtHR). The team of researchers developed a model that could predict the decisions of this Court with 79% accuracy, given the fact that cases which had not passed the admissibility stage were excluded

---

and the conclusion is that the magistrates stress the need to regulate their design and support their use. Link to the document: http://www.gip-recherche-justice.fr/publication/comment-le-numerique-transforme-le-droit-et-la-justice-par-de-nouveaux-usages-et-un-bouleversement-de-la-prise-de-decision-anticiper-les-evolutions-pour-les-accompagner-et-les-maitriser/. Last accessed 17 Dec. 2019.

15. Dyevre, Arthur and Wessel Wijtvliet, 'Measuring Judicial Ideology in Economic Cases: An Expert Crowdsourcing Approach,' revise and resubmit at *European Political Science Review* (2019).

16. N. Aletras, D. Tsarapatsanis, D. Preoţiuc-Pietro, V. Lampos, Predicting judicial decisions of the European Court of Human Rights: a Natural Language Processing perspective, 24 Oct. 2016, https://peerj.com/articles/cs-93/.

from the research material. They examined decisions regarding torture, degrading treatment and privacy. The study concluded that facts happen to be the most relevant criteria to forecast the outcome.

But, as we know by now, ML algorithms have to be trained, and since humans will be in charge of their training, there is a risk that, as K. Lum[17] says, 'encoded bias will reproduce, not eliminate bias'.

Regarding empathy, we should be aware of the existence of a discipline called Artificial Empathy (AE) or Affective Computing (AC) with the purpose of developing AI systems, such as companion robots, capable of detecting and responding to human emotions. Maybe the distance between companion robots and robot judges might not be too long.

Concerning the second set of questions, the report is very clear in stating the dangers derived from a machine delivering Justice, when it points out that 'it should be obvious to everyone that justice cannot and should not be predicted, and at a minimum this term should be replaced, for example, by the term "legal hazard quantification"'.

The report indicates as well that 'in our context, "predicting justice" means that we could, using an algorithm, "guess" the decision that would be made by a judge on a given case. It is important to understand that the concept of predictive justice is not only meaningless but also dangerous. It is also dangerous because it is misleading: indeed, if we imagine that one day a computer will be able to predict a decision, a moment's reflection is enough to understand that in reality, it will prescribe this decision: it is the machine that will state the law.'

Undoubtedly, the application of AI for judicial prediction has several advantages in terms of transparency, predictability and standardization of case law. But it can also be argued that it has the limitations and the reasoning bias of the software currently available in the market. The study included as an appendix of the Ethical Charter[18] adopted by the European Commission for the Efficiency of Justice (Council of Europe European Commission for the efficiency of justice (CEPEJ)) of the Council of Europe, which is the first European text setting out ethical principles relating to the use of artificial intelligence (AI) in judicial systems, includes the following concerns: 'the effect of these tools may be not only to provide incentives but to be almost prescriptive, creating a new form of normativity, which could supplement the law by regulating the sovereign discretion of the judge, and potentially leading, in the long term, to the standardization of judicial decisions based no longer on case-by-case reasoning by the courts, but on a pure statistical calculation linked to the average compensation previously awarded by other courts'.

In summary, in this case, the benefits of the application of IA to the prediction of results in the trial are not so obvious. While some, as we will *see* below, consider that it allows to obtain information that may infringe rights, such as, for example, the

17. Kristian Lum, Limitations of mitigating judicial bias with machine learning, Nature Human Behaviour volume 1, Article number: 0141 (2017).
18. European Ethical Charter on the use of Artificial Intelligence in judicial systems and their environment, CEPEJ, (Council of Europe Portal, 4 Dec. 2018) https://www.coe.int/en/web/cepej/cepej-european-ethical-charter-on-the-use-of-artificial-intelligence-ai-in-judicial-systems-and-their-environment.

freedom to pass sentence. Others believe that if machines are well trained, they could perhaps be more just than judges. It is clear that machines which are capable of comparing the decisions of judges can also identify patterns and, within these, biases. Moreover, judges get tired, have grown up in different settings with distinct ideologies and beliefs, whether they believe it or not. Hence, the debate is served.

§11.03 ROBOT, JUDGES AND ROBOT JUDGES

The use of AI in judicial systems of European countries is very uneven. As pointed out in the study included as an appendix of the Ethical Charter 'many European countries seem to have already developed an extremely advanced approach to using practical applications (in terms of both technology and legal support), while for others, this is still just an emerging issue and the focus is solely on effective IT management. For the time being, judges in the Council of Europe member States do not seem to be making any practical and daily use of predictive software'.

In 2018, the use of AI algorithms in European judicial systems remained primarily a private-sector commercial initiative aimed at insurance companies, legal departments, lawyers and individuals wanting to reduce legal uncertainty and the unpredictability of judicial decisions. The study adds that 'Nevertheless, public decision-makers are beginning to be increasingly solicited by a private sector wishing to *see* these tools – which are often "beta" versions which will evolve over time – integrated into public policies.'

As previously mentioned, within the hype that AI is currently experiencing, one of the headlines that has appeared in more than one publication refers to the possible future replacement of judges by robots. The truth is that this replacement is already taking place in some countries. An example is that provided in an article of Wired[19] magazine referring to the city of Chongqing where 4,589 cases involving credit card disputes where using an AI-enabled smart trial platform. The use of this robot judge was alleged to be saving up to twenty-seven working days on average to financial institutions which avoid having to appear in court by filing their lawsuits and submitting evidence online. The same article disclosed the plans of Estonia to use AI to decide on some small claims cases. The projected 'robot judge' would adjudicate small claims disputes of less than EUR 7,000.

A third example of this kind of projects, studied by NADAK, VAN DEN HERIK, JONGBLOED AND SALEM[20] is the Online private court of The Netherlands. This system solely based on AI was set up to offer fully digitalized court proceedings, and

19. Eric Niiler, 'Can AI be a fair judge in court? Estonia thinks so', Wired Business, https://www.wired.com/story/can-ai-be-fair-judge-court-estonia-thinks-so/ (25 Mar. 2019), last accessed 17 Dec. 2019. *See also*, Joe Pinkstone, 'Estonia creating AI powered judge', (Daily Mail Online, https://www.dailymail.co.uk/sciencetech/article-6851525/Estonia-creating-AI-powered-JUDGE.html), (26 Mar. 201), last accessed 17 Dec. 2019.

20. Henriette Nakad-Westrate, Ton Jongbloed, Jaap van den Herik, Abdel-Badeeh M. Salem, *Digitally Produced Judgments in Modern Court Proceedings*, (International Journal of Digital Society, Volume 6 Issue 4, (December 2015).

since 2011, it has also solved debt collection proceedings. In these kinds of proceedings, the parameters that judges have to take into consideration to adopt a decision are very limited, namely: the claim and all that relates to it, such as the amount, due date, interest with a due date, percentage and proportionality with regard to the claim amount, personal data on the parties, the costs of debt collection and the course of the proceedings. Nevertheless, the Dutch experience shows that humans could not fault the digital judge's decision-making, but several human errors did occur in terms of data input. There has not been a single case where clerks were able to improve the decision of the digital judge while, apparently, several human errors did occur during the process of entering data into the system. Thus, we could assess that the system is not flawed but humans are. Additionally, the authors point out three advantages of the e-Court: its speed, its impartiality and its capacity to avoid miscalculations.

In the opinion of *HERNÁNDEZ GIMENEZ,*[21] the characteristics that a robot judge capable of replacing humans must necessarily possess are:

(a) The functional capacity to recognize the parties in a trial, as well as interested third parties, to observe evidence, to interpret the law and the basic principles of law, as well as to weigh them adequately when applying them to facts. In short, it must be able to adapt to legal reasoning.
(b) The ability to follow the rules: While humans adapt their behaviour to rules autonomously, robots accept rules by the mere fact that they are programmed to accept them.
(c) An internal point of view about rules: Robots need to decide while a judge adopts decisions based on their internal point of view, motivated because they have a commitment to a standard or a pattern of general conduct. This pattern leads to social practice. *This willingness to act according to certain rules is not a characteristic that, until now, robots can develop, so the robot of the experiment does not meet this characteristic either,* points out *HERNANDEZ JIMÉNEZ.*

For robot judges to become a reality, the legal system must recognize its capacity to judge. In the case of the e-Court of The Netherlands since the Dutch did not provide for the possibility of a digital judge, the robot judge renders the verdict in the name of the human judge.

But the possibility of robots replacing judges is questioned in the report Comment le numérique transforme le droit et la justice vers de nouveaux usages et un bouleversement de la prise de decision,[22] where it is stated that robots '...can apprehend the

21. HERNÁNDEZ GIMÉNEZ, M., Inteligencia artificial y derecho penal, Intelligence and Criminal Law, Actualidad Jurídica Iberoamericana N° 10 bis, ISSN: 2386–4567, pp. 792–843, (June 2019).
22. http://www.gip-recherche-justice.fr/publication/comment-le-numerique-transforme-le-droit-et-la-justice-par-de-nouveaux-usages-et-un-bouleversement-de-la-prise-de-decision-anticiper-les-evolutions-pour-les-accompagner-et-les-maitriser/.

facts and organize them according to the appropriate rules of law, but a judge is also able to empathize with the feelings of both parties when making his/her decision, seeking beyond the rule of law a fair solution, which a machine cannot do to date'. Modelling the legal reasoning does not seem achievable at the moment; and even if it were, a deterministic approach (which would be naive to believe is really based on a syllogism, which is mainly used for the legal justification of the decision) would not be desirable, as it could not take into account the non-quantifiable variations between very close cases, which results in what appears to be an irreducible uncertainty about the outcome of a trial. Situations involving an inherent hazard are common in various fields, such as meteorology, medicine or finance. The scientific approach commonly used to treat this type of case is called probabilistic modelling.

But as pointed in the Appendix to the European Ethical Charter, 'Judicial decision processing by artificial intelligence, according to their developers, is likely, in civil, commercial and administrative matters, to help improve the predictability of the application of the law and consistency of court decisions, subject to compliance with the principles set out below. In criminal matters, their use must be considered with the greatest reservations in order to prevent discrimination based on sensitive data, in conformity with the guarantees of a fair trial. Whether designed with the aim of assisting in the provision of legal advice, helping in drafting or in the decision-making process or advising the user, it is essential that processing is carried out with transparency, impartiality and equity, certified by an external and independent expert assessment.'

Therefore, our view is that despite the resistance currently made by part of the judiciary, the truth is that the use of robots to solve conflicts may be the best solution to solve some of the most relevant problems of Justice, such as the delays and the lack of consistency amongst resolutions. Limiting the competence of the robot judges to specific matters seems to be the least risky solution, at least until AI probes to be a valid solution to the administration of Justice in any kind of case.

§11.04 THE IMPACT OF OPEN DATA REGARDING JUDICIAL DECISIONS IN AI DEVELOPMENT

Any AI solution is made out of several ingredients, of which the basic is the human brain, and dedication, data and algorithms. Therefore, an essential condition for the development of AI is the existence and availability of data. This is one of the main reasons why in most countries and in most cases, AI is being hindered.

Judicial data is not always open nor even well-collected and organized. It is important to realize that setting up a judicial resolutions database is a complex project that demands high investments. The Spanish CENDOJ explains in its judicial decisions portal that all decisions have to be submitted to the following workflow: Digitization → Structuring the body of the sentence → Making of text formats → Extraction of resolution fields → Dissociation of personal data → Marking of reference to legislation and jurisprudence → Develop Legal analysis.

For this reason, projects that aim to develop AI that do not need real judicial data, such as the textualization of audiovisual media, the transcription of court hearings or witness statements, or dictation systems, or identification of people by biometrics, are already successfully operating in several countries. On the other hand, projects that need real judicial data to start, such as those AI tools that serve to classify, anonymize or extract the content of documents; jurisprudence and legislation expert systems; cognitive virtual assistants; intermediation platforms in family issues, detection of possible false testimonies, etc., are encountering various difficulties to become a reality.

Consequently, an open data approach to judicial decisions is a prerequisite to the existence of Legal Tech devoted to predictive justice. As stated in the above-mentioned report of CEPEJ: 'The availability of data is an essential condition for the development of AI, enabling it to perform certain tasks previously carried out by humans in a non-automated manner. The more data available, the more AI is able to refine models improving their predictive ability. An open data approach to judicial decisions is, therefore, a prerequisite for the work of legal tech companies specializing in search engines or trend analysis ("predictive justice"). Processing of these data raises a number of issues, such as changes in the formation of case law and protection of personal data (including the names of professionals).' Judicial data is available at different conditions throughout European countries. While some countries have a real open data policy, others[23] only offer free access to data. These are different approaches with different consequences. While the first might promote the development of Legal Tech for judicial purposes, the second limits it since the data is not available for handling. The possibilities span from the need to pay a fee for the resolutions,[24] to the free disposal of the dataset of the whole repository of resolutions available. What varies as well from country to country is the amount of resolutions which are made available.

23. According the CEPEJ report in 2016 mentioned in footnote *supra*, all these countries still have free access policy regarding their judicial data but, not an open data policy: Armenia, Belgium, Bosnia and Herzegovina, Luxembourg, Russian Federation, Spain, Turkey.

24. This is the case of Spain where despite the richness in resolutions of the c institution in charge of judicial documentation, Centro de. Documentación Judicial(CENDOJ) when one enters its website, a pop up shows the following warning 'The user of the database will be able to consult the documents as long as he does so for his particular use. The use of the database for commercial purposes is not permitted, nor is the massive downloading of information. The reuse of this information for the creation of databases or for commercial purposes must follow the procedure and conditions established by the CGPJ through its Judicial Documentation Centre. Any action that contravenes the above indications may lead to the adoption of appropriate legal measures.'

In some countries, such as Spain, all superior courts' case law is published.[25] In France, the report *L'open data, des decisions de Justice,*[26] describes the situation of judicial open data in this country, where Articles 20 and 21 of the Law of 7 October 2016 for a digital republic established the provision of all judicial and administrative court decisions free of charge (in 'open data'), specifying that they should be made 'with due respect for the privacy of the persons concerned' and be 'preceded by an analysis of the risk of re-identification of persons'. The report makes solid and binding recommendations for the normative and technical implementation of this open data. Moreover, a total of twenty recommendations are provided amongst which one is the regulation in the use of new so-called predictive justice tools by the enactment of an obligation of transparency of algorithms, the implementation of flexible control mechanisms by public authorities and the adoption of a quality certification system by an independent body.

In Germany, the percentage of resolutions available is reported to be very limited. These differences in the amount and quality of the datasets available have a direct impact on the technology that can be developed.

§11.05 THE FRENCH CASE: A VETO TO PREDICTING CASE LAW TOOLS TO PROTECT JUDGES' FREEDOM OF DECISION

In March 2019, the *Loi n° 2019-222 du 23 mars 2019 de programmation 2018–2022 et de réforme pour la justice*[27] was published in France. Its Article 33[28] states that the identity data of magistrates and members of the Judicial Office may not be reused for

25. In Spain is the Judicial Documentation Centre (CENDOJ), in compliance with the competence granted to the General Council of the Judicial Branch by Article 560.1.10 of the Organic Law of the Judicial Branch, the technical body of the General Council of the Judiciary charged with the official publication of case law, as well as other competences in the field of documentation and knowledge management services. It also offers support and information services to members of the Judiciary, providing them with access to all types of document sources used when carrying out their judicial activity. The CENDOJ carries out the compilation, treatment and dissemination of the Jurisprudence of the Supreme Court and other Spanish Courts bodies (Audiencia Nacional (AN); Tribunales Superiores de Justicia (TSJ) and Audiencias Provinciales (AAPP)), as well as a growing selection of resolutions of unipersonal bodies whose importance and doctrinal interest justifies their dissemination, in compliance with the provisions of Article 619 of Organic Law 6/1985 of 1 July, of the Judicial Power. Likewise, CENDOJ manages the supply of sentences and other resolutions dictated by the Spanish Courts to various reusers, also attending to requests that do not constitute reuse, in accordance with the criteria established in the Law on the Reuse of Public Sector Information (LRISP).
26. http://www.justice.gouv.fr/publications-10047/rapports-thematiques-10049/remise-du-rapport-sur-lopen-data-des-decisions-de-justice-31165.html.
27. JORF n°0071 du 24 mars 2019.
28. « Les données d'identité des magistrats et des membres du greffe ne peuvent faire l'objet d'une réutilisation ayant pour objet ou pour effet d'évaluer, d'analyser, de comparer ou de prédire leurs pratiques professionnelles réelles ou supposées. La violation de cette interdiction est punie des peines prévues aux Articles 226-18, 226-24 et 226-31 du code pénal, sans préjudice des mesures et sanctions prévues par la loi n° 78-17 du 6 janvier 1978 relative à l'informatique, aux fichiers et aux libertés. »;.

the purpose or effect of evaluating, analysing, comparing or predicting their actual or presumed professional practices.

As described by McDonnell and Traynor,[29] 'France now requires that judges' decisions must be published in a manner such that the names and surnames of the parties, and of any third parties, are hidden and anonymized prior to being made available to the public. By extension, where a publication is likely to undermine the security or privacy of the parties or third parties, any element within the decision that would allow for their identification, including the identities of the judges and members of the court registry, must also be obscured.'

And what has shocked even more the legal community is that the infringement of the precept could constitute a crime for illegally obtaining and processing personal data, with penalties of up to five years in prison and fines of up to EUR 300,000.00, for which legal persons can also be held liable.

For a better understanding of the reasons behind this prohibition, we recommend reading the testimony of Michaël Benesty, published at Artificial Lawyer[30] where he explains in detail the facts that in his opinion led to the decision of the French Parliament to prohibit the use of predictive tools for case law. Benesty was a tax lawyer who decided to develop a project in 2016 to find French legal cases where the tax administration lost. Having found some very large discrepancies among judges, he created a website called SupraLegem (unpublished today) to let anyone using the tool for whatever bias they wanted to find. It was a non-commercial project. He published some articles with names and information on the decision-making of some specific judges. He concluded that Article 33 is the main consequence of what happened in 2016, at a time where no one had a real experience of ML applied to legal cases. No one expected these consequences. In his own words, *my understanding is that both French Supreme Courts are not against these statistics (if well done) as they help in some way to normalize the jurisprudence at the level of the country, and in some way it helps with their mission. But lower courts judges do not agree with this position, as they want to stay as independent as possible (which may sound like not accountable to some lawyers).*

This is the first regulation of its kind. It has been discussed throughout Europe and abroad. AI defenders dislike it since it limits the potential of this technology in favour of an arguable capacity to limit the independence of the judges' decision-making capacity.

§11.06 THE PSA: AI ASSISTING JUDGES IN THEIR PRETRIAL DECISIONS

The Public Safety Assessment (PSA), funded by the Laura and John Arnold Foundation, is an algorithmic pretrial risk assessment tool that helps judges making more informed pretrial decisions, for instance, when determining whether a defendant

29. Andy McDonnell and Stephen Traynor, France Bans Analytics of Judges' Decisions, France 21 Jun. 2019.
30. https://www.artificiallawyer.com/2019/06/07/the-judge-statistical-data-ban-my-story-michael-benesty/.

should be released before trial. The tool is being used by many of the US jurisdictions, including the states of Arizona, Kentucky, and New Jersey, and some of the largest cities in the country, such as Phoenix, Chicago, and Houston.

The foundation proved in a research that the pretrial decision-making process often results in high-risk defendants being released from jail to await trial, while low-risk defendants are frequently detained. In other words, rich people who are a danger to society can pay their way out of jail, while poor people who pose no threat to the community cannot. This has negative consequences for individuals, families, and communities, and it disproportionately impacts minority communities and low-income individuals. When analysing the system, they found that judges do not often have access to basic information, such as the defendant's criminal history, and decisions are frequently made in an entirely subjective manner or with the use of fixed bail schedules.

The PSA was created using the largest, most diverse set of pretrial records ever assembled: 750,000 cases from approximately 300 jurisdictions across the United States. Researchers analysed the data to determine which factors are most predictive of new criminal activity, new violent criminal activity, and failure to appear. The research team identified and tested hundreds of factors, which fell into broad categories, including prior arrests and convictions, prior incarceration, pending charges, prior failures to appear in court, drug and alcohol use, mental health, employment, and residence. Historical and prospective validations were conducted to determine how well the PSA performed by race and gender and to ensure that the PSA calculation did not promote bias. Ultimately, the team isolated nine factors that most effectively predicted new criminal activity, new violent criminal activity, and failure to appear.

The PSA's[31] nine factors are answered using administrative data from a defendant's criminal history, and they do not include other factors such as questions about race, gender, ethnic background, income, substance abuse, mental health, employment status, marital status, or any demographic or personal information other than age:

(a) The person's age at the time of the arrest.
(b) Whether the current offence is violent.
(c) Whether the person had a pending charge at the time of the current offence.
(d) Whether the person has a prior misdemeanour conviction.
(e) Whether the person has a prior felony conviction.
(f) Whether the person has prior convictions for violent crimes.
(g) How many times the person failed to appear at a pretrial hearing in the last two years.
(h) Whether the person failed to appear at a pretrial hearing more than two years ago.
(i) Whether the person has previously been sentenced to incarceration.

31. More detailed information on the PSA's development is available here: https://www.psapretrial.org/about/background last accessed 17 Dec. 2019.

By the time of closing the last version of this book, we were obliged to update certain parts due to last-minute events, being this section one of them. The reason: the announcement by the Petrial Justice Institute[32] that their Petrial Risk Assessment Tools *can no longer be a part of our solution for building equitable petrial justice systems*. The justification alleged ...*these tools are derived from data reflecting structural racism and institutional inequity that impact court and law enforcement policies and practices. Use of that data then deepens the inequity.*

§11.07 ETHICS APPLIED TO AI IN JUDICIAL SYSTEMS

As pointed out in *Comment le numérique transforme le droit et la justice vers de nouveaux usages et un bouleversement de la prise de decision,*[33] the use of AI in judicial might need a legal framework. But this framework does not exist so far, and its development will still probably demand some more years until the rule-maker achieves its goal. In the meantime, proposing ethical codes is a good solution to offer some guidance to all parties involved.

On 3rd December 2018, the CEPEJ[34] adopted at a plenary meeting The European Ethical Charter on the use of AI in judicial systems. The Charter contains five principles on the Use of AI in Judicial Systems and their environment. It is intended for public and private stakeholders responsible for the design and deployment of AI tools and services that involve the processing of judicial decisions and data (ML or any other methods deriving from data science). It also concerns public decision-makers in charge of the legislative or regulatory framework, of the development, audit or use of such tools and services.

(1) Principle of respect for fundamental rights: that aims to ensure that the design and implementation of AI tools and services are compatible with fundamental rights.
(2) Principle of non-discrimination: that prevents the development or intensification of any discrimination between individuals or groups of individuals.
(3) Principle of quality and security: with regard to the processing of judicial decisions and data, use certified sources and intangible data with models elaborated in a multi-disciplinary manner, in a secure technological environment.
(4) Principle of transparency, impartiality and fairness: make data processing methods accessible and understandable, authorize external audits.
(5) Principle 'under user control': preclude a prescriptive approach and ensure that users are informed actors and in control of the choices made.

32. Link to the position: https://www.pretrial.org/wp-content/uploads/Risk-Statement-PJI-2020.pdf, last accessed, 15 Jan. 2020.
33. http://www.gip-recherche-justice.fr/publication/comment-le-numerique-transforme-le-droit-et-la-justice-par-de-nouveaux-usages-et-un-bouleversement-de-la-prise-de-decision-anticiper-les-evolutions-pour-les-accompagner-et-les-maitriser/ last accessed 17 Dec. 2019.
34. CEPEJ stands for CEPEJ: https://www.coe.int/en/web/cepej/about-cepej last accessed 17 Dec. 2019.

§11.08 THE LOOMIS CASE: AI'S BLACK-BOX AND ITS EFFECTS IN JUDICIAL APPLICATION

In the following paragraphs, we will analyse the so-called black-box effect in AI, and we will do it with the help of the Loomis case. The interest of this case relies on the fact that it has been the first case where a court gives its opinion about the use of an AI tool in a judicial proceeding.

The name of the tool is COMPAS. Northpoint is the company that owns COMPAS, which did not disclose its algorithm, alleging that it is a trade secret. This raised a debate on whether a private company AI tool should be adequate to administer Justice. For some, the answer is that for judicial purposes, the algorithm should always be transparent; thus, privately owned tools are inadequate.

In the Loomis case, the defendant claimed the algorithm's report violated his right to due process, as there was no way to examine how the report was generated. The judges considered that a trial court's use of an algorithmic risk assessment in sentencing did not violate the defendant's due process rights even though the methodology used to produce the assessment was not disclosed to the court nor to the defendant. The reason alleged was that the assessment was not the sole basis for the decision and courts could at their discretion disagree with the assessment. The court also explained that risk scores might not be used 'to determine whether an offender is incarcerated' or 'to determine the severity of the sentence'.

Accordingly, courts cannot evaluate 'how the risk scores are determined or how the factors are weighed'. A solution to this kind of situations would be the filing to the court of what is called an AMICUS Brief. Something which in the Loomis case was denied to COMPAS. Most systems that use AI are opaque to all but its developers, not letting others know how a specific output, recommendation, or assessment is produced. This is called the black-box effect on AI. There are currently only a few studies analysing these assessments in part because the lack of methodological transparency from data assessment companies has made this difficult.

There are some interesting learnings to be extracted from this judgment.

(1) Judges must proceed with caution when using such risk assessments and must explain the factors other than the assessment that supports the sentence imposed.
(2) Only those jurisdictions that 'have the capacity for maintaining [risk assessment] tools and monitoring their continued accuracy' should use these tools.
(3) The reports Tests (PSIs) that incorporate a COMPAS assessment must include five written warnings for judges, in order to make them fully aware of the potential and limitations of these AI reports:
    (a) The 'proprietary nature of COMPAS' that prevents the disclosure of how risk scores are calculated.
    (b) That COMPAS scores are unable to identify specific high-risk individuals because these scores rely on group data.

(c) That although COMPAS relies on a national data sample, there has been 'no cross-validation study for a Wisconsin population'.
(d) That there are studies that 'have raised questions about whether [COMPAS scores] disproportionately classify minority offenders as having a higher risk of recidivism'.
(e) And finally, that COMPAS was developed specifically to assist the Department of Corrections in making post-sentencing determinations.

§11.09 CONCLUSIONS

As in other aspects of law, the application of AI to the judicial field is beginning its journey, and it is not encountering an unhindered path. On the one hand, professionals are often reluctant to change. On the other, the legal framework is not yet adapted to a new reality. Additionally, there are other challenges which derive from the lack of preparation and knowledge of people. Fear, caution, mistrust coexist with curiosity and the interest generated by a technology that only a few still feel that it will not completely transform the administration of Justice in a few years.

In this context, the first applications of AI are already being implemented by the judicial powers of different countries. We have seen examples from China, with a robot lawyer functioning for minor cases, and the USA, where AI is being used by judges as an assisting tool for pretrial decision making. We have also discussed the case of Estonia, which is investing in the development of robotic judges for minor cases and that of the Netherlands, where an online court is already being supported by AI.

In some countries, such as France, a debate is currently taking place for which we do not know what the outcome will be and whether or not the so-called robot judges are a solution. For now, the balance seems to be tilted towards disqualifying them on the grounds that with existing technology, they would not be able to perform some of the essential functions performed by a judge. Interestingly, it is in this same country where the first rule prohibiting the use of AI to predict the possible outcome of a trial has been enacted. The reasons that justify this rule: the protection of personal data of French magistrates and their right to pass sentence without the yoke that could derive from the existence of this type of tools. This rule has shocked many and probably calmed the spirits of others.

We have also analysed the very relevant role of judicial data, without which there is no possibility of developing AI. We have also differentiated between open judicial data and open judicial policy. These data are not available in all countries and in those where they are, sometimes only for consultation, but not for reuse. Fostering open data has, therefore, become the first battle to be won by those who wish AI to offer its full potential.

In relation to the use of tools to support decision-making, the challenges that arise derive from the fact that those used are privately owned and their owners thus protected by their right to trade secrets, and it is a non-governmental organization

(NGO) who detected the existence of the bias. This type of situation generates mistrust in the use of AI in a phase in which it still needs to gain the trust of politicians, judges and the justiciable and a logical debate: is it fair that a secret algorithm is used to administer Justice? This and many other questions still need to find an answer, and we legal professionals can help to find the proper one.

CHAPTER 12

Final Conclusions

María Jesús González-Espejo & Juan Pavón

Artificial Intelligence (AI) is being applied in most areas of our lives, and its impact needs to be analysed from different perspectives: social, economic, ethical, legal, etc. On the one hand, AI impacts in many ways in the legal system. On the other, AI can be useful to support legal practice. Some tools are already in use, such as the ones that analyse massive amounts of documents to extract conclusions from the content, the ones that help lawyers predict the outcome in judicial proceedings (*see* Chapter 11), or the ones that help them in the editing of legal documents. Additionally, it is also necessary to reflect on how AI should be regulated and the new kinds of legal cases that could be derived from its use.

Chapter 1 explains the history of AI and the different waves it has gone through. At present, we are going through probably the most relevant wave, largely sustained by machine learning (ML) and Big Data. The current wave is the result of an evolution from the paradigm based on the symbolic or knowledge-based approaches (as expert systems), to the data-driven approach, well represented by ML techniques. This evolution has been made possible by hardware advances which have allowed the storing and processing of huge amounts of data.

It is important to note that this data comes from heterogeneous sources – initially from the web, which continues to grow at an increasing rate with the activity derived from social networks, as well as with the use of mobile devices and geo-localization. Big Data will increase even faster with the information obtained from the sensors that shape the IoT, a phenomenon that will sustain our smart environments and smart cities.

Data is presented in many forms such as text, audio, video, and geo-localization (where the data comes from) and personalization (who or what is generating the data). So, it is not only the rise of AI but also of accompanying technologies that allow high distribution, mobility and ubiquity of information, knowledge and services. All of them reinforce each other, and their integration is encouraging the growth of several forms such as the IoT and Industry 4.0.

We have seen how ML, and more specifically, deep learning, is the main AI paradigm in this revolution. These techniques have achieved certain goals that were unforeseen just a decade ago, mainly in speech, image and video recognition, as well as the ability to acquire non-explicit knowledge. Note that expert systems (the previous generation of AI) facilitate knowledge management, but that knowledge was explicitly coded. ML takes raw data and can extract features from this data and classify it. Deep learning goes further than other ML techniques as it can learn complex representations from simple ones. The breakthrough came with AlexNet,[1] when in the ImageNet Large Scale Visual Recognition Challenge of 2012, got a top-5 error[2] for classification of images of 15.3%, significantly much better than previous systems. Currently, deep learning systems have surpassed human beings (we have around a 5.1% error rate), with values as low as 3%, so (we might assume) the challenge is over. For speech recognition, humans have a word error rate of 2–4%, and systems like Google Assistant and Microsoft are getting values close to 5%.

However, there are still relevant issues that must be understood in order to assess the capabilities of deep learning. On one side, there is the availability of data for training and testing the deep neural networks. There are big collections such as ImageNet[3] with more than 14 million hand-annotated images (remember that images have to be labelled initially by human beings, in order to specify what do they represent, so they can be used to train the ANNs), or the Google Open Images Dataset V5 + Extensions,[4] with more than 15 million. However, it is precisely on training data that there is a great risk of bias on the results of the intelligent system, and many cases have been illustrated in previous chapters.

We have also analysed the limitations of AI systems. As we have noted in Chapter 1, we can build an intelligent machine that can win world champion of chess or Go, but such machine cannot do other things that are quite normal for human beings (this is the Moravec paradox, *see* section §1.02). Furthermore, there is currently a big problem with deep learning systems, which is the ability to learn incrementally new things, as they suffer what is called the *catastrophic forgetting* issue. This means that a deep learning network that has been trained to recognize dogs if it is later trained to recognize cats, it forgets how to recognize dogs. The only solution is to train it again to recognize both dogs and cats. This is a limitation when a system must learn from experience, especially in changing environments, and is one of the main research challenges nowadays. In fact, the ability of an intelligent system to react to an

1. This is a convolutional neural network, one of the most common types of deep neural networks, especially for image recognition. Alexnet is the work of the thesis of Alex Krizhevsky, 'ImageNet Classification with Deep Convolutional Neural Networks' (available at http://www.image-net.org/challenges/LSVRC/2012/supervision.pdf, Retrieved 16 May 2019).
2. The system calculates the probabilities of an image being of some category (e.g., a dog, a cat, a car) in a set (for the ILSVR challenge there are 1000 categories). The top-5 error means that the correct category has not been in the first five predictions of the system. It is possible to consider also top-1 error, which considers whether the first prediction is not the right one.
3. http://image-net.org/. Retrieved 16 May 2019.
4. https://storage.googleapis.com/openimages/web/index.html. Retrieved 16 May 2019.

unexpected event, something for which it has not been trained, is still far for being achieved.

In all areas of application, where AI is used to make decisions that affect people and society, AI reasoning must be able to take into account societal values, moral and ethical considerations, weigh the respective priorities of values held by different stakeholders and in multiple multicultural contexts, explain its reasoning, and guarantee transparency. As the capabilities for autonomous decision-making grow, perhaps the most important issue to consider is the need to rethink our responsibility with respect to AI systems. It must be clear that whatever their level of autonomy and social awareness and their ability to learn and adapt to a changing environment, AI systems are artefacts, constructed by people to achieve some human purpose.

Chapter 3 discusses theories, methods, algorithms that can integrate societal, legal and moral values into AI systems considering the whole system life-cycle (analysis, design, construction, deployment and evaluation). These frameworks must deal both with the autonomic reasoning of the machine about such issues that we consider to have an ethical impact, but most importantly, we need frameworks to guide design choices, to regulate the reaches of AI systems, to ensure proper data stewardship, and to help individuals determine their own involvement. Chapter 3 proposes ways to ensure responsible and trustworthy AI during design and development processes (Ethics IN Design), as part of the behaviour and functioning of the system (Ethics BY Design) and as an integral part of education and commitment of developers and researchers integrity (Ethics FOR Design).

AI is not always visible. On the contrary, we are unaware of their existence of many AI solutions, but that does not mean that they do not affect our lives. This reinforces the need to establish a legal framework. In Chapter 2, we have analysed the feasibility and need for regulation through legally binding instruments, beyond the field of ethics. History shows what can happen if the State withdraws and allows private companies to set their own exclusive regulatory standards. We have a unique opportunity to create laws and principles governing AI on a common basis and with an indispensable public-private partnership that should preferably be international in scope with the leadership of the UN or, failing that, at least at European level led by EU institutions, as they had already achieved in the areas of privacy and data protection.

Although there are many committees at national and international level trying to establish some norms or guidelines for the evolution and use of AI, as explained in Chapter 2, it is still not clear whether they will end up being part of some well-established legislation.

On their side, the main AI companies are pushing towards self-regulation practice, but it is also questioned by many whether this soft law system is enough to guarantee human rights. More and more experts believe that regulatory action should be taken, and such regulation should have a global scope. This is obviously not going to be an easy task, but there are some relevant initiatives, such as the IEEE Global

Initiative on Ethics of Autonomous and Intelligent Systems[5] or the Asilomar AI principles,[6] propelled by the research community in this direction.

Having analysed the impact that AI has privacy and personal data protection wise, it is also worth highlighting the opportunity that AI, in combination with other technologies such as Big Data, IoT or Blockchain, offers society to rethink how technology should impact their lives. It is time to start a new balancing exercise to determine what should be acceptable or unacceptable in the future.

The development of AI should not only comply with current ethical standards and be subject to already consolidated values and principles but also demand a proper policy framework[7] that provides legal certainty for future technological developments.

It is also time to reconsider the limits that define some fundamental individual rights *versus* collective or general interests in respect of the rights to privacy, to personal data protection or to non-discrimination. Let us recall the phenomenon known as 'privacy paradox' and reconsider what are also the duties of individuals regarding the protection and processing of their privacy and their own data. This also refers to the need to articulate the way to deal with the fact that, in real life, due to the power of technology, data cannot clearly be split into personal or non-personal, data are not pseudonyms or anonymous for everyone equally, data are not private or public (recall the meaning of 'wholelife'), data is not offline or online (illustrated by the 'onlife' concept discussed above), data is not only owned by their data subjects but also by their generators, controllers and processors (as reflected in the taxonomy of data as per their origin mentioned above) and, finally, data is not immutable but can change from one type to another throughout their life-cycle.

It is time to evolve and incorporate new ways, such as the chance to self-sovereign identity *versus* personal identification, the importance of autonomy of will *versus* data control, the focus on cybersecurity *versus* developing security guarantees in the form of merely formal requirements. If an adequate policy framework is to be established, it would be helpful to use a proportionate[8] and new values balance-based approach, as well as to seek cooperation between most important global players.

AI can also be a way to reinforce cybersecurity as well as a tool to create new threats. AI applications in cybersecurity, which are reviewed in Chapter 9, are at different stages of maturity, ranging from the well-established techniques used to identify malware and malicious URLs, to the initial demonstrations of human-in-the-loop interactive defensive frameworks. Given the shortage of cybersecurity professionals anticipated for the next years, AI holds the promise of empowering defensive strategies to counteract even more proficient and sophisticated adversaries.

5. https://standards.ieee.org/industry-connections/ec/autonomous-systems.html. Retrieved 16 May 2019.
6. https://futureoflife.org/ai-principles/. Retrieved 16 May 2019.
7. Such as the European Commission Draft 12/12 Structure for the White Paper on Artificial Intelligence – A European Approach. https://www.epic.org/banfacesurveillance/EU-AI-white-paper.pdf, accessed at 28 Jan. 2019.
8. European Data Protection Supervisor, Guidelines on assessing the proportionality of measures that limit the fundamental rights to privacy and to the protection of personal data, available at https://edps.europa.eu/sites/edp/files/publication/19-12-19_edps_proportionality_guidelines2_en.pdf, accessed at 28 Jan. 2019.

The advent of technology has brought about substantial changes in the paradigm to which we have all become accustomed in the field of competition law. AI has supplanted people in the decision-making process in real markets, and companies are increasingly relying on digital tools to act with and against their competitors. If uncertainty is a critical element of the market, has technological development succeeded in reducing it, controlling it, and subduing it? Perhaps the paradigm shift has an even higher dimension than initially thought. What is the impact that technological innovation will have on competition laws? It is not that technology changes the rules, it is that perhaps the great agents of competition must adapt to a new environment to survive. Competition Law prohibits price-fixing, abuse of dominant position or market-sharing, but what happens when the algorithms have made the decisions? Should bots and AI learn the law before putting them on the market to ensure compliance? In Chapter 6, we have analysed the current situation and the challenges that AI poses to free competition and existing markets.

There is an important characteristic of intelligent systems that raises several concerns that must be addressed as well by legal professionals, their autonomy. Autonomy is a fundamental property that distinguishes intelligent agents from conventional software, as they have the capacity to make their own decisions, without explicit intervention of a human. This raises issues concerning the corresponding liability (*see* Chapter 8) and the ownership of their creations (*see* Chapter 7).

Legal liability of intelligent systems (agents) relies strongly on several aspects of their design as well as on the data that are used for their training. Therefore, a relevant issue is transparency and explainability of these systems, which is a complex issue not yet resolved, especially when using ML approaches. How this can be addressed in the development of legal regulations is still an open question that requires the collaboration of AI engineers with legal professionals.

The development of AI technologies is also challenging IP regulation. AI agents (developers, investors, etc.) are using traditional legal tools (e.g., patent, copyright, trade secrets, trademarks, etc.) to protect the vast advances in AI technologies. A recent report of the WIPO shows that the number of patents related to AI has grown exponentially since 2013 and according to the market experts, the AI industry will be worth around 4 trillion dollars by 2022. A lot is at stake, and the protection of the AI technologies is a pillar for the sustainability of this multimillion industry.

But the current existing European and others' regions IP legislation does not offer conclusive protection tools. For example, the fuel of this industry, algorithms, cannot be protected by copyright, nor by patent rules. A still unsolved additional question on AI and IP is whether these technologies and applications can become creators or inventors. We still do not have an answer to this set of questions: who can or would be considered the creator (copyright) or the inventor (patents)? Who holds the corresponding rights (and obligations)? All these questions will become more relevant as the AI's grow its capacity to create in an autonomous way.

The current principles related to copyright and patent law will have to evolve or probably change. And what if robots get a legal personality? Although there are recommendations, no one has yet amended the IP regulation in the light of the AI industry requirements. Some voices argue that these intelligent agents could have some kind of legal personality because of their autonomy during the creative process. However, from an engineering point of view, this is rather questionable because, in the end, the agent has to be given a goal. Such original goal (stated by its creator or owner) makes the agent work towards its satisfaction. Although the agent works autonomously and takes some decisions in this process, it does because it has a goal. Also, upon creation of a work, the owner of the agent can claim that it made it with some support of the agent. Determining whether the product has been made by the agent or a human becomes a kind of Turing test.

An important application area where AI is being used and that also raises several questions from a social and legal perspective is taxation (*see* Chapter 5). AI is transforming this field of practice. It is already assisting tax authorities to detect tax fraud, predict market patterns, optimize tax structures, and improve collection capacity. It is also improving the relationship between taxpayers and tax administrations through intelligent virtual assistants capable of offering immediate and cheap responses through chatbots based on natural language and with the aim of collaborating in the compliance of the obligations of the former, reducing or eliminating errors, while the virtual assistants learn automatically based on each individual needs.

Additionally, tax experts should start reflecting on how the implementation of AI solutions in the job market will impact tax collection. There have already been proposals with different approaches to this matter. Some believe that corporations using AI should assume new taxes. Others propose a tax on the salary assigned to robots with tax withholding at source, as well as on the robot's contribution to the Social Security. They believe that robots should pay VAT or that there should be a new tax on the ownership of these machines or taxes for their registration and control. However, all these solutions do have a problem: they suppose a penalty to innovation and consequently, entail a loss of competitiveness for those businesses that invest in them.

Others propose that society as a whole should bear the cost of robotization, applying the principles of economic capacity and progressivity, increasing the collection of Corporate Tax, removing favourable treatment for capital income, cutting tax benefits and reviewing the taxation on Wealth, Inheritance and Environment, and contributions to health services and pensions.

The attribution of legal personality to robots for tax and civil liability purposes is a solution that is being considered by some, in case they attain a financial autonomy comparable to that of human beings: receiving a salary, providing services as businesspersons or professionals, although, as mentioned above, giving such legal personality is highly controversial.

This discussion is quite related to the impact of AI on the labour market, a subject of high controversy, as discussed in Chapter 4. It is clear that AI implies a new era of automatization, not only of mechanical tasks, also cognitive. Therefore, many current jobs that perform repetitive tasks will be assumed by intelligent machines. The conception and maintenance of these systems will, on the other side, be a source for new kinds of jobs. We have discussed how this affects labour law and practice, and we see new opportunities on the use of AI as a tool that can support human resource managers. This view of AI as a complement to our professions may seem quite optimistic for many, but the pace of evolution of AI has not given rise to the disasters that some predicted. Anyway, AI poses challenges in the labour market, with more need to adapt workers for changes, demand for new skills, and the creation of new professions. Some countries are evolving more quickly than the majority, so they will achieve an advantageous position in the future. Governments have a responsibility in designing the politics and strategies to drive this evolution in close relationship with enterprises, while still taking care of social inclusiveness and sustainability.

As in other fields of law, the judicial is also a field of experimentation for those who develop solutions based on AI. The judicial function also requires the analysis of data, the understanding of information (laws, facts, judicial precedents, personal data, etc.), the drafting of documents that include arguments that support certain theses, the making of fair decisions without bias. AI responds to many of these needs and is already being used for these purposes. In Chapter 11, we have seen that there are already at least three use cases of what have been classified as *robot judges* and that the results obtained are rather satisfactory. In all three cases, these are trials in which the aspects to be analysed in order to adopt a decision and to pass sentence are based on objective questions such as the existence of certain documents and the occurrence of certain facts.

We have also seen that there are AI solutions that support the judge in his or her decision-making. However, we have also analysed a challenge that arises when introducing AI-based tools into the field of justice delivery, and that is the so-called *black-box* effect. The question is whether, in this area, the opacity of an algorithm that deprives an individual's liberty should be allowed. Using AI tools developed by private companies to deliver justice is a topic that needs to be openly discussed. Privately owned applications may not want to disclose the secrets behind their machines, but justice without transparency is a risky business.

On the other hand, the debate has already arisen in France on whether AI can be applied to the analysis of court decisions. In 2018, the processing of data regarding judges' decisions was banned by law in order to ensure their safety. In other countries, these predictive or, more accurately, probabilistic tools are being used mainly by lawyers who are helped in formulating strategies to defend the interests of their clients. Should judges be protected from judgment on their judgments, let them be fairer in the future, or should citizens be entitled to know more about judges' views?

The development of AI applied to the judicial sphere is a concern for regulators, which is evidenced by the fact that codes of ethics have already been published that apply specifically to this type of tool, something that has not yet happened for AI intended for other purposes.

The development of AI applied to the judicial field will depend mainly on the following factors: the judges and the policies that their governing bodies decide to have towards AI; the availability of the necessary data relevant to the judicial function and key to developing these tools and finally, the policies of national governments and international bodies, such as the EU, the OECD or the UN.

We believe that AI can do much to make justice better, more transparent, equitable and efficient. Hopefully, the interest that will influence decision-making in the coming years will be the 'public' and not others, such as the preservation of strongholds of power, the false belief that human beings are superior to machines or that the current systems that most countries have to solve conflicts are the only one possible.

AI should not only support the legal system we have today but also revise and rethink it: could AI help us, for example, to prevent as many disputes coming to court; could it improve the quality of laws; could courts be made up of a staff of judges and robot judges?

We are privileged to be able to experience one of the most exciting moments in the development of humanity and the delivery of justice.

An Interview With

Bryan Khun

General Manager and Vice President, Digital Strategy & Solutions at Elevate Services

Why Should Legal Professionals Understand What AI is?

Legal professionals should make an effort to understand AI for several reasons:

(a) Your Clients Are Using It: As in other industries, the legal services industry has evolved from organizational centricity, in which law firms defined which services to offer and market to clients, to individual centricity, in which empowered legal consumers demand insight-driven, customized experiences. If you work for a law firm, many of your clients are already using AI across multiple internal business lines in non-legal scenarios; your clients' use of and experience with enterprise-grade AI has two major implications for you. First, their general success with AI will transform their expectations of the level of service that you provide (i.e., AI enables your clients to do more on their own, in turn increasing their expectations). Second, to the degree that your clients' use of AI results in business risk (i.e., a poorly installed solution that produces insights resulting in legal liability), you will be called upon to offer legal guidance and support;

(b) You Need a Strategy: Lawyers are challenged to extract the maximum potential value from their AI tools. In a rush to compete and optimize, lawyers often apply technology without an accompanying business-aligned strategy, including but not limited to identifying a business-justified starting place for AI, determining minimum viability, determining success metrics, formulating a governance model for data quality, ensuring that a vendor's underlying ML models are trained by qualified subject matter experts, and weighing the choice between custom solutions that provide company or firm-specific insights versus point solutions based on crowd-sourced data. Also, and critically, one-size-fits-all ML models are of limited value; due to the contextual nature of language, a ML model trained to analyse IP-related contracts will be much more powerful than a model trained to analyse multiple types of contracts simultaneously. With so many moving parts, success depends on formulating an AI strategy.

(c) Overwhelming Choice of Vendors: In a legal tech environment with low barriers to entry, many excellent startups have emerged to augment the delivery of legal services, both empowering law firms and facilitating law department self-service. However, there are also a significant number of AI startups that have over-promised and under-delivered. The legal tech space is crowded with new entrants offering parallel capabilities. Too often, vendors implement solutions without an understanding of customers' unique business problems and experiences, producing limited results. Given AI's increasing ubiquity across industries, lawyers in firms and law departments must become educated consumers and look outside the legal industry to examples of AI success that can be learned from and repurposed;

How will AI Impact the Legal Profession?

As AI continues to be adopted throughout the legal profession, it will allow legal organizations to repurpose, learn from and monetize *their own* historical know-how in alignment with their current challenges or their clients' challenges. In other words, AI that efficiently produces organization-specific insights (i.e., versus crowd-sourced models) securely trained on organization-specific data is the key to impactful legal tech. The consequence will be a massive cost reduction for law departments and net new revenue for law firms:

In Which Fields do You Expect AI will Have More Impact?

AI will have the most impact on augmenting the delivery of high-volume legal services.

How do you advise legal professionals to acquire the necessary knowledge on AI?

Look outside the legal industry for examples. The use of AI in the legal profession is not substantially different than the use of AI in other language-intensive professions, such as healthcare and accounting.

Can You Explain Your Professional Relationship with AI?

I founded and led a global digital strategy consultancy for IBM called Watson Legal. Based on conducting over 160 use case identification workshops to take the measure of the market for AI in legal tech, my team and I develop solution 'frameworks' based on common industry problems, then use consulting principles to wrap those frameworks around our clients' business needs, creating custom strategies and custom AI solutions for them.

How and Why did You Get into the Field of AI?

I find AI personally fascinating. It has the potential to enhance what is ultimately the most important element of legal services: the client's results.

Do You Want to Tell us Anything Else About Your Job or the Future of AI?

Late last year, IBM publicly showcased an experimental project called *Project Debater*. Debater's goal is to help professionals and policymakers make better decisions when situations are not black and white. The system was pitted against an expert human debater; each side made an opening statement, followed by a rebuttal and a closing summary. The topic was whether or not we should increase the use of telemedicine (i.e., healthcare from a distance). The system listened to its human opponent's opening remarks, then parsed that data and created a persuasive argument on the fly that highlighted and attempted to debunk information shared by the human opponent. The system had access to approximately 300 million news articles, but ... and here's the exciting bit ... *it wasn't trained on the topic of debate*, just the *structure* of formal debate generally. In other words, Debater was creating its own unscripted narrative, training its own models, and interacting with its environment in real-time.

About Bryan Khun

Bryan is responsible for developing and leading Elevate's Global Digital Strategy & Solutions business, one of the first in-industry digital strategy consultancies serving the global legal industry. As a former practicing attorney and founder of the IBM Watson Legal business, Bryan has deep experience helping customers develop transformative digital strategies that optimize the use of technology to address underlying business objectives.

Daniel S. Acevedo Sánchez

Daniel is the Strategic Projects and Innovation Manager, Galicia Abogados S.C. and Founder of Legaltech en Español.

Why Should Legal Professionals Understand What AI is?

The usual answer, albeit somewhat useless, is because it will change the way lawyers practise their profession through the next ten years, both in practice itself and in the legal challenges from society. The problem with this is that nobody explains how these changes will occur. This happens because talking about 'Artificial Intelligence' seems impossible since there is no such thing as 'Artificial Intelligence.' What we know as AI is actually a set of tools that allow the automatization of tasks that any human being can perform and, in some specific cases, the machine is able to perform faster or for a longer period of time than humans since it is not restrained by biological limitations.

Bearing this in mind, lawyers should understand the technologies that are understood as AI because, one way or another, the machine will take over the execution of their tasks in a much more efficient manner. Therefore, being competitive in the future will not be measured by how much legal knowledge a person has, but rather how proficient the professionals are in the use of tools that automate some of their tasks, and therefore free to focus on higher-value responsibilities.

How will AI Impact the Legal Profession?

As I mentioned before, this impact can be seen in two ways: (i) in the legal challenges set by the implementation of AI in society, such as AI-driven cars; and (ii) in the specific activities from a lawyer that can be automated. I will focus on the latter.

Truly, there is no magical tool that allows us to identify which activities can or cannot be automated or if an automated activity falls into the category of AI technologies. In fact, in the world of AI research, there is something known as 'The AI Effect' or 'The Tesler's Theorem' that states that people usually call things as 'Artificial Intelligence' just because they don't fully understand how they work, but when this hypothesis stage is overcome and replaced by the discovery stage, we are no longer talking about AI but rather about technical solutions for a particular problem, such as 'image recognition' to differentiate, for example, whether there is a dog or a cookie in a picture.

That said, where I really believe that AI will have a greater impact on the legal practice is in those areas that have shown room for automatization, meaning that the machines will carry out the tasks faster or with more precision:

- Applied ML to text analysis that allows the identification of clauses that do not meet certain established criteria (legal or business-wise).
- Cognitive computing like Natural Language Processing (NLP) that allows a client to 'talk' with a machine to get a quick answer on a specific legal issue.
- Forecast models using a deep learning algorithm that can predict the probability of winning/losing a trial and the estimated amount of damages.
- Data analysis and data visualization for legal research that helps lawyers do legal research in a more efficient manner.

In Which Fields do You Expect AI will have More Impact?

Understanding the word *field* as industries or sectors of the economy, I believe there will be a greater impact in those with a lesser burden of analysis and thus, following the previous line of thought, can be automated. I fully agree with the findings and predictions of Carl Benedikt and Michael Osborne in their research article *The Future of Employment: How susceptible are Jobs to computerisation?*, published by Oxford University in 2013, where they establish the probability, from 0 to 1, that some jobs are bound to disappear as a result of automatization. Some of these are listed below:

- Telemarketing.
- Tax preparers.
- Sports referees.
- Restaurant hostesses.
- Real estate brokers.

- Administrative assistants.

On the other hand, if we understand *fields* as areas of the Law, I think there will be a greater impact in those services where the work of a lawyer is more operational rather than analytical, again, more susceptible to being automated. From my point of view, I believe that the following services and areas will be the most affected:

- Intellectual Property, especially everything related to trademark registration.
- Commercial Law, especially company incorporation, and drafting and analysis of standard commercial agreements.
- Civil and Family Law, especially drafting of wills and succession procedures.
- Litigation, especially those that come from a series of events, say, related to the recovery of banking assets and repossessions.
- Banking and Finance Law, especially what is related to the analysis of documentation to establish the risk of insolvency of a borrower, whether it is a company or a person.

How do You Advise Legal Professionals to Acquire The Necessary Knowledge of AI?

My best advice would be to understand perfectly what happens outside of the technology, i.e., every activity that is undertaken in the legal services, including those that are not directly related to Law itself, such as the billing process. In other words, you should have the architecture of your business processes clearly identified, laid out and analysed. Why is this my best advice to learn about AI? Because AI is about automating activities, and if you don't know how what is to be automated really works, you are bound to implement technology chaotically, and that is always a bad idea. However, once the processes have been understood, people interested in learning how most of AI technologies work may begin their approach by learning statistics and probability, which are the most important conceptual tools from most AI systems.

Can You Explain Your Professional Relationship with AI?

My role inside companies, especially Law firms, is to understand what the company processes are; then, identify those that can be fully or partially automated and estimate the financial benefits of this automatization to establish the viability of a project. I also identify the databases that may contain the answer to the problem and then find the technology that can best carry out this automatization process. In some cases it might be a voice recognition and speech-to-text tool; in other cases, it could be a ML tool to recognize written patterns in certain types of documents, or a chatbot that recognizes a text input, reads a question and offers an answer. Sometimes it may even be necessary to combine two different types of technology to achieve the desired results. Identifying the problem and designing the solution is what is known in engineering as a solution architect. Once this happens, we enter a stage of prototype development and, depending on the project management methodology, the architect takes over the role of the product owner in the software development process, although they are not the ones that do the coding.

How and Why did You Get into the Field of AI?

Because of the eagerness to find a more efficient way to get the job done. In my case, it all started with the analysis of processes to find a more efficient way to do my work as a lawyer, representing insurance companies in Colombia. To me, it was unbelievable how again and again the same patterns would repeat themselves during a trial, but each time we had to manually search for jurisprudence, write the response to the suit, etc. So, I started acting as a process analyst and with time I found that, although I could make them more efficient in theory, the only way to actually take our processes to the next level was by applying technology. Even if the solution wasn't as sophisticated, it solved the need and an out-of-the-box tool was enough. In other cases, we had to design our own tools because there wasn't any solution at our disposal in the market.

Thanks to this experience I realized that there was no one in the legal services market (in Colombia or even Latin America) that were focused on the design of process optimization solutions through the application of information technology, so in 2014 I took a leap of faith and changed careers to become a consultant in operational excellence for the legal sector. In 2017, with the 'overpopulation' of AI technologies, I started to research how these technologies worked and how they might help me in my crusade for the greatest optimization of the work of a lawyer. My arrival in this field was a natural evolution of my work as an analyst and process designer.

Do You Want to Tell us Anything else About Your Job or the Future of AI?

I do not doubt that all technological tools, and not only those related to AI, can be very beneficial to the legal practice, but it must be clear to us the reason why we are acquiring or developing these tools. Alex Smith, head of innovation at iManage and the person in charge of the AI division (previously RAVN systems), recently mentioned in a conference the importance of bringing up the conversations of boring topics. In fact, #bringbackboring was trending on Twitter, emphasizing that it is quite easy to give in to the temptation of developing 'hot IT topic projects' (AI, blockchain, you name it) but that this vision of developing 'just because' is highly dangerous in the long term because, without doing the 'trimming' first, the development of technology will probably do the business more harm than good. That said – and this is actually part of my job – I will add this: just because a supplier knocks on your door with a shiny new IT thing does not mean you should purchase it, even if your competitor also has it. You should know your operation first, properly diagnose it, and only then you can establish which is the tool (or the toolkit) that may bring more value to your business in the medium-term.

About Daniel Acevedo

He is a strategic advisor in innovation and technology applied to legal services and the analysis of the future of law. He is the Manager of Strategic Projects and Innovation at Galicia Abogados S.C. (Mexico) and is responsible for the redesign of the firm's business model with a focus on digital product development. Daniel is also the founder and host of *Legaltech en Español*, a podcast on the legal implications and uses cases of technology and innovation in the digital society and the legal services industry. Daniel is a lawyer from Icesi University and is pursuing a master's degree in Technology & Business from Universidad de Los Andes. Daniel combines his professional practice with his passion for teaching, leading workshops on agile project management, pricing strategies, process optimization – among other topics – in Law Schools in Colombia, Peru, Guatemala, Mexico and the United States, and is also the author of multiple articles related to the transformation of the legal services industry. Before joining Galicia Abogados, Daniel was the Director of the Business Transformation Department in Gómez-Pinzón Abogados (Colombia), and an independent consultant in strategic planning and technology architecture design for law firms in Latin America, among other positions.

Petra Arends-Paltzer

Founder of Davos Digital Forum and Co-Founder Swiss Legal Tech Conference

Why Should Legal Professionals Understand What AI is?

The concept of AI influences various aspects of future business and society – to mention a few – healthcare, finance, education, workplace procedures, and basic business management. This will directly affect legal professionals in their day-to-day work. AI is beginning to transform the legal profession in many ways; several applications like Due Diligence, Prediction technology, and document automation are already available and will fundamentally change the work of legal professionals. Legal professionals who want to act in new business areas driven and created by AI must at least know the underlying basic techniques.

How will AI Impact on the Legal Profession?

On the one hand, AI will support legal professionals to manage a laborious task, and this will lead to a reduction in several legal roles. On the other hand, AI will support legal professionals to conduct and streamline work processes; i.e., it will make their lives easier. AI will also create new jobs in and for the legal ecosystem.

In Which Fields do You Expect AI will Have More Impact?

Human-Machine Cooperation/ Medical Diagnostics, for example. A computer has millions of records available to perform the desired analysis in a fraction of the time, with high accuracy and broad coverage of the possible factors to be diagnosed.

How do You Advise Legal Professionals to Acquire the Necessary Knowledge of AI?

Join the relevant conferences to get to know the legal tech innovators. Watch the films on information pioneers like Ravn, HighQ (now Thomson Reuters); iManage, Leverton, eBrevia, Kira Systems to name a few, which are provided for free.

Can you Explain Your Professional Relationship with AI?

I co-founded the Swiss Legal Technology Conference, founded the Davos Digital Forum (a Think Tank) and wrote a book on digital transformation for legal professionals. I don't work in AI myself, but I know the international (AI) players and their products. AI is surely one of the most interesting future topics.

Do You Want to Tell us Anything else About Your Job or the Future of AI?

AI and related techniques will contribute to democratizing the world. Thanks to new technologies, millions of people will be able to gain access to basic information and rights such as medicine and education.

About Petra Arends-Paltzer

She is an experienced banker and lawyer. For several years, she specialized in the area of digitalization. During this period, she organized several conferences and events that generated wide publicity. For these efforts, she received in 2018 the award 'Woman of Legal Tech 2018'. She founded 'Davos Digital Forum', and then co-founded 'Swiss Legal Tech Conference'. She has a deep understanding and extensive knowledge in the current digital marketplaces and landscapes, especially in Legal; Gov + Reg Tech. She is a keynote speaker and a participant in international conferences and seminars/panels. In addition, she is the co-author of a bestselling book 'Digital Transformation and Legal Transformation'. She is personally interested in topics that centre around democratization through digitization.

Markus Hartung

Bucerius Center on the Legal Profession at Bucerius Law School, Hamburg, Germany

Why Should Legal Professionals Understand What AI is?

AI, or innovative and sophisticated software in general, will more and more impact on our life. Law and the legal profession is no exception. For lawyers, it is of utmost importance to understand what AI/software can do and cannot do in order to provide better services to clients and to stay competitive in the legal market.

How will AI Impact on the Legal Profession?

With AI software, processes can be automated, and large amounts of documents (data) can be reviewed, far more effectively, and cost-efficiently than humans can do this. Plus, AI software is better positioned to undertake research and provide meaningful results.

In Which Fields do You Expect AI will have More Impact?

Document review and analysis, contract review and management, automation. Later: analysis of complex and seemingly unsolvable situations and proposals on how to act under given circumstances.

How do You Advise Legal Professionals to Acquire the Necessary Knowledge of AI?

With patience. Actually, you have to cut it into smaller chunks. We all tend to overestimate the capability of the software, and that stands in our way when we try to understand it. It is very much explanation, concrete use cases, best practices etc.

Can You Explain Your Professional Relationship with AI?

Mostly academic and as a consultant. Adding to that, I am part of a new project with a legal tech-based law firm where we want to develop an algorithm to achieve better results for clients.

About Markus Hartung

Markus Hartung is a lawyer and mediator (www.markushartung.com). He is founder of the Bucerius Center on the Legal Profession (CLP) at Bucerius Law School, Hamburg. From 2010 to 2019, he was managing director of the CLP. Today, as Senior Fellow, he continues his research focusing on market development and trends, management and strategic leadership as well as corporate governance of law firms and business models of law firms with regard to the digitalization of the legal market. He is Chair of the Committee on Professional Regulation of the German Bar Association (DAV) and Co-Founder of ELTA – The European Legal Technology Association. As a lawyer, he focuses on conflict management, regulatory matters and professional indemnity issues. In addition, he advises law firms in strategy and management questions and coaches partners in management functions. Recently he co-founded the CHEVALIER Law Firm, which is a Legal Tech Firm focusing on employment law exclusively for employees. He is a regular lecturer and conference-speaker on leadership, management topics and professional ethics and has written numerous articles and book chapters on these topics. He is Co-author of 'How Legal Technology Will Change the Business of Law', a joint study of The Boston Consulting Group and the Bucerius Law School (available here: http://www.bucerius-education.de/english/lawport/projekte/studien-analysen-und-veroeffentlichungen/). His recently co-published and co-authored book 'Legal Tech. How Technology is Changing the Legal World. A Practitioner's Guide' is the first comprehensive analysis of the impact of Legal Technology on the legal profession.

Ricard Martínez

Ricard Martínez is an Assistant Professor Doctor in the Department of Constitutional Law, Political and Administrative Sciences of the Universitat de Valencia

Why Should Legal Professionals Understand What AI is?

AI is the next frontier for law. It will oblige us to define the principles and applicable values of the legal framework. It is a challenge. Projects are underway, technology is advancing, and companies and public bodies need answers now with the tools we have, which are not suitable ones.

How will AI Impact on the Legal Profession?

In my opinion, in two ways. First, it will make *Iuscybernetics* a reality. I am referring to the tools that support the work of legal professionals. This includes categories of technology such as the ones that allow automation in case management and resolution or those that serve to appraise risks in compliance or generate digital evidence. Second, it will demand changes in the way we do things. Legal professionals will have to adopt a technological culture and operate as engineers, the legal engineer. We must learn to iterate.

In Which Fields do You Expect AI will have More Impact?

Some of these fields have already been identified. Human rights, the right to data protection, or the determination liability, etc. Concepts such as the legal personality of AI are also discussed, as well as transhumanism. However, I am more concerned about the impact of AI as a process. That is to say, each AI can have an instrumental relation to the area in which it carries out its activity: healthcare, the right to education, labour relationships. Therefore, the challenges affect the whole legal framework.

How do You Advise Legal Professionals to Acquire the Necessary Knowledge of AI?

The answer is really simple: study, study, study. But above all, they must have a proactive attitude, an open mind, a permanent curiosity. And if I may say so, they must awake to reality. The challenges derived from AI are for sure not solved from the distance of a chair in a law firm.

Can You Explain Your Professional Relationship with AI?

My relationship is two-fold. On the one hand, I have dedicated my career as a researcher to the field of Constitutional Law and more specifically, to the impact of information technologies on fundamental rights and especially in the right to privacy. Studying the impact of AI was a natural step. On the other hand, I work on research projects in the area of healthcare whose purpose is precisely to develop data analysis through ML and contribute to programming decisional models of assisted diagnosis. As I have said before, I believe that it is essential to put your hands in the dough.

How and Why did You Get into the Field of AI?

I lead the chair on privacy and digital transformation Microsoft-Universitat de València, and it is thanks to this position that I needed to enter this field. In the last two years, we decided to focus on this matter. So far, our more relevant achievements are that we have set up a community of 300 people that includes scientists from all areas, developers, industry and the representatives of the different administrations. It has been an intense and accelerated dive into the sea of IA.

Do You Want to Tell us Anything else About Your Job or the Future of AI?

I just want to share a thought. We cannot approach AI from the perspective of fear. Nor can we accept a model where AI can develop without limits or human and legal values. We must invest in the deployment of operational solutions. We have to use data for the common good. Our task is to help set up a future where AI is respectful with human rights, and at the service of mankind.

About Ricard Martínez

Ricard Martínez is a Doctor in Law from the Universitat de València. He has dedicated his research to study fundamental laws concerning data protection and also different issues related to the effects of information and communication technologies and private life. He is currently an Assistant Professor Doctor in the Department of Constitutional Law, Political and Administrative Sciences of the Universitat de Valencia. He is included in the Work Group concerning Digital Rights of Citizens of the Ministry of Energy, Tourism and Digital Agenda. He coordinates the Work Group constituted by the Principals' Conference of Spanish Universities (CRUE-TIC) for the boost of the General Regulation of data protection. He has worked as a delegate of data protection in the Universitat de València and has been head of the Transparency Service of the Valencian Provincial Council and President of the Professional Spanish Association of Privacy. He has collaborated with different universities as a Professor in Degree and Postgraduate Studies and has been responsible for the Studies Area of the Spanish Agency of Data Protection. He has written different monographs dedicated to this issue – 'Tecnologías de la Información, Policía y Constitución', 'Una aproximación crítica a la autodeterminación informativa'– and has participated as an author and coordinator in different comments to the Development Regulation of the Organic Law of Data protection, and monographs about Law and Social Networks or Cloud Computing among others. He is a member of the Academic Council of Fide and co-director of its Data Protection Forum.

Juan Gustavo Corbalán

Director of the Innovation and Artificial Intelligence Laboratory of the Law School University of Buenos Aires. Co-Creator of the artificial intelligence PROMETEA, at the service of rights

Why Should Legal Professionals Understand What AI is?

Technological disruption has arrived in all sectors, and the legal one is no exception. Although many areas have already incorporated successful technologies, the legal world is usually one-step behind with those changes, as a traditional profession, all changes tend to encounter greater resistance. However, the new paradigm puts us in a position in which lawyers have a new science to be acquainted with, to a greater or lesser extent, depending on their speciality. By saying this, I do not mean that all lawyers should know how to program or how to develop an expert AI system (although some definitely do), but in general, they should have enough knowledge in the most used technologies (Big Data, AI, Blockchain, etc.).

There are two fundamental issues related to professional practice, which demonstrate why lawyers should have technological knowledge. The first one has to do with lawyer's work itself, especially corporate ones, as more companies are incorporating these technologies and doing business with them. How can a lawyer without knowledge in these matters advise a client properly? How can you even understand legal problems that arise around technologies you do not know? How can you deal with liability issues if you do not have a global idea of the risks that are involved? However, these questions can also be applied to other legal professionals such as judges and prosecutors. How can they carry out an investigation or decide a conviction on issues of this nature? Alternatively, in consumer-related cases, how can issues related to electronic payments or e-wallets be addressed if they do not know how do they work? And I could go on. Many examples and situations justify why it is essential for lawyers to have knowledge of technology. The second reason why lawyers should have technological knowledge lies in the fact that the incorporation of technology allows them to work more efficiently and achieve greater productivity in fewer work hours: automate documents, control deadlines with an intelligent calendar, among many other benefits of AI.

How will AI Impact on the Legal Profession?

Even though AI and emerging technologies are transforming a large number of professions, this shouldn't alarm anyone, at least not in the legal field. Some trades and professions will gradually disappear, while new ones will emerge. However, AI will not replace lawyers, but it will convert tasks. Contrary to what we may think, this is not a bad thing. Converting tasks will allow a resignification of the lawyer's future profession. Nowadays, many of the tasks a lawyer does are repetitive, based on a constant copy-paste of data and information. A great amount of time is spent on these tasks, which do not add value to the work itself. We actually have enough technology that allows for task automation of document generation of statements of claim, judgments, etc., and in some cases, predictive systems are available. The incorporation of these technologies will allow lawyers to focus their efforts on those tasks that due to their complexity require their specific know-how, in which lawyers can really apply their technical knowledge gained during their years of study and specialization.

In Which Fields do You Expect AI will have More Impact?

AI is generating changes in all fields since it is not a new phenomenon; on the contrary, it has been present in the industry since the 1980s. There is a recent milestone that is relevant when assessing impact: today, human beings are able to develop algorithms that far exceed human intelligence. The capability of human beings to create and adjust algorithms has increased and consequently, the impact they have on the economy, employment, public policies, spheres of government, citizen-state relationship; in law, health, the protection of the environment, and also in the personal sphere of citizens, in their way of choosing and making decisions, etc. Almost by accident, we use AI to make decisions, or we even allow AI to make them for us, such as Spotify and Netflix. AI has already interfered in all sectors – and will continue to do so – by being a key piece in all areas where human beings work.

How do you Advise Legal Professionals to Acquire the Necessary Knowledge of AI?

In the first place, I consider that legal professionals should acquire knowledge in emerging technologies and AI within the first years of university, and these topics should be incorporated into regular degree programs. In fact, I believe these technologies are so integral that they should even be studied from elementary through to high school. Traditional law subjects are no longer sufficient as lawyers need to have knowledge of technologies and AI in order to address multidisciplinary issues, which touch different areas of law. For instance, the potential to optimize rights, issues of responsibility for the use of robots and intelligent systems, smart contracts and their execution, AI solutions applied to public policies, among many other issues of high impact.

Moreover, it is important for professionals to be trained in legal issues related to innovation and emerging technologies through postgraduate courses, which should remain current as technology is continuously changing. Following this premise, since last year, I have been leading different postgraduate courses at *Universidad Austral* (Argentina), which focuses on both, lawyers of the private and public sector. This year, we have started with the first Latin American 'Law 4.0' Diploma, which has a totally innovative and disruptive approach.

Can You Explain Professional Relationship with AI?

Since 2017, I have dedicated myself to investigating issues related to AI and law, always having in mind that in order to work on these issues, it is necessary to understand such technologies, their benefits, strengths and weakest aspects. I have specialized in this area and have written a series of articles related to the application of AI within the public sector and the future of employment, among other issues.

In the Public Prosecutor's Office of the City of Buenos Aires, where I am currently serving as Adjunct Deputy Attorney General, I have led a project named 'PROMETEA', which is the first Latin American predictive AI system applicable to justice. Together with Luis Cevasco (Deputy Attorney General of the City of Buenos Aires), we have decided to create an AI system with the ability to prepare legal opinions.

We started by working on data governance to prepare the Attorney General's Office for the implementation of AI. The result was so successful that we achieved a 96% success rate in just a few months. Based on this experience, we created the Innovation and AI Laboratory of the Law School of the University of Buenos Aires (IALAB).

PROMETEA was also applied in other areas of the Public Prosecutor's Office and in other public entities associated with to law. In this line, we have worked on a pilot test with the Inter-American Court of Human Rights, where PROMETEA was trained to work as an intelligent notifier and as an advanced search tool. Moreover, we have recently applied PROMETEA in the Constitutional Court of Colombia, as an innovative 'smart detector' which in a few seconds detects priority and urgent cases for the highest Court of Colombia (in the pilot test, PROMETEA automatically detected 32 urgent cases out of the 1400 cases analysed).

In the field of civil justice in Argentina, we have developed functionality that allows PROMETEA to detect if the causal link has been interrupted or not, in just a few seconds. To make this possible, the AI was trained with 366 cases; PROMETEA was able to predict in 89.34% of those cases (327 judgments), and its prediction was right in 87.16% of those cases. Apart from applying PROMETEA in different concrete projects, at the IALAB we have also mapped AI systems of greatest impact linked to the achievement of the sustainable development goals (SDGs). For further information, you can visit IALAB's website: https://ialab.com.ar/.

Academically, as I have already mentioned, I believe that lawyers need to acquire knowledge in these fields. Consequently, I decided to direct the postgraduate courses in Innovation 4.0, Administration and Justice 4.0 and the Law 4.0 Diploma of the *Universidad Austral*, with great interest and acceptance of students. In addition, I have provided lectures, participated in international events on these topics and I am a visiting professor at the Master's Degree in Digital Law of the University of Paris 1 Panthéon-Sorbonne. In May of this year, we were invited to present PROMETEA at the AI for Good Global Summit; the leading United Nations platform for global and inclusive dialogue on AI, in Geneva, Switzerland. Last year, PROMETEA was presented in the Organization of American States (OAS) in Washington D.C., in the Inter-American Development Bank (IBD), as well as in many Latin American and European universities. More information can be found on the IALAB's website as well.

How and Why did You Get into the Field of AI?

I was always interested in technology in general and AI in particular. However, one day, I realized that only thinking with a lawyer's mind was not enough to address complex legal issues in this new paradigm. To move forward, we must find interdisciplinary solutions. Law is related to almost all sciences, and technologies can be a great ally to fully achieve rights efficiency. That was my main motivation.

About Juan Gustavo Corbalán

Juan Gustavo Corbalán is a Doctor of Legal Sciences; currently, he is a postdoctoral student and visiting professor in the Master's Degree at Digital Law of the University of Sorbonne / Paris 1; he is a Professor of Administrative Law at the University of Buenos Aires; he is a Director of the Innovation and AI Laboratory of the Law School University of Buenos Aires. He is a Co-Creator of the AI PROMETEA, at the service of rights; he is a Contentious Administrative and Tax judge of the City of Buenos Aires, currently serving as Deputy Attorney General in Administrative and Tax Litigation before the Superior Court of the City of Buenos Aires; he is also the author of four books; he is a participant in the publication of the study section of the French State Council; he is a lecturer at the World Summit of AI for Good in Geneva, at the United Nations (UN headquarters Vienna), at the Permanent Council of the Organization of American States (OAS), at the French State Council, at the Protection Agency of Fundamental Rights of the EU, at the University of Oxford, among other national and foreign universities and institutions.

Erick Richard Rincon Cardenas

Professor at Universidad Law School and President of Colombia Fintech.

Why Should Legal Professionals Understand What AI is?

AI enabling legal tech solutions will allow human lawyers to complete more work with a higher degree of accuracy, freeing up bandwidth to focus on different and/or more complex types of work that can create substantial value for their companies and clients.

AI Won't Replace Lawyers, but Lawyers Who Use AI Will Replace Those Who Don't.

How will AI Impact on the Legal Profession?

Some may say that its impact is disrupting, whereas some may argue it to be useful. AI is helping legal professionals in many ways, such as with research on legal cases. AI will also be able to handle repetitive tasks of increasing complexity, especially in data extraction, which will require new systems to be built to extract value out of new kinds of data.

In Which Fields do You Expect AI will have More Impact?

Within the next few years, we will find ourselves on the cusp of a revolution in the practice of law led by the adoption of AI – in particular, by in-house lawyers. Much like email changed the way we do business every day, AI will become ubiquitous – an indispensable assistant to practically every lawyer. Those that do not adopt and embrace the change will get left behind. Those that do will ultimately find themselves freed up to do the two things there always seems to be too little time for thinking and advising.

How do You Advise Legal Professionals to Acquire the Necessary Knowledge on AI?

To maintain the requisite knowledge and skills, a lawyer should keep abreast of changes in the law and its practice, including the benefits and risks associated with relevant technology.

Gain knowledge by attending AI-focused sessions and panels like conferences and webinars. The legal professionals will not become data scientists but can acquire the structural think to understand the way that can group, sort and organize the legal data, to minimize the effort for a data scientist to build models and to obtain better results.

Can You Explain Your Professional Relationship with AI?

As a legal support professional, I was kept busy conducting due diligence to uncover background information on behalf of customers. This work included confirming facts and figures and thoroughly evaluating the decisions on prior cases to effectively provide counsel to customers. AI tools can help to conduct due diligence more efficiently and with more accuracy since this work is often tedious for humans.

How and Why did You Get into the Field of AI?

The evolving of the technology pushed me into several different fields related to 4IR, as a legal counsel in several technologic companies and organizations like Fintech, Legaltech, Insurtech and Data Administration. AI creates a need to be vigilant in the legal field and is a 'must have' skill, for lawyers specialized in legal technology advice.

Do You Want to Tell us Anything else About Your Job or the Future of AI?

The future is imponderable related to AI, but in the short term will continue evolving in the uses related to performs due diligence, legal analytics (tied to Big Data), Document automation, Chatbots & Voicebots, Smart Contracts (By joint the AI with Blockchain technologies). In the long term, concepts like strong AI, Transhumanism, Superintelligence, which are really creepy in the sci-fi movies will require the definition of limits in the ethical and legal point of view.

About Erick Richard Rincon Cardenas

He is a lawyer of the Universidad del Rosario (Colombia) with postgraduate degrees in Financial Law and Contractual Law from Universidad del Rosario; he holds a Master's Degree in Commercial Law from the Universidad Alfonso X of Spain; he is also a Doctor in Law from the European University of Madrid. He was General Manager of Certicámara and Legis and currently is a Professor of Law in the Universidad del Rosario.

Manuel González Bedia

Professor in the Department of Computer Science at the University of Zaragoza

Why Should Legal Professionals Understand What AI is?

For many reasons, but fundamentally because Technology Corporations are promoting the self-regulation as opposed to a normative intervention from Governments that limit the potential of innovations in AI. However, polluting industries should not establish the limits of atmospheric emissions any more than technological companies should regulate the effects of their software developments. It is obvious that many of the limits to be imposed on intelligent technologies should come from law and regulation. In order to do this, legal professionals should understand AI and its characteristics. Only with legal rules, rights and obligations can regulation be guaranteed, and legal responsibilities assumed.

How will AI Impact on the Legal Profession?

AI can have an impact because new rights will be needed in order to respond to new challenges, as happened in the past with labour or environmental rights. In some cases, intelligent technologies are designed to create addiction, social polarization or fake news with consequences on the degradation of democracy. Others are designed to capture our attention and to exploit psychological vulnerabilities. In these situations, the law must be worried about how to preserve values such as dignity, autonomy, privacy and non-discrimination in the new technological contexts.

In Which Fields do You Expect AI will have More Impact?

AI will produce effects in all industrial and commercial domains, in public issues such as Health or Education, and in social environments, including political institutions. Intelligent technologies are General Purpose technologies, i.e., technologies that have a high potential in several issues, rapid growth, high impact, rapid diffusion and whose presence in one field can be reoriented or recombined to explore new opportunities in other related domains. They are technologies that will generate radical innovations with associated socio-economic changes.

How do You Advise Legal Professionals to Acquire the Necessary Knowledge of AI?

I think that the best way is the formation of interdisciplinary teams (with technical, legal and sociological profiles) to understand difficulties and challenges at all stages of the development of new advances. Perspectives from social sciences or humanities in the design and in the orientation of new developments, co-defining methods of analysis, would be a good way to understand AI in order to know how to regulate it.

Can You Explain Your Professional Relationship with AI?

I am currently part of the team that is preparing the Spanish AI Strategy (SAIS). In this strategy, we want to define the responsibilities that Public Institutions should have in this context, for example, avoiding knowledge asymmetries between suppliers and consumers, anticipating the effects on unemployment, or supporting technological diversity by preventing the closure of alternative trajectories. The SAIS, therefore, wants to determine what political orientations should be followed in order to optimize social benefits and the opportunities that these technologies offer.

How and Why did You Get into the field of AI?

I have a PhD in AI, and I am Lecturer in the Department of Computer Science at the University of Zaragoza. For more than a decade, my research and academic activity have focused on understanding the mechanisms, organization and adaptive principles in natural or artificial systems in order to use this knowledge in the design of intelligent applications, expanding their fields of application. Recently, I became a scientific advisor in the Office of the Minister of Science, Innovation and Universities, where one of my responsibilities is the design of the Spanish National AI Strategy.

Do You Want to Tell us Anything else About Your Job or the Future of AI?

It is difficult to make predictions about the future of AI. We have three possible approaches, but we do not know which of them will be true. On the one hand, a techno-optimistic position that defends that technology will automate professions but that, on average, the current amount of jobs will not be lost. On the other hand, a position that argues that the changes brought about by digitization will not generate enough employment to compensate for the jobs that will be lost. Finally, a third opinion that believes that the AI revolution is overvalued because the real technological revolution occurred at the beginning of the twentieth century with electricity, telephone and the extension of cars. We do not know what will happen, and we will have to wait to *see* what prediction is right.

About Manuel González Bedia

He is a Professor in the Department of Computer Science at the University of Zaragoza (Spain). He has a degree in Physical Sciences, a Master in Social Studies of Science and a Doctorate in Computer Science from the University of Salamanca. For several years he worked in the field of business R&D (in England and Spain) and in the field of technological innovation management. For more than a decade, his research and academic activity have focused on understanding the mechanisms, organization and adaptive principles in natural or artificial systems in order to use this knowledge in the design of intelligent applications, expanding their fields of application. He has been professor/researcher at the universities of Salamanca, Complutense de Madrid and Carlos III de Madrid, and postdoctoral researcher at the universities of Edinburgh and Sussex (Brighton). He is a co-founder of the 'Spanish Network of Cognitive Sciences', a thematic network that constitutes an interdisciplinary research framework in the field of natural and artificial cognitive systems. Since 2019, he is a scientific advisor in the Office of the Minister of Science, Innovation and Universities.

Selected Bibliography

Ajay Agrawal, Joshua Gans & Avi Goldfarb. *Prediction machines: the simple economics of artificial intelligence* (Harvard Business Press, 2018).

Vincent Aravantinos, *Traceability of Deep Neural Networks* (2018), https://arxiv.org/abs/1812.06744v1 (accessed 22 March 2019).

Kevin D. Ashley, *Artificial Intelligence and Legal Analytics. New Tools for Law Practice in the Digital Age* (Cambridge University Press 2017).

Moisés Barrio, *Legal Tech. La transformación digital de la abogacía* (Kluwer, 2019).

Alain Bensoussan & Jérémy Bensoussan, *IA, robots et droit* (Bruylant, 2019).

Valéry Bonneau, *Mon collègue est un robot* (Alternatives, Gallimard, 2016).

Nick Bostrom, *Superintelligence: Paths, Dangers, Strategies* (Oxford University Press, 2014).

Rodney A. Brooks, *Elephants don't play chess*, 6 Robotics and Autonomous Systems 3–15 (1990).

Ryan Calo, A. Michael Froomkin & Ian Kerr (eds.), *Robot Law* (Edward Elgar Publishing, 2016).

Jacques Crémer, Yves-Alexandre de Montjoye & Heike Schweitzer, *Competition policy for the digital era – Final report* (European Commission 2019), http://ec.europa.eu/competition/publications/reports/kd0419345enn.pdf (last access, Dec. 2019).

Daniel L. Chen, *Machine Learning and the Rule of Law, Computational Analysis of Law*, Santa Fe Institute Press, ed. M. Livermore and D. Rockmore, Forthcoming (2019).

Silvia Díaz Alabart, *Robots y Responsabilidad Civil* (Ed. Reus, 2018).

Luciano Floridi, *The Onlife Manifesto. Being Human in a Hyperconnected Era*, Springer (2015).

Jason Furman et al., *Unlocking Digital Competition, Report of the Digital Competition Expert Panel, Report prepared for the Government of the United Kingdom, March* 2019.

David Gunning, *Explainable artificial intelligence (XAI)*, Defense Advanced Research Projects Agency (DARPA), nd Web 2 (2017).

Jaap Hage, *Theoretical foundations for the responsibility of autonomous agents*, 25 Artificial Intelligence and Law, 255–271 (2017).

Markus Hartung, Micha-Manuel Bues & Gernot Halbleib, *Legal Tech: a practitioner's guide* (Beck Hart Nomos, 2018).

Information Commissioner's Office (ICO), *Big Data, artificial intelligence, machine learning and data protection*, available at https://ico.org.uk/media/for-organisations/documents/2013559/big-data-ai-ml-and-data-protection.pdf, (accessed 15 September 2019).

IEEE Global Initiative on Ethics of Autonomous and Intelligent Systems, *Ethically Aligned Design: A Vision for Prioritizing Human Well-being with Autonomous and Intelligent Systems, Version 2* (2017).

Robert M. O'Keefe & Daniel E. O'Leary, *Expert system verification and validation: a survey and tutorial*, 7 Artif Intell Rev 3–42 (1993).

Alex Krizhevsky, Ilya Sutskever & Geoffrey E. Hinton, *ImageNet Classification with Deep Convolutional Neural Networks*, 60 Commun. ACM 84–90 (2017).

José Ignacio Latorre, *Ética para máquinas* (Ariel, 2019).

Logan Kugler, *AI Judges and Juries*, Communications of the ACM, Vol. 61 No. 12, 19–21 (2018).

Jie Lin, et al., *A survey on Internet of Things: Architecture, enabling technologies, security and privacy, and applications*. IEEE Internet of Things Journal, 4(5), 1125–1142 (2017).

Kristian Lum, *Limitations of mitigating judicial bias with machine learning*, Nature Human Behaviour volume 1, Article number: 0141 (2017).

Gary E. Marchant, *Artificial intelligence and the future of legal practice*, TheSciTechLawyer Fall 2017, 21–23, https://www.americanbar.org/content/dam/aba/administrative/litigation/materials/2017-2018/2018-sac/written-materials/artificial-intelligence-and-the-future.authcheckdam.pdf, (accessed 17 December 2019).

Decebal Constantin Mocanu et al., *Scalable training of artificial neural networks with adaptive sparse connectivity inspired by network science*, 9 Nature Communications 2383 (2018).

Hans Moravec, *Mind Children*, Harvard University Press (1988).

Allen Newell, *The knowledge level*, 18 Artificial Intelligence 87–127 (1982).

Ugo Pagallo, *The Laws of Robots. Crimes, Contracts and Torts* (Dordrecht: Springer 2013).

Frank Pasquale, *The Black Box Society, The Secret Algorithms That Control Money and Information* (Harvard University Press 2015).

Henry Prakken & Giovanni Sartor, *Law and logic: A review from an argumentation perspective*, 223 Artificial Intelligence, 214–245 (2015); Douglas Walton, Argumentation Methods for Artificial Intelligence in Law (Springer 2005).

Nadezhda Purtova, *The law of everything. Broad concept of personal data and future of EU data protection law*, Law, innovation & Technology Journal, Volume 10, 2018, available at https://www.tandfonline.com/doi/full/10.1080/17579961.2018.1452176 (accessed 15 September 2019).

Ana Ramalho, *Will Robots Rule the (Artistic) World? A Proposed Model for the Legal Status of Creations by Artificial Intelligence Systems*, Journal of Internet Law (2017).

Carlos Rogel Vide, *Los Robots y el Derecho* (Ed. Reus, 2018).

Stuart J. Russell & Peter Norvig, *Artificial Intelligence: A Modern Approach. Third Edition* (Prentice Hall 2016).

Herbert A. Simon, *Models of Man, Social and Rational: Mathematical Essays on Rational Human Behavior in a Social Setting*, 59 Journal of Philosophy 177–182 (1962).

Max Tegmark, *Life 3.0 Being Human in the Age of Artificial Intelligence* (Knopf 2018).

Alan M. Turing, *Computing machinery and intelligence*, LIX Mind 433–460 (1950).

Jacob Turner, *Robot rules: Regulating artificial intelligence* (Springer, 2018).

Rolf H. Weber & Studer Evelyne, *Cybersecurity in the Internet of Things: Legal aspects*, Computer Law & Security Review 32.5: 715–728 (2016).

Index

B

C

D

www.ingramcontent.com/pod-product-compliance
Lightning Source LLC
Chambersburg PA
CBHW071244230926
51849CB00001B/217
* 9 7 8 9 4 0 3 5 0 9 4 3 3 *